Affecting Change
Social Workers in the Political Arena

Third Edition

Karen S. Haynes
University of Houston-Victoria

James S. Mickelson
CHILDREN AT RISK, Houston, Texas

Foreword by Senator Barbara A. Mikulski

 LONGMAN

An imprint of Addison Wesley Longman, Inc.

New York • Reading, Massachusetts • Menlo Park, California • Harlow, England
Don Mills, Ontario • Sydney • Mexico City • Madrid • Amsterdam

**Affecting Change: Social Workers
in the Political Arena, Third Edition**

Longman, 10 Bank Street, White Plains, N.Y. 10606

Associated companies:
Longman Group Ltd., London
Longman Cheshire Pty., Melbourne
Longman Paul Pty., Auckland
Copp Clark Longman Ltd., Toronto

Executive editor: Pamela A. Gordon
Associate editor: Hillary B. Henderson
Production editor: Linda Moser
Editorial assistant: Jennifer A. McCaffery
Cover design: Kevin Kall
Production supervisor: Edith Pullman

Library of Congress Cataloging-in-Publication Data
Haynes, Karen S.
    Affecting change : social workers in the political arena / by
Karen S. Haynes & James S. Mickelson.—3rd ed.
        p.   cm.
    Includes bibliographical references and index.
    ISBN 0-8013-1620-0
    1. Social workers—United States—Political activity.   2. United
States—Social policy.   I. Mickelson, James S.   II. Title.
HV40.8.U6H39   1997
361.3'2—dc20   96-10447
                                                            CIP

4 5 6 7 8 9 10-MA-009998

To those social workers
who dare to enter the political arena
and translate their ideas and ideals
into actions
for the greater good

Contents

CHAPTER 6 INFLUENCE THROUGH LOBBYING 87

CHAPTER 7 INFLUENCE THROUGH ORGANIZING OTHERS 107

Foreword

Affecting Change: Social Workers in the Political Arena, Third Edition is a pragmatic guide that outlines, step-by-step, how social workers can become agents of change.

This book is just what social workers need to become effective political advocates. The third edition of *Affecting Change* offers practical self-help tools to help social workers influence public policy.

The authors, Karen Haynes and Jim Mickelson, look at politics through the eyes of a social worker as they offer practical political skills for BSW and MSW students.

But *Affecting Change* is not just for students. This book gives social workers a step-by-step guide to using their professional skills to influence social policy. It shows how the skills of social workers are also the skills of effective lobbyists or elected officials. The examples, assignments, and suggested readings both enhance social workers' skills and demonstrate the importance of social workers' participation in the political arena.

Affecting Change is a practical guide book to becoming a political advocate. It is helpful to those who are working with clients on a daily basis as it is to those who wish to seek elected office, including the United States Senate.

Social workers will return again and again to this book throughout their careers. It provides technical information, such as a glossary of terms. And it provides encouragement and motivation to social workers across the country who have already stepped forward to make a difference.

As we enter the twenty-first century, we face a time of complex problems. This nation is at a great time of change. There are doomsayers who say we are at the end of an era, but I believe that we are entering a time that could be one of great opportunity for every American.

I encourage all social workers to join in the political arena to help make the next millennium a time of prosperity for our nation.

We must join together to decide what kind of nation we want to be. We must ask ourselves, as a nation: Who are we? Where are we going? How do we get there?

I challenge social workers to join in this nation's political debate to help create a shared national vision to make the next century a prosperous time for America.

I challenge social workers to help meet the demands of the new century—to educate our workforce, to help create an opportunity structure for our future, and to restore character and value in this society.

We need a national vision to create good jobs and give help to those who work hard, play by the rules, and practice self-help. We need to create a new state of mind that—as Americans—we can solve our nation's problems together.

These problems all call out for the leadership skills of social workers to help guide us into the next millennium through political activity.

My own experiences as a social worker, as a community activist, as a member of Congress, and as a U.S. senator convince me that it is possible to beat City Hall, and then help lead it on a better course.

Barbara A. Mikulski, MSW
United States Senator, D-Maryland

Preface

We take the request to write a third edition of *Affecting Change: Social Workers in the Political Arena* as a mixed message. We are pleased that it continues to be adopted and read, but remain somewhat disheartened that 15 years since we had the idea, 20 years since we individually became angry at the profession for its "dispassionate, objective, and apolitical stance," there is still a great need for this kind of message.

This edition has several new and unique features not found in the previous two editions. The first is this preface with its inclusion of suggested uses for this text. Another is a new chapter 2, "The Debate," which we hope adds credence to the currentness of this professional argument and portrays a strong response to it. Chapter 12 is significantly changed to include "rules for advocacy" and advice from advocates. Throughout we have updated the references and data, included some new case illustrations, and, perhaps more importantly given this topic, added the importance of technology.

As we reviewed the places where we should insert information about the use of technology, we realized that the magnitude of its influence is so great and so fluid that we could never adequately integrate it within this text. "Every 18 months or so a new chip will be designed that can do twice as much as the best chip before it. Every decade, computers will be about ten times as powerful as computers at the beginning of the decade and available at the same cost."[1] However, we have done our best to reference the use of and importance of technology in many chapters.

---

[1] Sterling, Bruce. "Year 200 & Beyond: Information Technology for Social Work: Vision, Choices, Ethics," in *Proceedings of the Ninth Annual Social Work Futures Conference*, May 1994, Travis Courville and Paul Raffoul, eds. Sponsored by the Graduate School of Social Work, University of Houston and the Houston Unit of the Texas Chapter of National Association of Social Workers.

We have seen progress related to social work advocacy in the political arena and will note that progress throughout this text. However, the last 15 years have not been positive ones for our clients nor for our profession and we will continue to make this book a call to action. Our intention from the beginning is that this book would be a practical guide to skill development within the political arena and would serve as a justification for those activities. We never intended this to be a primary text; we never intended this to be highly theoretical nor used predominantly as a history text. Our intention is not simply to describe political action skills and political processes, but also to pave the way for the integration of recognized political skills within traditional social work skills, thereby creating an effective and viable advocacy model.

We do not want advocacy to be left only to the "advocates"; we want professionals, current and future ones, to see the compatibility of social work values as an impetus to enter the political arena. We hope that advocacy becomes the central mission of our professional association, a mandated standard for all social work practice, and a daily part of every social worker's experience.

We do not argue that some social workers have taken an active part in social reform during this century and we know that it would be naive to suggest that individual social workers have not engaged in a variety of political activities. However, throughout more than 70 years of formalized social work education in the United States, political content, strategies for political intervention, and the related skills have not consistently been included in social work curriculum. Accreditation standards for graduate and undergraduate social work programs still speak only in generalities about such course content and coverage.

Furthermore, many have pointed out that the drive toward specialization and professionalization in social work may be one of the factors responsible for the lack of interest in (or even antagonism to) social action. In either case, a lack of knowledge and training in the strategies and techniques fundamental to effective social change intervention must be rectified. A commitment to social change without the means to achieve it is futile in any profession. We hope that this book is one mechanism to fill in the knowledge and skill gaps.

Although it seems evident that social workers would be the logical professional group to defend and support human service programs, such support has seldom been forthcoming from either individual social workers or social work organizations. Even today some still question whether social workers should be politically trained at all. Those who do support political training of social workers are left with the question of how, by whom, where, and for what particular political positions.

There are many more arguments, along with the aforementioned, for including political content in the curriculum of social work schools and departments. There are also distinct advantages to having politically knowledgeable and active graduates. The most obvious advantage is the accumulated potential for creating progressive social policy to deal with unmet needs, resolve social problems, or ameliorate unjust or inequitable conditions in society. The second is the ability to amass political strength for the promotion and protection of professional standards for human service personnel.

Finally, because the majority of social work programs are publicly funded, a politically effective profession can be a positive influence on human service funding during the budget allocation process. Although this point may appear self-serving, one should remember that without sufficient funds to hire professionally trained social workers, human services will be poorly delivered.

There are several ways in which social work education can interject political skills, experiences, and activities into the curriculum without shifting its emphasis. The first prescription for social work education at any level would be to include a political action course in the policy sequence: rather than teaching the subject descriptively and historically, policy skills for practice would be taught. This would in no way run counter to the accreditation standards established by the Council for Social Work Education (CSWE) for bachelor of social work or master of social work programs. What would be a logical extension for some graduate programs would be the creation of specializations in political social work such as the University of Houston's Graduate School of Social Work has done.

Given that we intended this book to be a secondary text for several different courses, we have decided to be bold in this third edition and suggest where and how it might be used. We envision that this text could be used for both BSW and MSW programs, potentially with an introductory course, a history course, a policy course, or a practice course. Therefore, it would be possible (although, we admit, highly unlikely) for a student to purchase this book and read sections of it for several courses.

If used for an introductory course, our suggestion is that chapters 1, 2, 3, and 5 would be the most instructive such that the debate could be framed, a brief history of advocacy included, the compatibility with the profession's values noted, and the practitioner's influence on policy discussed. If used to compliment a history course, chapters 1, 2, and 12 would frame the historical debate, provide a brief history of advocacy, and suggest ways to begin advocacy efforts.[2]

The text is probably most useful for policy and macro courses. For policy courses, chapters 1 through 6, and 8 would have the greatest applicability. Once again, framing the debate and a brief history of advocacy would be pertinent to a policy course (chapters 1 and 2). Values and models are extremely important content in policy courses (chapters 3 and 4) and the unique contributions of chapter 5, the practitioner's influence on policy, and lobbying and monitoring the bureaucracy (chapters 6 and 8) are usually not covered within traditional policy texts. For practice courses, chapters 1, 2, and 3 set the stages, but chapters 5 through 11 really provide the specific roles and skills for political practice.

Chapters are short, user friendly with examples and case illustrations, and include assignments and suggested readings for the professor or student who wants to augment the basics provided here. A brief synopsis of chapters follows.

Chapter 1 provides a brief history of social work political action so that readers will appreciate the origins of political advocacy. Chapter 2 frames the debate about the profession's mission and the inclusion of advocacy within that

---

[2] Mickelson, James S. "Advocacy." In *Encyclopedia of Social Work,* 19th ed. (Washington, D.C.: NASW Press, 1995), pp. 95–100.

mission. It is a new chapter, made essential out of the continued critical nature of the professional debate. Chapter 3 illustrates the compatibility of social work values with political action. Chapter 4 examines several policy models that provide guidelines for examining policy and suggest interventive strategies appropriate to each model.

The way in which a practitioner's daily activities can culminate in significant input to the political process is discussed in chapter 5. The more traditional approach of lobbying is presented in chapter 6, whereas chapter 7 addresses changes in policy by organizing others. Chapter 8, "Monitoring the Bureaucracy," reviews the implementation of and subsequent adherence to legislative intent. Chapter 9 focuses on political action committees as another more specialized means used to influence the political process. Chapter 10 presents an overview of campaigning in order to enable the social worker to assist in the election process. Chapter 11 discusses the unique concept of affecting change as a politician within the political system. The last chapter, substantially revised, provides both a summary and some pointers for getting started.

We have continued to include a glossary to assist social workers with political jargon. Suggested assignments with varying degrees of difficulty, complexity, and involvement are found at the end of each chapter to assist in the development of political skills. Because this book may be used as a supplementary text, suggested readings are provided for further exploration of a given area.

ACKNOWLEDGMENTS

No book is solely the product of its authors, nor is a book, even a third edition, the product of single experiences. This book is now the cumulative product of over a decade of dialogues, student interaction, collegial challenge, and political observation.

This third edition was written because events and changes in the profession and in the political times mandated an update; because it continues to remain, we believe, a unique contribution to our professional literature; and because our belief that social workers must be a positive force for change has not wavered.

We thank Senator Barbara Mikulski for being such a public and positive role model for social workers in the political arena and for writing a forward of such encouragement to our readers.

We thank the social workers quoted throughout this edition who took time from already hectic schedules to talk with us, share their stories, and provide useful advice and challenges.

We thank and acknowledge the following reviewers who took the time to provide useful and insightful comments:

Margaret Jane Allen, Eastern Kentucky University
Michael P. Connolly, Barry University
David P. Fauri, Virginia Commonwealth University

Sue Henry, University of Denver
Alice Lieberman, University of Kansas
Michael Reisch, University of Pennsylvania
Jennifer R. Stucker, Eastern Washington University
Kenrick S. Thompson, Northern Michigan University
Daniel Weisman, Rhode Island College
Joseph Wronka, Springfield College

Although not all comments are included in this third edition, we have retained the advice for a future edition and for our own professional teaching and service activities. Also, the staff at Longman have remained commited to this text from its initiation and have worked with us within an abbreviated time frame to bring this to production quickly.

We finally thank all of you who read this book and take away a stronger notion of "political social work" because the writing of this book fulfills our belief that each of us can truly make a difference.

chapter 1

The Emergence of a Social Work Polity

You take people as far as they will go, not as far as you would like them to go.*

Jeanette Rankin

Jeannette felt the cool fall winds of Montana on her face as she walked through the park, thinking about her past and about what the immediate future would bring. In just a few moments, the course of her professional life could alter dramatically.

She had known she was in the right profession when she received her degree in social work from a New York university. Yet, after practicing in various agencies, she had begun to develop mixed feelings about her work. She liked children and found meaning working with orphans and abused children, but more and more she felt empty and confused. Some difficult questions were on her mind: Why are children abandoned? Why are orphans treated poorly in institutions? Why are so many women beaten and left homeless by their husbands? Could one social worker really make a difference?

Jeannette understood that people have problems in the course of their lives, but it perplexed her that society didn't seem to care. Why did the government spend so much money on the military and so little on what she considered to be the country's greatest asset: the welfare of its children?

Jeannette knew she was good at her profession, but now she wasn't sure whether the new direction in which her career was heading would bring

---

* Josephson, Hannah. *First Lady in Congress: Jeannette Rankin.* Indianapolis, Ind.: Bobbs-Merrill Company, Inc., 1974, p. xii.

about help for the children. She was taking a hard road, yet she was convinced that it was necessary. She recently had spent many months traveling around the state discussing the problems that she encountered.

She knew that she could not continue working at the Children's Home Society. She found the job of locating homes for orphans intolerable. Seeing her clients traded like cattle or living under the deplorable conditions that existed in institutions, she became increasingly frustrated with the necessarily slow and singular efforts she made on behalf of these children. As an advocate for these defenseless and unloved children, she could not help but to realize that many of the institutions' policies negated the positive changes she could make. She had come to know that the greatest possibility for reform was through influencing the laws that govern social institutions.

It seemed like only yesterday she had filed with the election commission to run for Congress, yet here she was today on her way to learn the election results. Competing with seven men had definitely been an uphill battle, but her background and knowledge of social problems had made a difference. If elected, her hard work in campaigning would pay off.

It took several days to tally all the votes, and in the end the Democrats swept the election except for one instance: Jeannette won her congressional seat by only 7,567 votes. On April 2, 1917, at the age of 36, Jeannette Rankin was installed as the first woman and the first social worker in the United States Congress (Lavassaur, 1984).

For Rankin, case advocacy for children led to a career in class and legislative advocacy. She lost her bid for reelection in 1919 because of her controversial vote opposing the United States' entry into World War I. Hers was the only opposing vote. The defeat did not stop her political activities, however, and she continued to work hard for women's suffrage and for reform of government policies toward children. She was reelected in 1941, only to vote again against American entry into another war, this time against Japan. She left her imprint on this country and its policies, on the peace movement, and on women's rights.

Jeannette Rankin portrays the transition and movement from individual to political reform today. Embodied in her, and in many of the early social workers of this period, is the simultaneous growth of social conscience, "Scientific methodology," and macrolevel reform that logically emanate from individual problem solving. Her career exemplifies the fact that involvement in social action to meet human needs and improve social functioning is a logical outgrowth of social work practice. Clearly, today's social workers are the heirs of a powerful tradition of social action.

Although social action is not synonymous with political intervention, social action strategies, when used to intervene in the affairs of government, are political strategies. Furthermore, although social workers have been influential in the political arena, politics has not consistently been a central arena for social work practice. Consequently, an historic and ongoing dynamic tension exists between the two institutions.

During the decades of professional development following World War I the main body of social work may have turned away from its tradition of reform, but social workers never totally abandoned this tradition. In fact, the intensity of the debate over social reform changes with the general social climate. A lessening of disagreements among social workers on this issue not only will contribute to the unification of the profession, but could produce a multitude of interventions aimed at the formation and renovation of public policy.

No profession is in a better position to judge the impact of social policy than is social work. Although other professions direct their services toward specific problems, social work as a profession is involved with the overall impact on both the individual and the community of unemployment, inadequate health care, lack of education, poor housing, and insufficient income. Nonetheless, the social work profession has not systematically and consistently sought, nor has it been asked to take, a significant role in the planning of social programs or the formulation of social policy. Currently there is increasing emphasis on professionalism within the field. Social workers should not be criticized for their efforts to attain professional standing, because acceptance of social work as a profession is basis for achieving the respect and authority necessary to effectively meet its obligations to those it serves. But the drive toward professionalism seems to have paralleled the profession's weakening concern with social reform.

> The coalescing and maturation of the trends in social work, in terms of the performance of a function rather than a cause, in emphasizing methods and techniques rather than goals, and in grasping for higher professional status . . . appear to be commitments of the process of professionalization itself in the United States, but if this complex of trends continues, where are we headed? Three consequences are likely to follow. First, a continuing de-emphasis on the controversial social action which has broad social implications; second, a related lessening of attempts to influence social policy and the acceptance of the role of technician's implementor, and third, change in the ideology of social work that will lessen the gap between its system of ideas and that of the dominant groups in society. (Bisno, 1969)

Indeed, social action has been de-emphasized to the point that many question whether it really is the business of social work. In a 1972 study of 51 schools of social work, the majority of social work graduate students and educators did not consider social action or the initiation of social change to be a primary function of the profession (Carlton and Jung, 1972). A mid-1980s survey of undergraduate and graduate bulletins of schools of social work found there was minimal inclusion of course titles or descriptions that reflect political content or terminology (Haynes and Mickelson, 1985). A review of MSW program concentrations indicated that five had community organization concentrations, two had community or social development concentrations, one had social strategies, one had social justice, and one had political social work. Therefore, less than 10 percent of the accredited MSW programs self-describe anything resembling a "politicized" social work concentration. Add to this the data that approximately only 5 percent of MSW students in these ten programs are likely enrolled in these political concentrations, and it is clear that we are not, in the mid-1990s, preparing many political social workers (Haynes, 1996).

Although these findings may reflect the professional MSW program's traditional bias toward the direct-service method of intervention, this bias has also been found in many of our professional journals. A passionate but uninformed quest for relevance in activism is noted in one such journal as a factor responsible for the deprofessionalization of social work. Another journal asserts that "an activist spirit in social work downgrades professional practice." However, an optimistic prediction for increased political awareness is the fact that a few more schools are including political content and courses and are promoting, or at least allowing, political placements. Additionally, recently the social work literature appears to contain a renewed focus on advocacy, empowerment, and political social work.

Some examples of this new or renewed focus are found in the works of Burghardt (1982), *The Other Side of Organizing*; Fisher (1984), *Let the People Decide: Neighborhood Organizing in America*; and Reeser and Epstein (1990), *Professionalization and Activism in Social Work*. If one adds some of the empowerment-oriented and feminist scholarship that affirms the linking of the personal with the political, then one can refer to the works of Bricker-Jenkins and Hooyman (1986), Friere (1973), Gutierrez and Lewis (1990), Gutierrez and Nurius (1994), and Van DenBergh and Cooper (1986). Other materials directly connecting micro and macro practice such as Rees (1991) and Wakefield (1988a, b) provided additional support for this argument. In fact, Rees (1991) provided a model of social work education grounded in four key assumptions, all of which promote political social work. These four assumptions are (1) all social work is fundamentally political; (2) social work education must focus on power; (3) social work education must include skills that range from engaging with individuals in a collaborative practice to organizing communities and winning elections, and (4) all good social work practice must recognize that policy and all forms of practice are inextricably interdependent.

The works of Carniol (1990, 1992), LeComte (1990), Moreau (1990), and Wharf (1990), although Canadian, advocate a politicized model of social work education and trace their structural framework back to the practice of settlement workers in the United States and the radical tradition of social work in the United States and Great Britain. "Acknowledging the limits of the social work profession, they argue that effective social work education must include an analysis of power and political dialogue as integral aspects of the social worker-client relationships" (Fisher et al., 1994). However, the authors would contend that despite this increased literature, political social work or politicized social work practice is still viewed as atypical, aberrant, temporary and/or nonprofessional in the mid-1990s.

Professional education's stress on specialization, as well as some realistic legal restrictions (Hatch Acts), has affected social work's participation in social action. According to a recent labor force study, in the early 1990s, the majority (57 percent) of social workers function as direct service workers. The small minority (33 percent) who practice at a "macro" level do so as managers, administrators, planners, or program evaluators. Indeed, there is little provision for operating at a level beyond or outside direct service treatment and management. Only community organization work includes as a primary area of responsibility the taking of action to improve social conditions, and unfortunately, as noted earlier, training in this orientation is no longer provided in most social work graduate programs. While advocacy may be an underpinning for BSW programs, the reality is still that content, placements, and curriculum space are devoted more to direct practice, which is where the majority of BSW-level jobs will be.

Generally, professional schools do not furnish training in the strategies and techniques fundamental to effective implementation of social reform. The option of social action simply is not offered to most social work students, and a commitment to social change and reform without the means to achieve these ends is useless. Studies have suggested that holders of BSWs and MSWs rank social policy and social legislation as among the least important areas of knowledge and skill (Biggerstaff and Kolevzon, 1980). Reeser and Epstein's (1990) survey concludes that there have been significant changes in social workers' social action attitudes and behaviors since the 1960s, with the 1980s social workers being more activist oriented, a finding contrary to the primary argument being made in this book. However, they also argue that social workers in the 1960s did not support conflict strategies for the profession. Also, not surprisingly, both groups (1960s and 1980s) strongly preferred consensus to conflict models of resolution, and view adaption to the environment rather than structural change of the environment as the profession's primary mission.

The failure of the social work profession to assume a position of leadership in the movement for social reform is inconsistent with its historical and philosophical background. The relatively nonactivist professional of the 1980s exists in stark contrast with turn-of-the-century reformers. A major characteristic of social workers of yesteryear were their efforts to direct the attention of the public toward social injustice (Meyer, 1970, p. 20), whereas a frequently noted characteristic of social work since the 1970s is its failure to speak out about the inadequacies of welfare and other programs in urban communities as well as in the rest of the United States (Ginsberg, 1970, p. 19). Clearly the profession's apparent reticence to address social problems that undermine the self-respect and morale of the individual is incongruent with its belief in the dignity and worth of human beings. How can a profession that regards the welfare of the individual or group as its primary obligation fail to speak out for social change?

It is our contention that professional social workers must oppose social injustice and, more importantly, intervene to right social wrongs. However, we repeat: It is insufficient and futile to promulgate moral imperatives without sensitizing professionals to these issues and providing them with techniques for successful intervention.

THE REFORM PERIOD

The Progressive Era (1895–1915) often is hailed as a proud moment in social work history. Early figures in social work have been lauded for their efforts on behalf of social action, and Jane Addams frequently is chosen as a model of the "involved" social worker. Caseworkers from charity organizations and settlement houses that existed in that era are heralded for having been in the vanguard of social reform. However, even though advocacy once occupied a prominent place in social work practice, and this function was highly visible early in the history of social casework, in examining the actions and interventive styles of this era in more detail, one notes that many social workers honored advocacy more with rhetoric than with practice.

Not only was the Progressive Era a prominent time for social work advocacy, these also were the years during which social work became established as an identifiable vocation. This era probably was the liveliest period of social reform and political advocacy in the history of the social work profession, as well as in the history of the United States. Thus it is not coincidental that the social work profession began with a focus on social reform. This was a direct result of the larger societal political climate at the time.

Social work during this period emerged from two separate interacting movements, both of English origin: the Charity Organization Society movement, which began in this country in the late 1870s and spread rapidly, so that by 1900 it had made its way into virtually every major American city and many smaller ones as well, and the settlement movement, which took root in the United States in the 1880s and spread just as quickly.

By 1900 both of these movements were solidly established. Although their overall goals were essentially the same (protecting individual initiative and freedom), each movement's short-range goals and methods were quite different and frequently in conflict. The Charity Organization Society movement sought to reform on an individual level the character of those who were "losers" in society, whereas the settlement movement worked to reform the social environment that made people "losers." The Charity Organization Society movement was not as oblivious to reform as this oversimplification might suggest, but social reform was never its dominant theme, nor was the idea of reforming an individual's character totally absent in the settlement movement.

Furthermore, a gap apparently existed between what was said by the Charity Organization Society's leadership and what was done by its staff and volunteers. The principles of scientific charity were never uniformly diffused or implemented. Although articles and agency records from this period contain some statements by social workers impatient to see the day when charitable relief, with all its humiliations and harrowing uncertainties, would be replaced by a fairer distribution of income and a complete system of social hygiene, education, and insurance, the society's handbook seems insidiously pervaded by nineteenth-century Darwinism. It suggests, for example, that only two possible reasons could explain why a family with a father present would be in need of assistance: Either the father is physically or mentally incapacitated, or he is handicapped by some defect of character or temperament (Lloyd, 1970; Sears, 1918).

Even during this period the social worker seemed to play more the role of facilitator or broker than of advocate. Although references to professionalization abounded in publications of the era, settlement workers were indifferent or even antagonistic to proposals for formalizing methods for helping. For this reason, their activities notwithstanding, settlement house workers did not significantly contribute to the development of social work methodology, but were more engaged in activities such as promoting factory legislation, better housing, adequate wages and working hours, arbitration of labor disputes, and providing free employment services. A passage from Jane Addams's *Twenty Years at Hull House* notes,

> We found ourselves spending many hours and efforts to secure support for deserted women, insurance for bewildered widows, damages for injured operators, furniture from the clutches of the installment store, constantly acting between the various institutions of the city and the people for whose benefits these institutions were erected. (Addams, 1940, p. 167)

Case-level advocacy was prevalent within the settlement movement. Particularly in view of its espoused objective of improving living conditions, the settlement movement epitomized the idea that a social agency should serve as an arena for the conversion of private troubles into public issues.

In summary, even during the Progressive Era reform period, case rather than class advocacy was the primary strategy of social workers. Furthermore, the translation of these skills into more formalized methodology did not materialize. Consequently, the decade of the 1920s left social work open to psychoanalytic theory and technique.

THE NEW DEAL AND BEYOND

With the New Deal era of the 1930s came another wave of political involvement by social workers. Although social action strategies were not necessarily well developed or formalized, the widespread recognition of social problems and the simultaneous identification of the public's responsibility for them provided broad opportunities for public policy intervention.

The massive social problems created by the depression encouraged the development of a coalition of spokespersons for the poor, many of whom had been apathetic or even hostile to the idea of public welfare. Consequently, during this era the social work profession became enmeshed in the national swing toward radicalism that was evident at the time in political parties.

By the 1930s, professional schools of social work provided a forum and a focus for critical thought about social service administration and the broader vistas of social welfare. However, their curricula were still somewhat disorganized and their primary emphasis was still on casework. The social work profession was not the leading faction in the nation's political-social reform movements, but a participant. Political activity was viewed by the profession as a short-term requirement for achieving its reform goals, but not as a legitimate social work method.

It was, however, during this period that Harry Hopkins, a social worker and political adviser, attained recognition as the controversial administrator of the first federal relief program in the history of the United States. His ascent from an administrator of a temporary state emergency relief fund in New York (at the time the largest state relief fund ever created) to head of the Federal Emergency Relief Administration and then of the Works Progress Administration was unprecedented.

Although unfortunately he came to symbolize the lavish use of federal funds, Hopkins contended that these thousands of projects had not only fed the hungry, clothed the needy, and sheltered the homeless, but also had enriched the economy, ultimately affecting the lives of 15 million Americans. Because of his policies and programs devoted to mobilization of human labor power, he often has been hailed as the first national conservator of human resources in the United States. There were also other social workers during this period, such as Frances Perkins and those in the Children's Bureau and the Women's Bureau, who furthered important social causes.

THE WAR ON POVERTY

From the time of the New Deal through the 1950s, social work matured as a profession. During these years, the social casework method was refined and ego psychology became its dominant approach. United community charities and councils were developed to provide an organized method of meeting community needs. World War II and economic resurgence reemphasized individual dysfunc-tioning and, consequently, micro-level interventions. Social action was not a major emphasis during this period. Its absence set the stage for the subsequent renewal of professional interest in social action, which began to increase in the 1950s, as professional social workers saw that many of the issues that concerned them could not be dealt with through individual therapeutic methods. Social workers issued calls to undertake social action against the erosion of civil liberties under McCarthyism and against the arms race, and to support the developing fight for civil rights. Demonstration projects sponsored by the federal government and by foundations in the 1950s and early 1960s, such as the Grey Areas Project and Mobilization for Youth, provided a testing ground for new directions in community programs and new social work roles.

The mid-1950s were a landmark time for social work activity. The National Association of Social Workers was formed from the merger of several professional organizations, including the Association for the Study of Community Organization. The 1954 amendments to the Housing Act of 1949 required citizen participation in the formation of urban renewal plans, a requirement that set the stage for citizen participation clauses in other federal legislation. At the same time, a militant phase of the civil rights movement in the South introduced freedom rides, sit-ins, strikes, and protest marches.

Nonetheless, social action still was not emphasized in social work education, despite its use and partial legitimization in social work practice. Only a few practitioners and educators expected social action to become a major theme in social work education. As interest in social change spread, community organization became the focal point for students, practitioners, and educators oriented toward social change. Although community organization became a recognized methodological specialization built on a social action and class advocacy model, the general social worker's role was further removed from political involvement and intervention.

In the early- to mid-1950s less than 2 percent of all students enrolled in social work programs specialized in community organization. Community organization training was concerned with social welfare organization as a method of bringing about and maintaining adjustments between social welfare needs and social welfare resources. Preparation was primarily for practice in community welfare councils.

In 1955, Murray Ross presented community organization as a process in which community cooperation and collaboration could be built around problem solving. His formulation added new dimensions to community organization theory and practice. To the role of resource coordinator, popular in community welfare organizations, was added the enabler role. This practice method stressed helping communities to establish cooperation and reach goals by providing them with information and services in an objective manner (Ross, 1955).

Social Action Models

Attempts to respond to social changes gave rise during the 1950s to three models of social action in social work: citizen social worker, agent of social change, and actionist. The first model of social action, that of citizen social worker, is the oldest of the three. It calls for the professional social worker to use the information and knowledge gained through work with individuals and groups to inform the larger society of needed programs and policies. The citizen social worker confronts the problems of civil rights, international peace, equality of opportunity, expansion of social programs, automation and mechanization, suburbanization, and the need for preventive services as a concerned citizen, not as a professional obligation.

Many social workers came to embrace this model. Noting the professional social worker's responsibility for social action, Youngdahl (1966, p. 132) states,

> First, we must have knowledge and fact, then we must derive our convictions based on these facts, this is followed by zeal to do something about them. It is not one or the other, that is, case work or social action; rather, it is taking advantage of every opportunity to be helpful to people as individuals, groups, or in society as a whole.

He goes on to say that social work, in trying to understand the individual, has made efforts to get at the causes of situations, and that our experience in dealing with numerous individuals has brought us to advocate certain social policies that will remove these causes and prevent the same thing from happening to others. This accounts for social work's broad interest in social legislation pertaining to housing, nutrition, recreation, and migrant workers, among others. However, according to this model, the primary reason social action is taken is because the social worker is an informed citizen.

The second model—agent of social change—developed in the late 1950s. Within this model, social action is defined as efforts toward purposeful change. The goal is to achieve desirable social goals utilizing well-developed and well-formulated theoretical systems as a guide to action.

This model developed new roles for the professional practitioner that emphasized active participation in an organization's political process. It suggested that social workers should be directly involved in political action and social policy formulation. These new roles were intended to produce change in institutional relations and policies via nondisruptive tactics.

Calls for more aggressive professional stances in policy formulation were extended during this period. Many theories suggested that social workers should enter the political arena and learn to deal more effectively with the community power structure.

In this model, the importance of working within agency or community structures is emphasized. The use of disruptive tactics, such as protests or strikes, is viewed as action that prevents the target system from continuing to operate as usual, and thus, is counterproductive.

The third social action model is that of the actionist. Actionists share the traditional social work concern for client groups but reject the detachment, insistence on societal sanction for the profession, and the belief that rational planning and cooperation are possible. They believe that social change, particularly for disaffiliated people or groups, can be achieved only by developing and using political, economic, or social pressure.

The actionist role is one of involvement with the client group the actionist seeks to help. The goal is to bring about desired changes based on what the client group identifies as its needs. The selection of tactics or strategies is determined by whether they will be effective in achieving the desired goal.

The social actionist operates to a great extent on the basis of general principles, value considerations, and some operational instructions deduced from practice. The social actionist role is epitomized by the work in Chicago of Saul Alinsky (not a social worker by professional training) and the People's Organization in the 1960s. The primary ideology of that organization was that "all groups are moved by self-interest, the poor and the nonpoor alike; as soon as the poor and the victimized learn to see it that way, they'll be able to get power and control their destiny" (Alinsky, 1971, p. 41).

The actionist, although not opposed to using cooperation and collaboration as strategies, has more often been identified with attempts to develop power strategies. Actionists reject as confining the professional's identification with organizations and with social sanctions, and they tend to view conflict and bargaining as the best method to bring about desired change.

What is important to actionists is the sanction of the group with which they are identified rather than the social sanction of their profession. The actionist model stresses ideological identification of social work with society's victims: the poor, the mentally ill, the unfortunate. Central to this method is the need for social work to support the attempts of the disaffiliated to develop power and fulfill their needs.

Although the preceding three models provided direction and sanction for an array of social action strategies for social workers, the first and last models are not based on a social action orientation for the social work profession as a whole. Rather, they focus on the social worker as an informed and politically active private citizen and as a member of a temporary coalition.

With the national rediscovery of poverty in the late 1950s and the packaging of an array of federal programmatic responses to "cultural deprivation" and "pockets of poverty" growing out of the 1964 Economic Opportunity Act, social work once again had the methods and social sanction to engage in social reform. Community organizing, local community needs assessments, welfare rights advocacy groups, and "maximum citizen participation" clauses in federal legislation gave increased impetus to macro-level interventive techniques. Schools of social work developed a community organizing curriculum, social workers were active in antiwar, civil rights, and welfare rights organizations, and black social workers such as Whitney Young were active in the political arena.

FEDERALISM

During the early 1970s, some of the reform ideologies and movements of the 1960s continued. Unfortunately, however, as the decade progressed and the War on Poverty programs became increasingly bureaucratized, social work practice and social work education turned their focus toward management and administrative theories and techniques, losing sight of advocacy and reform goals. As federal monies dwindled, competition for funds increased and skills in grant writing, planning, and financial accountability took on more importance.

Despite some shifts away from social action, in a 1970–71 report entitled "Social Work Education in a Period of Change," Arnulf Pins, executive director of the Council on Social Work Education, made the following comments:

> Our nation, along with the rest of the world, is facing major social problems. Large segments of our population suffer from neglect, physical and mental illness, poverty, discrimination, and racism. Government leaders, citizen groups, and all professions must give immediate attention to the solution of these social and human problems. Social work has a unique role and opportunity. Consequently, social work education

has a special responsibility and challenge, for it must prepare social work personnel with the commitment, knowledge, and skills needed: (1) to recognize and call attention to social needs, human injustices, and dysfunctional systems for service delivery; (2) to plan and bring about needed changes; and (3) to provide and administer social services in a more humane and effective way. (Pins, 1971)

Additionally, the leadership of the Council on Social Work Education testified in the early 1970s before the Senate Finance Committee, highlighting deficiencies in existing family assistance plans and seeking the inclusion of funds for labor power development in a proposed companion social services bill.

Furthermore, Daniel Thursz exhorted fellow social workers to consider one of a number of social action strategies. He debunked the common myths that have kept social workers from participating in many common social action strategies: the limits set forth by federal and state "Hatch Acts," and false notions related to the profession's expertise, status, or dignity. In addition to the social action models of the previous decades, Thursz added civil disobedience, disruption, and "watchdogging" (Thursz, 1975).

The term *civil disobedience* refers to "any act or process of public defiance of a law or police enforced by established governments authorities, insofar as the action is premeditated, understood to be illegal or of contested legality and carried out for limited public ends through carefully chosen and limited means" (Thursz, 1975). The important aspect of this definition is that civil disobedience is a method of social action to be used by persons unwilling to accept the rules of the system as a whole. Consequently, the social worker who participates in civil disobedience, regardless of the motive, must be ready to pay the price imposed by society.

Most professional social workers do not condone violence. Disruption, however, is a social action technique that should not be confused with violence. Disruption may serve to call public attention to a cause and may serve as a prelude to new negotiations and advances in the relationship between an institution and the population it is expected to serve. The emergence of the National Welfare Rights Organization is a good illustration of this.

The watchdog role that Thursz describes, also called monitoring, is a social action strategy aimed at keeping institutions and their administrators faithful to a mission or policy objective. Administrators making complex determinations to establish criteria, determine eligibility, assess capability, evaluate past performance, or set a range of permissible experimentation have the power to advance or to thwart policy goals, to benefit or not to benefit the intended service recipient, and to realize or to subvert the democratic will. According to Thursz, social workers should be watchdogs of administrative regulations to ensure their consistent adherence to policy goals.

During the 1970s social work practice and education changed in three important ways. First, with the increased emphasis on program and financial accountability, training in macro-level skills, particularly at the graduate level, was directed toward management, budgeting, and program evaluation. Second, a baccalaureate-level, professionally trained social work force emerged with the accreditation of BSW programs nationally. Third, doctoral education in social work experienced unparalleled growth.

These changes forced consideration of the differential use of social work labor power, as well as reconsideration of the core skills taught at all educational levels. The BSW core skills included linking, advocating, and brokering master's level specializations were either clinically or managerially oriented, and doctoral education focused on research and education. Consequently, as the profession entered the 1980s, social workers continued to play a minimal role in the political arena and to view political activity as the result of individual, idiosyncratic preferences rather than as a clearly stated objective of social work education and training.

However, some professional developments did occur during the 1970s that signaled the profession's reemerging awareness of political activities and processes. These included the National Association of Social Workers' (NASW) development of the Education Legislation Action Network (ELAN) and Political Action for Candidate Endorsement (PACE). These subdivisions of NASW were created to affect legislative processes. ELAN was to do this through lobbying and PACE through the election of prohuman service candidates.

The primary strategies of these two organizations were to educate social workers through the dissemination of information about both legislation and candidates, and to encourage social workers to support prohuman service issues and candidates and to oppose antihuman service issues and candidates. These efforts slowly filtered down to the state level, with parallel functions being performed by autonomous state organizations. Although both of these organizations have matured during the last decade, in 1990 they were still in the early stages of development. In fact, in some states neither of these organizations exist.

THE NEW FEDERALISM

The 1980s and the election of President Reagan began the era that, once again, shifted societal and, consequently, social service concerns toward fiscal conservatism and privatization. The expansion of public and federal programs evidenced throughout the decades of the 1960s and 1970s was blamed for increasing the federal deficit, was hearkened as the harbinger of encroaching socialism, and did not "cure" poverty or social problems in this country.

Probably most significant, long-lasting, and symbolic of this retrenchment was the Gramm-Rudman Balanced Budget and Emergency Deficit Control Act of 1985. This legislation was enacted to enforce substantial reductions in the amount of the annual deficit permitted in each of the ensuing five years, declining to zero in 1991.

While the figures were clear that the deficit had increased in less than five years by $130 billion, the reason was not largely due to expenditures in social services, but to enormous increases in military spending and to substantial reductions in federal taxes. Placing the burden of deficit reduction on domestic programs, primarily social services, was not only unreasonable, but inhumane and shortsighted.

The shortsightedness is marked by the fact that poverty, by any measure, increased by more than 27 percent in the 1980s, disproportionately affecting women, minorities, children, and the elderly. Moreover, the ranks of the working poor are considerably larger in the 1990s than in the late 1970s. Since these policies also simultaneously cut education funds, these two forms of budget reduction together have increased the problems of illiteracy, unemployment, family dissolution, homelessness, hunger, and domestic violence.

These policies have returned the focus to moving public assistance recipients off welfare roles and into employment. However, they have largely ignored another major segment of the poverty population—the working poor—and have ignored the social supports necessary to effectively move people into productive, and not marginal, employment.

Further, the expectation that the private, philanthropic arena would replace these federal and state dollars was not achieved since greater unemployment leaves fewer individuals to contribute, and more problems strain the private sector as well.

However, these issues helped to develop the establishment of Human Serve, a national organization created in 1984 that employs a grassroots empowerment strategy. It targets increased voter registration and reduction in barriers to voter registration, as well as educational outreach on selected issues. As social workers nationally became engaged in strategies to enfranchise their clients, an important, if unintended, consequence was the finding that many social workers themselves were not registered voters.

Perhaps another consequence of this reduction of federal dollars and the return of decision making to local entities has been the increased incentive within the social work profession to examine accountability strategies and to describe outcome effectiveness along with humane solutions. Further, toward the end of this decade, with the pendulum swing back to greater interest in social problems, more students enrolled in social work programs and became more politically active.

Unfortunately, the 1980s caught the profession short of social workers trained or even interested in some form of political activity, either as a professional career choice or at least as an adjunct activity to clinical practice (Witherspoon and Phillips, 1987; Wolk, 1981). It continues to be true that legislators do not have an accurate perception of who social workers are and what they do, indicating the continued necessity to educate them in order to increase social work's potential influence and impact in the future (Mathews, 1982). Social work education needs to continue its role in fostering political activism and related skills (Hull, 1987).

When President Reagan's second term ended, the same popular platforms of reduced taxation and antiwelfarist attitudes swept George Bush into office with a mandate to continue the reforms of the previous eight years. As noted earlier these were (1) to decrease social spending; (2) to build up the military; and (3) to reduce taxes. While many authors concluded that the decade ended with the welfare state intact, the damage done to the New Deal legacy may be permanent (Midgeley, 1992).

THE 1990s

Although President Bush lost his bid for reelection and the Democrats won the presidency with Bill Clinton, the Republicans took the leadership in both houses of Congress for the first time in decades and thus could attempt to continue the Reagan priorities. The success of this continuous campaign against the welfare state is, in large part, due to the fact that costs have increased and there are still problems and poverty. However, the opposing voices were few or were silent. The argument that costs have increased over time not because people have gotten lazier but because our population has increased, because competition in our industrialized and urbanized nation has increased, because social problems have changed, and perhaps, more importantly, because public responsibility has always been seen as gap filling, last minute, remedial and because prevention was never publicly funded was never made (Haynes and Mickelson, 1992).

What is important about the "Contract with America" is that it contains provisions that ensure that progress is not made; it protects and further supports the widening gap between the classes and makes individual, not societal or structural, change the cure. And, the authors contend, it has been and may continue to be implemented and effective if social workers do not increase their political action.

For example, the provision to balance the federal budget may not be a bad idea. Although some economists would argue it is a fiscally poor idea and impossible, it cannot be done through only domestic social service cuts. Increasing military spending during peace time should be questioned. The anticrime package to strengthen penalties, fund additional prison construction, and cut social spending contained in the Crime Control Act is yet another example of "individuals at fault," and it is an economically expensive choice given that institutional care versus prevention and/or outpatient care is always the most expensive alternative.

The current welfare reform proposal—the "Personal Responsibility Act"—seeks to deny benefits to poor children born to unmarried mothers younger than 18, as well as to poor children whose paternity has not been established; it would eliminate benefits for almost all legal immigrants, and would significantly reduce assistance for low income children and their families. In other words, we will "blame the victims" and further impoverish women and children, not provide women with employable skills, not provide women with young children with affordable and quality day care, and call these women lazy and immoral. It will not end the cycle of poverty.

This contract also includes a variety of proposed tax cuts for middle and upper income individuals that will not only reward the already economically advantaged, but also make little fiscal sense in a time of proposed federal budget reductions. So, if these proposals make no sense, fiscally or humanely, why have they continued to receive such support during the last 15 years and over four presidential elections?

Additionally, the decade of the 1990s may be described as the erosion of some significant human rights. With arguments and appeals to turn back Affirmative Action legislation, state referendums to deny benefits to illegal aliens, the "new education initiatives" to provide vouchers so that there can be enhanced choice to improve educational possibilities, basic human rights and basic human dignity are in jeopardy. The very values that social work has always supported and which undergirded the Social Security Act, the Medicare and Medicaid bills, the integration of neighborhoods and public schools, and opportunities and access for women and persons of color will be lost if social work voices are not raised.

While social workers and the social work profession cannot and should not be held as the only group at fault, the authors point to this as a glaring example of the unpreparedness and the unwillingness of social workers to get involved. It is true that the NASW endorsed President Clinton early, that the NASW drafted and promulgated health care legislation, and that more social workers ran for office in 1990 and won, but our contention is that it is too little, too late.

CONCLUSION

The examination of 100 years of social work history suggests that over the years the profession has used a variety of political action strategies and activities. Playing roles that range from social worker as informed citizen to active lobbyist to federal or state administrator to politician, social workers have been engaged in political activity. Whether or not it is part of their formal role or training, political action has been part of social work history and will be part of its future.

Just as Jeannette Rankin made history as the first social worker elected to Congress, there are social workers today who are making history and are part of the continuing efforts of the profession to affect change in the political arena. The following is one such social worker.

> In 1969, I was a struggling social worker with a social conscience. I had a master's degree from the University of Maryland School of Social Work (1965) in community organizing and social planning. I was busy trying to decentralize the local welfare department. Then I got a call that started me on the "road" to the U. S. Senate.
>
> A community group had learned that a highway project was going to destroy the East Baltimore neighborhood where my family settled when they first came to this country. I also knew that there was an expressway coming through the west side of Baltimore that was going to take out the first black home ownership neighborhood in Baltimore City. The road was going to take the homes of a lot of people in Baltimore's proud neighborhoods—Polish, Italian, Greek, and Black—and give them almost nothing in return. And

it threatened the most historic neighborhood in Baltimore, Fells Point, where good and solid citizens had lived and worked since before the Revolutionary War.

I got fired up. "We didn't let the British take Fells Point, we didn't let the termites take Fells Point, and we're not going to let the state roads commission take Fells Point," was what I said when I found out that their idea of community input and community participation was choosing the color of the planning grid and the kind of stone we wanted the guard rail made of.

We talked to the planners, the architects, and the politicians. We organized the neighborhoods and we challenged the cost-benefit analysis. We ran bake sales so that we could rent buses to take us to City Hall, the State House, and Washington, D.C. We put our mimeograph machine borrowed from the Holy Rosary Society up against their $5,000 audiovisual equipment, and our coalition up against their design concept team.

And today, when people talk about the wonderful, new downtown Baltimore, they are seeing a "revitalization" that began with a citizen protest movement and an organized community. Because we won the fight against the road commission, we won the fight for Baltimore's neighborhoods.

And I decided it was time to quit knocking on City Hall's doors, move inside, open them up, and let the people in. I announced my candidacy for the Baltimore City Council. Running against an established political machine, I did what I know best: grassroots organizing. Through the summer of 1971, my team and I went door to door. I knocked on 15,000 doors that summer, wore out five pairs of shoes, got mugged by fourteen Chihuahuas, and I won my seat on the city council.

In City Hall, I took my social worker's skills and made the personal political. From potholes to public education, I worked to save neighborhoods one person and one problem at a time. And at every step, I was trying to do more good for more people.

In 1976, I ran for the U.S. House of Representatives. Going back to my training, I went back to the community and that grassroots organization. And I carried the same skills and values to Washington when I won.

After ten years in the House, I ran for the U.S. Senate. After a tough primary against another sitting congressman and the sitting governor, I had a general election campaign for the history books. For the first time, both parties nominated women candidates for the U.S. Senate. Expanding my grassroots organization statewide, I ran a people-based campaign and won decisively.

In the Senate, I have achieved a number of firsts: the first Democratic woman to hold a seat not previously held by her husband, the first Polish-American to serve in both houses of Congress, the first woman to chair a subcommittee on the powerful Appropriations Committee.

Being the first, however, is not the most important thing. Although I am honored, I know there will be many more who follow in my footsteps. I worked hard to get seats on important committees, committees where I can make a real difference for people's day-to-day lives and needs.

There is one first, though, that has meant a real difference: I am the first social worker in the U.S. Senate. Now I have a caseload of four million Marylanders! And though I am practicing in a different forum, those skills and values I learned as a community organizer on the streets of Baltimore are what make me an effective leader in the corridors of Congress.

Barbara Mikulski, MSW
U.S. Senator (Maryland)

Although it was seventy years from Jeannette Rankin's election to Congress to the election of Barbara Mikulski to the U.S. Senate, there is no clearer indication that social workers are achieving a greater political influence than to see them elected and accepted to one of the nation's highest representative offices.

ASSIGNMENTS

1. Choose a period in U.S. history in which a major piece of social work legislation was passed. Identify the role of the profession or of the individual social workers, or both, in its introduction or passage.
2. Choose one notable social work activist and trace his or her educational and experiential background.

SUGGESTED READINGS

Cohen, Wilbur. 1966. "What Every Social Worker Should Know about Political Action." *Social Work* II (July): 3–11.
Davis, Allen F. 1982. "Settlement Workers in Politics, 1890-1914." In *Practical Politics: Social Work and Political Responsibility,* M. Mahaffey and J. W. Hanks (eds.), pp. 32–45. Washington, D.C.: National Association of Social Workers.
Gilbert, Neil, and Harry Specht. 1976. "Advocacy and Professional Ethics." *Social Work* 21 (July): 288–293.

REFERENCES

Addams, Jane. 1940. *Twenty Years at Hull House with Autobiographical Notes.* New York: MacMillan.
Alinsky, Saul. 1971. *Rules for Radicals.* New York: Random House.
Biggerstaff, Marilyn A., and Michael S. Kolevzon. 1980. "Differential Use of Social Work Knowledge, Skills, and Techniques by MSW, BSW, and BA Level Practitioners." *Journal of Education for Social Work* 16 (3): 67–74.
Bisno, Herbert. 1969. "How Social Will Social Work Be?" In *Perspectives on Social Welfare,* Paul E. Weinberger (ed.), pp. 304–318. Toronto: MacMillan.
Bricker-Jenkins, M., and N. Hooyman (eds.). 1986. *Not for Women Only: Social Work Practice for a Feminist Future.* Silver Springs, MD: National Association of Social Workers.

Burghardt, Steve. 1982. *The Other Side of Organizing*. Cambridge, MA: Schenkman.

Carlton, T. O., and M. Jung. 1972. "Adjustment or Change: Attitudes among Social Workers." *Social Work* 17 (6): 64-71.

Carniol, B. 1990. "Social Work and the Labor Movement." In *Social Work and Social Change in Canada*, B. Wharf (ed.). Toronto: McClelland and Stewart.

———. 1992. "Structural Social Work: Maurice Moreau's Challenge to Social Work Practice." *Journal of Progressive Human Services* 3 (1): 1-20.

Fisher, Robert, Karen S. Haynes, Jean Kantambu Latting, and William Buffum. 1994. "Empowerment-based Curriculum Design: Building a Program in Political Social Work." In *Education and Research for Empowerment Practice*, Lorrain Gutierrez and Paul Nurius (eds.). Seattle, WA: Center for Policy and Practice Research.

Fisher, Robert. 1984. *Let the People Decide: Neighborhood Organizing in America*. Boston, MA: Twayne.

Friere, P. 1973. *Education for Critical Consciousness*. New York: Seabury Press.

Ginsberg, Mitchell. 1970. "Changing Values in Social Work." In *Social Work Values in an Age of Discontent,* Katherine S. Kendall (ed.), pp. 13-34. New York: Council on Social Work Education.

Gutierrez, L., and E. Lewis. 1990. "A Feminist Perspective on Organizing with Women of Color." In *Organizing with People of Color: Changing and Emerging Communities*, J. Erlich and F. Rivera (eds.). Needham Heights, MA: Allyn and Bacon.

Gutierrez, Lorraine, and Paula Nurius (eds.). 1994. *Education and Research for Empowerment Practice.* Seattle, WA: Center for Policy and Practice Research.

Haynes, Karen S. 1996. "The Future of Political Social Work." In *Future Issues for Social Work Practice,* Paul R. Raffoul and C. Aaron McNeece (eds.). Needham Heights, MA: Allyn and Bacon.

Haynes, Karen S., and James S. Mickelson. 1985. "Social Policy: The Hidden Power Base." Presentation at the Council of Social Work Education Annual Program Meeting, Washington, D.C.

Haynes, Karen S., and James S. Mickelson. 1992. "Social Work and the Reagan Era: Challenges to the Profession." *Sociology and Social Welfare* XIX (1): 169-183.

Hull, Grafton. 1987. "Joining Together: A Faculty-Student Experience in Political Campaigning." *Journal of Social Work Education* 3 (23): 37-43.

Lavassaur, Jean M. 1984. "Jeannette Rankin: Political Social Worker." Paper presented at Political Institute, Michigan State University.

LeComte, R. 1990. "Connecting Private Troubles and Public Issues in Social Work Education." In *Social Work and Social Change in Canada*, B. Wharf (ed.). Toronto, Canada: McClelland & Steward.

Lloyd, Gary. 1970. *Charities, Settlements, and Social Work: An Inquiry into Philosophy, and Method, 1890-1915*. New Orleans: Tulane University School of Social Work.

Mathews, Gary. 1982. "Social Workers and Political Influence." *Social Service Review* 56 (4): 616-628.

Meyer, Carol. 1970. *Social Work Practice—A Response to the Urban Crisis*. New York: Free Press.

Midgeley, James. 1992. "Society, Social Policy and the Ideology of Reaganism." *The Reagan Legacy and the American Welfare State, Special Issue of the Journal of Sociology and Social Welfare* 19: 13-29.

Moreau, M. 1990. "Empowerment through Advocacy and Consciousness Raising: Implications of a Structural Approach to Social Work." *Journal of Sociology and Social Welfare* 17: 53-67.

Pins, Arnulf. 1971. *Social Work Education in a Period of Change.* New York: Council on Social Work Education.

Rees, S. 1991. *Achieving Power: Practice and Policy in Social Welfare.* North Sydney, Australia: Allen and Unwin.

Reeser, L. C., and I. Epstein. 1990. *Professionalization and Activism in Social Work: The Sixties, the Eighties and the Future.* New York: Columbia University Press.

Ross, Murray. 1955. *Community Organization.* New York: Harper & Row.

Sears, Ameba. 1918. *The Charity Visitor: A Handbook for Beginners.* Chicago: Chicago School of Civics and Philanthropy.

Thursz, Daniel. 1975. "Social Action as a Professional Responsibility and Political Participation." In *Participation in Politics,* T. R. Pennock and John W. Chapman (eds.), pp. 213–232. New York: Leibor-Atherton.

Wakefield, J. C. 1988a. "Psychology, Distributive Justice, and Social Work, Part I." *Social Service Review* 62: 187–210.

———. 1988b. "Psychology, Distributive Justice, and Social Work, Part II." *Social Service Review* 62: 353–382.

Wharf, B. (ed.). 1990. *Social Work and Social Change in Canada.* Toronto, Canada: McClelland and Stewart.

Witherspoon, Roger, and Norma Kolko Phillips. 1987. "Heightening Political Awareness in Social Work Students in the 1980s." *Journal of Social Work Education* 23 (3): 44–49.

Wolk, James. 1981. "Are Social Workers Politically Active?" *Social Work* 26 (July): 284–288.

Van DenBergh, N., and L. Cooper (eds.). 1986. *Feminist Visions for Social Work.* Silver Springs, MD: National Association of Social Workers.

Youngdahl, Benjamin E. 1966. *Social Action and Social Work.* New York: Association Press.

chapter 2

The Debate

In a democracy, where every vote and voice count, doing nothing is a political act.

Nancy Amidei*

"All social work is political." Would you find this a brash and unfounded statement or an historical truth? Are social workers agents of social change or are they agents of social control? A profession's credibility necessitates objectivity and neutrality, or does it? Although we have just described more than 100 years of social work activity that we define as political, you would likely find it a difficult leap to the above statement.

Although formalized social work practice is well over 100 years old in the United States, these debates flare up and then quiet down, but professional consensus has never yet been achieved. This debate is still current and extremely critical in our profession as we approach the twenty-first century.

The first half of the 1990s has, in the authors' opinion, heightened the need for political social work practice. The continued attack that government intervention is the problem, rather than the solution, that the marketplace can and will address our growing economic and social problems, that when only 26 percent of the electorate vote, theirs represents the mandate for these changes, will, if unchallenged by the social work profession, leave us with an impossible task and in an undefensible posture in the future.

While the attributes of professionalism that we ascribed to 80 years ago may, to some, support an apolitical posture, the very elements of our profession compel us to enter the political arena. Those elements that Flexner originally

---

* Nancy Amidei is a senior lecturer at the University of Washington School of Social Work.

described as essential attributes of a profession and to which social work has directed its attention for decades—(1) a scientific knowledge base, (2) autonomous practice, (3) a code of ethics, (4) a professional association, and (5) public sanction (Flexner, 1915)—do not necessarily prescribe an apolitical posture. In fact, it is indeed possible to describe each as mandating political action. For example, if the attribute of a scientific knowledge base includes and refers to standards for curriculum content, then social work within the Council on Social Work Education Accreditation Standards requires political knowledge and skills. In fact, since the 1982 CSWE Curriculum Policy Statement this has been true. The 1994 Curriculum Policy Statement describes the purpose of social work as:

> The pursuit of policies, services, resources, and programs through organizational or administrative advocacy and social or political action, to empower groups at risk and to promote social and economic justice. (CSWE, 1994, p. 97)

And, further, in the definition of social welfare policy and services mandates that

> Students must be taught to analyze current social policy within the context of historical and contemporary factors that shape policy. Content must be presented about the political and organizational processes used to influence policy, the process of policy formulation, and the frameworks for analyzing social policies in the light of the principles of social and economic justice. (CSWE, 1994, p. 102)

Autonomous practice, instead of being defined only as independent (private) practice should be regarded as self-sufficient and self-reliant. Autonomous practice need not, should not, describe the context of practice—solo and independent, group, agency—but the practice competencies and professional judgments that are sanctioned. The NASW Code of Ethics has undergone several significant revisions since it was originally adopted in 1960. The recent code (1980) notes that social work's primary obligation is "the welfare of the individual or group served, which includes action to improve social conditions. Therefore, a commitment to this code is a commitment to social action." In fact, the proposed Code of Ethics to be voted on in August 1996 includes even stronger prescriptive language regarding political action:

> "[S]ocial workers should engage in social and political action that seeks to ensure that all persons have equal access to the resources, employment, services and opportunities that they require in order to meet their basic human needs and to develop fully. Social workers should be aware of the impact of the political arena on practice and should advocate for changes in policy and legislation to improve social conditions in order to meet basic human needs and promote social justice." (*NASW News,* 1996)

The attribute of a professional association has been met for decades and does not include the purposes of the association except to further its development. Thus, it cannot be used to justify an apolitical stance. In fact, the authors would argue that if the professional association does not promote social action, it may retard that development. Also, it is quite evident in the context of the last several decades that the "real" professions of medicine and law have quite assertively entered the political arena through the use of political action committees, paid lobbyists, and the proposals of national and state legislation that would further the profession.

And the question for public sanction has been met via a number of indicators. The strategies that have absorbed our professional energy since the early 1970s have been the quest for legal regulation of social work practice. Now that all states have some form of legal regulation, this attribute, too, has been met. However, public sanction for our "unloved profession" may also be interpreted to mean public recognition and status. To the extent that some might argue that we have not achieved this yet, the authors would counter that it may be due to the absence of our political advocacy. If we permit, through the absence of our voice, the blame for a failed welfare system to fall on the profession of social work, then we may be contributing to the public's lack of regard for us.

Perhaps, additionally, in our quest to be like other professions, such as medicine, we lost track of those attributes of social work that distinguish it from other professions. Some of these distinguishing elements are (1) a systems approach that includes examination of the environment as a critical factor both in causing as well as in solving individual and social problems, (2) the importance of history in shaping the lives of people and of communities, (3) a respect for people, their strengths, and their problem-solving capacities, and (4) a belief in the inevitability and desirability of change (Reisch, 1995). Why has our profession focused on our similarities with other professions rather than on our uniqueness, thus perhaps minimizing these unique characteristics?

SOME PERSPECTIVES

Social work historically, as well as presently, depends upon heuristic frameworks that include interventions which range from consciousness raising to reallocation of resources, which are concerned with the attainment of basic needs as well as self-actualization, and which direct strategies toward individual as well as community and societal needs. Given the breadth of these targets of intervention that are derived from the goals of our profession, the authors have contended that political social work practice legitimizes social work's role in policy formulation as well as in the policy implementation stage (Haynes, 1996).

Probably nowhere is this debate as well articulated as in the Abramovitz/ Bardill debate (Abramovitz and Bardill, 1993). While both agree that the profession's mission is to "train students to become experts in individual and social change," both agree that the internal arguments between personal treatment versus social reform (micro/macro) are debilitating and divisive, that the "systems perspective" is a unique and useful one to maintain. However, they remain opponents because they appear to hold that there is a dichotomization and mutual exclusivity of direction and purpose of these two perspectives, that it is essential to accomplish only one of these, but not both, because in attempting both, both will be diminished. And the argument is waged that there is an ideological schism because social change ideology might mean a radical and partisan political basis.

It seems to be increasingly difficult to retain a professional posture of political neutrality and objectivity when the political agenda is to wage war with the profession of social work and with our clients. The choices, and they are the political choices, are choices central to the lives of our clients, and as such are choices about which the profession of social work ought to have a stake.

In chapter 1 we discussed the erosion of the welfare state and the urgency and centrality of political action. We would further note that midway through the 1990s, there appears to be a trend toward political activism, but that does not mean that the issue can be discarded. While there are more social workers working in politically related employment, and there are increases in the number of social workers running for political office, it is encouraging that political advocacy is being taught in more schools of social work, and that some agencies are beginning to emerge whose prime mission is to be very politically active in order to bring much needed policy changes for clients. But whatever measures of progress we might optimistically argue, there is yet no professional consensus. Given that we had to argue that there would be any demand for the first edition of this book in 1986, the request for the third edition is being considered a testimony to the increased attention to this important component of the profession.

However, others must keep the debate alive until political social work, by whatever terminology, is firmly entrenched in social work education and in social work practice. Until that time, the authors welcome the debate and even the controversy, for it is what will assure a socially relevant and credible profession. Given that debates serve this important purpose, the recently controversial position explicated by Harry Specht and Mark Courtney (1994) in *Unfaithful Angels* should be acknowledged as important in continuing the dialogue. Indeed, the book raised the level of the debate within the profession several decibels and many believe it was a healthy debate.

WHEN KAREN MET HARRY: *UNFAITHFUL ANGELS* DISPUTED

The following is the text from a speech given by Karen Haynes. It was to have been the keynote speech given by Dr. Harry Specht at the Texas National Association of Social Workers Conference in November 1994. However, Dr. Specht became ill. Dr. Karen Haynes, coauthor of this book, was asked to step in. While she agreed to present Dr. Specht's remarks, she did so only with the notion that she could debate them. All of Dr. Specht's words are those written by him for the intended speech.

Karen Frames the Debate

"Well, if you think that you're disappointed, so am I. Not only did I want to listen to Harry, with his acerbic humor, thought provoking message, and lengthy perspective on our history, but I had hoped to ask provocative questions. When I received the call asking if I could replace Harry, I knew that no one could replace Harry; be Harry; or dare to speak for Harry. But, I thought, maybe I could still have the conversation with Harry that I had wanted to have.

"Perhaps like many of you in the audience, I met Harry more than two decades ago through his written communications—articles, the initial edition of the infamous Gilbert and Specht Dimensions of Social Welfare Policy (Gilbert and Specht, 1986). Perhaps he was a bit less controversial 25 years ago, but I found his work interesting, as I was also concerned about the big picture and the long view.

"It was probably ten years later before I heard Harry give a speech at the Council on Social Work Education meetings, and I was intrigued by his quick wit and his enjoyment of controversy. You couldn't not react to what Harry said. Then I met him in closer proximity when I became a new dean. And in 1985 when I became a new dean, Harry was a senior dean, and not just any senior-dean, but Berkeley's dean. And he was saying outrageous things in deans' meetings.

"And then he and Mark Courtney published *Unfaithful Angels* and I was not surprised that it raised considerable controversy within the profession. I knew that was Harry's intent . . . to keep the debate alive. I read *Unfaithful Angels* and, not surprisingly, there was much in his perspective with which I heartily agreed. There were, however, a number of points of departure. Someday, I thought, I shall share these thoughts with Harry.

"So today, I have constructed a conversation with Harry about *Unfaithful Angels*. Harry's remarks are his own."

Harry Begins

"The profession of social work is somewhat more than 100 years old. In the 1920s it took a wrong turn in the direction of modern psychiatry and psycho-analysis. In the 70-plus intervening years, it has not veered from that path. Today, the profession is about to be engulfed by the psychotherapy industry. In 1991, 57 percent of the members of the National Association of Social Workers were engaged in for-profit practice doing psychotherapy at least part of their work week. That does not include another large proportion of social workers employed by public and nonprofit social agencies who use psychotherapy as their major mode of intervention. I am not alone in perceiving that our profession is fast being converted to a major battalion in the psychotherapeutic armies. In August 1993, the Associated Press released a story about the NASW Delegate Assembly, referring to NASW as 'a professional association of psychotherapists.' The group, they said, 'is made up of professional psychotherapists who work in a broad range of social work jobs. . . . Social workers provide psychotherapy and counseling. . . . Some 145,000 social workers are members of the group.'"

Karen Interrupts

"Harry, my version of history, not to mention causality, differs from yours. First, and this is my women's thing, Harry, is that if our profession significantly veered from its historical path in the 1920s it was because men convinced us what the tenets of professionalism were. We have, since our profession's beginning, allowed and even encouraged men to determine whether we are a profession at all. First Flexner in 1915, Greenwood, and Etzioni later, determined that social work wasn't and maybe never would be a profession and we have continued to believe that and have allowed it to push our national education and practice agendas for almost eighty years.

"Secondly, Harry, you seem to ignore the waves and cycles of social reform—the 1930s, 1960s, and perhaps, the 1990s? You seem to overlook the entrance of a significant group of professionals—the BSWs—who represent almost as large a cadre of students and practitioners as MSWs.

"And, thirdly, if we're looking at the same data set, only 11 percent of NASW members were engaged full time in private practice and 32 percent are not in direct practice at all. And, finally, I don't equate direct practice with psychotherapy."

Harry

"May I continue, Karen?

"Now before I go on, I want to emphasize that there is no single set of people responsible for the profession's drift into psychotherapy and private practice. The organized profession has endorsed it, the schools of social work have taught it, many social agencies have taken psychotherapy as their major intervention mode of practice, and community has always given only unwilling support to social work and public services in contrast to the great love Americans have for psychotherapy of all shades and varieties. It is for that reason that I addressed my book to a broad audience. The current state of social work and the social services is a community problem. One part of the problem is social work's abandonment of its mission; the other part is the deep and sincere belief the Americans have the utility and efficacy of psychotherapy. Let me speak to the latter problem first.

"Psychotherapy is a big enterprise. According to a study by the National Institute of Mental Health, 1990 spending on mental health care in the United States was $67 billion, approximately 10 percent of all spending on health care. Approximately $27 billion (40 percent) of these expenditures was for care of the hospitalized mentally ill. The remaining $40 billion was spent on outpatient care for a wide range of disorders, including depression, mania, panic attack, codependency, addictions, and dysthymia.

"A significant proportion of outpatient care is for people with mild kinds of mental health problems. This group can be characterized as 'the worried well'; 20- to 40-year-old professionals, primarily Caucasians, who are unfulfilled and searching for meaning in their lives and for ways to increase their self-esteem. While the exact amount of outpatient care devoted to this group is unknown, more than 20 percent of patients seen in community mental health centers were classified as suffering from 'social maladjustment,' 'no mental disorder,' and 'deferred diagnosis, nonspecific condition.' Adding cases classified as 'neuroses and personality disorders' brings the treatment of milder types of mental health problems up to more than 40 percent of community mental health center caseloads. Of course, private practitioners serve an even smaller proportion of chronically and severely mentally ill people than community mental health centers. The point is that if only 40 percent of outpatient care is devoted to treatment of the worried well, the bill comes to a whopping $16 billion annually, and that doesn't include the costs of educating the huge squadrons of psychotherapists, social workers, marriage and family counselors, and physicians who provide psychotherapy.

"Findings of the National Institute of Mental Health's Epidemiologic Catchment Area program (ECA) indicate that 44.7 million people (28 percent of the U.S. adult population) have some sort of mental/addictive disorder. (The ECA program is the largest and most comprehensive study ever done on the state of Americans' mental health.) The ECA figures are modest compared to some others. For example, Melody Beattle, a national authority on the problem of 'codependency,' says that 96 percent of all Americans suffer from it. But even the conservative ECA figures should cause us to wonder whether or not the mental health experts have created, at least in part, a phantom epidemic that society is attempting to eliminate at great cost and with decreasing success.

"The evidence for the efficacy of psychotherapeutic interventions to deal with these problems is not persuasive. Study after study indicates that there is little difference in the success rates achieved by one or another of many forms of psychotherapy ranging from psychoanalysis to humanistic psychology, gestalt therapy, rolfing, channeling, and primal screaming, to name only a few. And there appears to be little difference between success rates attained from treatments given by professionals compared to those given by nonprofessionals."

Karen

"But Harry, do we have valid and reliable measures of any kind of social work intervention, even today? Our 'welfare' programs have been repeatedly criticized for their ineffectiveness in eliminating poverty. Our public child welfare programs have measured increases in reported child abuse and neglect since the initiation of state's legislation in the 1970s, a finding which might be contradictory to a measure of success."

Harry, a Bit More Firmly, Notes

"But, the public doesn't enjoy welfare benefits or parenting classes.

"There is, though, clear evidence that patients like and enjoy psychotherapy, and that they like and enjoy their psychotherapists. The empathetic psychotherapist who gives you his/her undivided and sincere attention (for anywhere from $75 to $250 for 50 minutes) offers a sympathetic ear to what our British cousins call the 'chattering classes.' If you're feeling bad, they can help you recognize that this is because you have been abused, maltreated, misunderstood—generally victimized in any number of ways—by parents, spouse, boss, or teacher. The therapists are on your side for every good reason, you or your insurance companies are paying them a lot. They can persuade people that they have psychological problems because the psychotherapeutic process is designed to make the patient emotionally dependent on and eager to please the psychotherapist.

"Worst of all, psychotherapy is an essentially individualistic means of problem solving that has become the choice intervention for dealing with such social problems as alienation, loneliness, child abuse, economic dependency, and violence. But these are community problems and it is time to devote resources to enlisting the community in solving them. The fact that many people like and enjoy psychotherapy is no more of a reason to cover these treatments by public funds or insurance benefits than to cover massages or attending the symphony in order to relax. If the resources we now spend on radical individualistic treatments were devoted to development of social care, society would benefit enormously. Healthy people grow and develop in healthy communities, not in psychotherapists' offices. I believe, therefore, that it is time for Americans to consider a new approach in delivering social services to communities."

Karen

"Well, I certainly can't disagree with your basic premise—the growth in incidence, severity, and criticality of societal problems is frightening and can't entirely be solved by treating individuals. And, on this point we certainly agree that our profession is at least partly at fault.

"Given how dramatic these changes have been and how desperate troubles have become, it is amazing that it has taken us so long to speak out. I believe our silence during much of the last decade may have been viewed as consent. Our de-emphasizing of cause and focusing on function; our fixation on methods and techniques rather than on social goals, and our 'buy in' to the privatization model, which has created higher caseloads, volunteers functioning in professional roles, and marketplace models for low income and marginalized families, has helped contribute to the societal malaise. And for those of us who have not always kept silent, we have sometimes been rebuffed by our own colleagues. When I have spoken out repeatedly in the past for macro-level advocacy, I have been questioned about my political interests, I have been confronted about my professionalism, and it has been presumed that I devalue clinical skills and clinical practice. I not only get angry, I get confused. My vision of good social work practice has always been, and I don't doubt, will always be, one of advocacy with, and on behalf of, our clients toward the enhancement of individual social functioning and community empowerment. Isn't that your vision, Harry? I have believed, for as long as I can remember, that direct interpersonal involvement with people, families, and small groups who are in pain is essential. I equally strongly believe that political intervention and macro solutions might effectively achieve permanent goals that will also alleviate that pain and suffering.

"Yes, I still hear from some students and from some community practitioners the question, 'What does policy and political action have to do with what I'll be practicing?' In other words, 'What does private troubles have to do with public issues?'

"We must define private troubles as public issues right now. And you and I would agree, Harry, that it must be us not them who define those public issues.

"Does it make any sense for clinicians to spend hundreds of hours to keep a family together, only to watch public policy rip them apart again? Is it reasonable to work to empower parents to address the issues facing them, and then leave them with outdated and punitive policies that may destroy them? If we are willing to devote everything it takes to keep a family functioning and intact, then we must also be willing to turn our efforts to advocacy in the political arena.

"We must simultaneously pull our clients out of the destructive river *and* go upstream to prevent their being pushed in.

"And, before you remind me, yes, it is true that I have been dismayed that two-thirds of the legislative priorities of state chapters involved licensure or third-party payments.

"But I balance that anger with a great deal of pride that there are so many of us who devote professional lifetimes to HIV-infected persons, to victims of violence, to securing basic services for people—not the 'worried, well, or wealthy,' but the stigmatized, forgotten, and oppressed—that there are many who remained 'faithful' to our mission and who are uplifting spokespersons for us all.

"But, are we doing enough? Have we veered a bit from that mission? Yes!"

Harry

"Here we most assuredly agree, Karen. So, how did this happen? I believe it has to do with our mission. In truth, the mission of the profession has never been very clear in this country. Also in truth, the profession and social work education have never embraced the publicly supported social services as the major institutional area of social work as is the case, for example, in the United Kingdom, Canada, and Australia. To the extent that it is an area for social work jobs in the United States, it has been largely relegated to BSWs. This is unfortunate for many reasons: the public social services meet the needs of the poorest and most oppressed people in society; the public social services represent the most refined expression of the community's desire to help those in need; and, equally important, the public social services represent a much needed, powerful, significant, and natural constituency for our profession. There are not many powerful and significant people around who are ready to speak up for social work, and I believe the profession missed the boat on public social services. (I'll come back to this point later on.)

"Both Jane Addams and Mary Richmond began their careers in social work (in 1888 and 1889) with a much higher degree of clarity about their objectives than that which pertains in the profession 30 years later. They both began their work with a kind of missionary zeal. Their goal was to uplift the downtrodden. They were both guided by a Victorian morality and a desire for social justice. When you read their earliest works—Jane Addams's, *Democracy and Social Ethics* (1905) and Mary Richmond's, *The Good Neighbor in the Modern City* (1907)—you can hardly tell them apart. Here is an excerpt from one of them:

> Certain it is that no sufficient study has been made of the child who enters into industrial life early and stays there permanently, to give him some offset to its monotony and dullness, some historic significance of the part he is taking in the life of the community.

"And here in an excerpt from the other:

> I have said that the city might be made a much safer and more attractive place for children to grow up in. What might each one do to bring this about?
>
> In the first place, we might, instead of talking so persistently about the importance of keeping them off the streets, talk much more about the importance of making the streets cleaner places, in every sense, for the children to run about it. City children must be out of doors often if they are to be kept healthy, and the city's out-of-doors should be well enough policed, lighted, cleaned, and protected from illicit traffics of all sorts to be a fit place for children to spend part of each day.

"The first example is from Jane Addams, and the second is from Mary Richmond. You can see in these brief quotations the altruism and concern for the community betterment and social reform that they shared.

"Two great institutions grew up around these women in a relatively short period of time: the Charity Organization Societies (COS) around Mary Richmond and the Settlement Houses around Jane Addams. In that short period Richmond developed the idea of a 'social investigation' of the supplicants who came to the COS, and she described the procedure for a social investigation in great detail in her famous book, *Social Diagnostic.* She called what she did 'social treatment' and it later came to be called 'social casework.' Richmond had a deeply held belief that if you got all of the information about a person, the solution to his/her problem would become evident.

"Later on, Richmond came to be disappointed with the results of 'social diagnosis.' There didn't seem to be anywhere to go after the investigation. This was especially disappointing to Richmond and her colleagues because of Dr. Abraham Flexner's famous 1915 paper, 'Is Social Work a Profession?' Flexner answered his question with a resounding no; his primary reason for saying nay was that social work lacked a theoretical base. Well, in short order a set of theories arrived: first, theories of modern psychiatry in the 1920s and, second, psychoanalytic theory in the 1930s. These theories were interesting, compelling, gripping, and available for adoption. They were the wrong theories for social work, but, to put it simply, there was nothing better available. Mary Richmond was not happy about that. She was reaching for a different, more socially oriented set of theories. But the kind of theory she would have liked didn't start developing until the 1940s. These are the theories of social psychology. There is in social psychology a powerful set of theories for working with persons in the social environment: Examples are social exchange theory, symbolic interaction, attribution theory, and social network analysis. Social psychology's body of knowledge has been developing for over 50 years. It is quite substantial and it has been, for the most part, ignored by social work practitioners and educators.

"And what became of Jane Addams's perspective? Her view of social services was very close to the notion of community-based social care that I discuss in great detail in my book (*Unfaithful Angels*). But the settlements are largely out of business. Why did the form not became institutionalized in the United States? There are several reasons. First, Jane Addams, like Mary Richmond, did not believe in programs financed by governments. She largely ignored the New Deal programs. But the kinds of programs we need to serve American communities require public support along with volunteerism.

"Second, Jane Addams's views about professionalism differed considerably from Mary Richmond's. She was very cool toward professional education. The failure to build a professionalized workforce reduced the possibility of institutionalizing the social function of the settlements.

"Third, the settlement house arrangement of Jane Addams's day was based on very strong social class distinctions: middle-class settlement workers ministering to poor and working-class people. As the settlement house users assimilated, they moved up the social class scale and began to perceive of the settlement workers as patronizing and the settlement as a place for poor people.

"Fourth, the settlements had their greatest successes with immigrant communities that had a strong communal orientation and that were upwardly mobile. That was the Jews, Greeks, and Italians. The settlements had less success with the immigrant and in-migrant populations that replaced the groups originally served by the settlements, such as the Puerto Ricans and African Americans.

"Finally, there is the powerful force of American individualism. We are the most individualistic people on earth. We are a young nation and the sense of 'us' and 'them' pervades our thinking about our neighbors. (And, as we all know, the Reagan/Bush administrations served to undermine considerably whatever fragile and small sense of community Americans have.)"

Karen

"Well, Harry, I've been quiet for a while now, but I must interrupt. Let me see if I can keep my points straight.

"First, relative to public social services being 'relegated to BSWs'—one can look at that from a different perspective—that BSWs are educated to do generalist social work practice, which is congruent, in my view, to roles within many public social services. Also, still on this point, your language that 'public social services represent the most refined expression of a community's desire to help those in need' if true is a terrible indictment of community caring given the per capita expenditures for public social services in many states.

"Secondly, what happened to Mary Richmond's and Jane Addams's influence on our profession? Well, another take is that it's a women's issue again. You know, because you wrote it in your book, that both Addams and Richmond lost the 1923 election for president of the National Conference of Charities and Corrections, and it took that conference 37 years to elect a woman president and, when they did, it was Jane Addams who by then had won the Nobel Peace Prize.

"I'm not laying blame on any one single group either, but a theoretical base was not the only criteria that Flexner described—autonomous practice was another. Why did we allow a predominantly female profession to be so directed by a male medical model of practice?"

Harry

"I probably shouldn't respond to that, so let me turn now to our part of this century, I believe we must be concerned about the profession's drift toward psychotherapy, and especially about the increasing number of social workers engaging in the private practice of psychotherapy. Increasingly, over the last 20 years, both schools and the profession have become disengaged from those agencies serving the poorest and neediest members of society: the publicly supported social services. Under Presidents Reagan and Bush, federal social welfare programs suffered budget freezes and cuts. As jobs in government disappeared and working conditions worsened, even more social workers left public service for private practice."

Karen

"Harry, it's really never been clear to me that professionally educated social workers were ever in the public sector in large numbers, so I've always been a bit perplexed by the notion that we've abandoned that practice setting.

"But I'm willing to concede that those settings have not been appealing to many professionals—but let's not blame the victims. Caseloads are unconscionable, liability and public scrutiny are high, rewards are low, and the congruence with our mission of change and prevention is almost nonexistent.

"But have we focused our collective efforts to change these institutions and their practices? Only lately, and you, Harry, and your California colleagues have been a national exemplar."

Harry

"Thanks, Karen, but I see that the social work profession and social work education over these last 50 years has become increasingly engaged in a triple misalliance, the elements of which are science and empiricism in professional education, psychotherapy, and private practice. Correspondingly, we have failed to embrace our most natural constituency which consists of the professionals, administrators, and users of publicly supported social services."

Karen

"Unfortunately, I agree Harry that social work education bears some of the blame. The recent debate by Abramovitz and Bardill (1993) in the *Journal of Social Work Education* about the place of social change in social work curriculums clearly indicates that we remain divided."

Harry

"Karen, can I get back to my point?

"The twentieth century has given rise to a great new institution—the welfare state. It is a significant institution in modern society. However, social work has never perceived of the welfare state as its major institutional arena. Instead, the profession and social work education have responded to any and all demands made upon it for casework, group work, psychotherapy, group therapy, behavior modification, advocacy, planning, management, and other functions, fads, and fancies under public, voluntary, and for-profit auspices. At times, the profession must appear to outsiders to be a gigantic fuddle factory without a core. Frequently, social workers appear to be in competition with flocks of other professionals (e.g., psychologists, MFCCs, and physicians) to provide psychotherapeutic services that are of dubious social value to a population that is affluent. In that respect, social work as a profession does not have the integrity of some other professions because it lacks a clear institutional mission."

Karen

"Oh, Harry, I can't keep still any longer. I am baffled by the use of the word *integrity* with respect to other professions; to the notion that they have not followed leads and funding streams. Perhaps life is different in Berkeley, but I am hard pressed to see more of a central mission, or more integrity, in the professions of law and medicine than in social work today. In fact, I would vehemently argue that we in social work may have remained more steadfast than others about how we can help those in pain.

"Enough said . . ."

Harry

"Well, Karen, I am also concerned that social work's hard-won legitimacy in the university and the community will erode as the profession is less and less able to demonstrate that it has a significant service mission because universities are becoming more and more concerned with demonstrating their social relevance, and the community will give even less support than it does now to a social work profession that does not carry out a significant social function. This was pointed up very sharply to me in a review of my book by Jan S. Efrau (1994) in *Networker.* Efrau writes as follows:

> What may be needed is a new profession or calling that fills the void social work has left behind. It need not be connected with mental health, and its methods might have to be invented from scratch, the way Mary Richmond and Jane Addams carved out a model for social work 100 years ago. A number of years back, community psychology took a stab at such a project, but it failed miserably. This was partly due to a rapid change in the political climate, but it was also because of unclear goals, inadequate theory, and divided loyalties—it tried to be an amalgam of psychology, sociology, and political action, and it wasn't very good in any of those departments. Perhaps the next social reform attempt will be more successful. However, one thing seems painfully clear: the vitality needed for such a venture will not come from recruiting contemporary social workers to return to the fold.

"That is a rather harsh assessment of our profession's prospects for restoring a significant mission for ourselves. I hope Efrau is wrong."

Karen

"Harry, I believe he is wrong. I, too, have despaired that our profession may not always appear to see the big picture, to intervene in the public debates, to sit at the policy table.

"I was furious a decade ago when publisher after publisher refused *Affecting Change* because there were no social work courses in which political advocacy existed. I was dismayed 15 years ago in Indiana when the moral majority chose Dan Quayle to defeat Birch Bayh, Indiana's 18-year democratic prohuman service senator, and social workers weren't already positioned to fight this.

"I was dumbfounded in 1984 when NASW nationally refused to help me collect data about social workers in state and federally elected and appointed positions. I was surprised to hear, given that I began Indiana's PAC in 1979, that Connecticut was just now beginning one.

"But, Harry, times are changing . . ."

Harry

"Karen, that's what I'd like to talk about now before we're out of time.

"It is now time for social work to move on to the next phase of its connection to the community. The direction of the move must be outward to the systems of service that are directed at meeting the needs of the poor.

"A move in that direction is not a bad idea politically. As I said earlier, there is not, today, any significant constituency to speak in support of social work. The psychotherapy lobbies will not carry us over the long haul. Insurance companies and government are increasingly becoming disenchanted with the results of these interventions, and the competition from psychologists, physicians, MFCCs, and others is fierce. But there is no other profession that can match social work's capacity to be the major workforce in a welfare state that is committed to the provision of social care. The public services are huge agencies that manage enormous resources. The administrators of these agencies are well connected to legislators and other elected and appointed officials. The opportunities to do, and to fund, significant, relevant, and interesting practices, programs, and research on social programs are enormous if one tries to imagine an ideal kind of political, organizational, and economic support system for social services.

"If we, as a country, are to solve our major social problems, we must focus our efforts on the primary source of those problems—on the community, or perhaps more correctly, on the absence of community in American lives. To develop healthy communities we must build community systems of social care that will eradicate highly fragmented social services, education, child care, public health, recreation, job training and development, and criminal justice arrangements. The major objective of such a system will be to help Americans learn to live with, care for, and love one another. That is a very tall order. But it is a mission worthy of and appropriate for our profession."

Karen

"See, Harry, we do agree. The mission of this profession is, and always has been, to heal individual pain and create or maintain a just society. Jeannette Rankin, the first woman and the first social worker installed in Congress, in 1917, saw that vision and that connection.

"Today Senator Barbara Mikulski and Representatives Ed Towns and Ron Dellums share and operationalize that vision. And at least 165 social workers in elected office nationally do too.

"And, Harry, one of the most privatized and entrepreneurial cities in the United States—Houston, Texas—has a political social work concentration; the School of Social Work does not teach 'psychotherapy' as mainstream practice, but 'empowerment,' and that city has a multitude of community practitioners who engage in change efforts as part of their paid employment or in their volunteer time, and many of them are in direct practice."

Harry

"Well Karen, that's part of what I was going to say. . . .

"Fortunately, we have a new national administration that does believe in building community. Whether they will find the resources to fund it and can muster the political support for it remains to be seen. But there is the potential and the hope for a new day. Maybe we can build a twenty-first century system of community-based social care.

"In the meantime, I have three recommendations we can work on:

1. The profession and social work education must make a major commitment to build the professionalism of the public social services.
2. We must abandon clinical psychotherapeutic practice and begin to replace it with adult education, community work, and group work.
3. We must reform social work education. Education for psychotherapy must be replaced by education in law, community work, group work, and adult education.

"So, you see, we have a great deal to do."

Karen

"Well, Harry, I agree with professionalizing the public social services and reforming parts of social work education. I would not suggest the abandonment of clinical practice, nor do I see it as synonymous with psychotherapy.

"But, Harry, before we end our conversation, I'd like to just say thanks.

"Thanks for not backing away from controversy, for it is necessary to our professional growth and integrity. Thanks for feeling so strongly about our mission regarding society's most difficult problems and about our profession's commitment to offer solutions. And, thanks for being so angry that we may be veering too far off, that we may become too complacent, that we may forget our historical roots."

CONCLUSION

This book is not only intended to keep the debate alive, to clearly present arguments that "all social work is political," but to provide useful skills to practice political social work. On the eve of the twenty-first century the authors hope to continue to persuade colleagues and students that social work skills are extremely effective in the political arena and that political action is compatible with social work values.

To act to right social wrongs, to work to increase diversity and reduce discrimination, to expand choice and opportunity are the goals of social work. If and when these goals lead us to the political arena, we must follow them there.

ASSIGNMENTS

1. Review the recent social work literature and provide two illustrations of this debate continued.
2. Given this debate and the current political climate, make three recommendations to the professional association for policy endorsement.

SUGGESTED READINGS

Abramovitz, Mimi, and D. Ray Bardill. 1993. "Should all Social Work Students be Educated for Social Change?" *Journal of Social Work Education* 29 (1): 6-18.
Specht, Harry, and Mark Courtney. 1994. *Unfaithful Angels.* New York: Free Press.

REFERENCES

Abramovitz, Mimi, and D. Ray Bardill. 1993. "Should all Social Work Students be Educated for Social Change?" *Journal of Social Work Education* 29 (1): 6-18.
CSWE. 1994. Council on Social Work Education Curriculum Policy Statement. Alexandria, VA: Council of Social Work Education.
Efrau, Jan S. 1994. *Networker.*
Flexner, Abraham. 1915. "Is Social Work a Profession?" In *Proceedings of the National Conference of Charities and Corrections*, pp. 576-590. Chicago, IL: National Conference of Charities and Corrections.
Gilbert, Neil, and Harry Specht. 1986. *Dimensions of Social Welfare Policy,* 2nd ed. Englewood Cliffs, NJ: Prentice Hall.
Haynes, Karen. 1996. "The Future of Political Social Work." In *Future Issues for Social Work Practice,* Paul R. Raffoul and C. Aaron McNeece (eds.), pp. 266-275. Needham Heights, MA: Allyn and Bacon.
NASW News. "Revision of the Code of Ethics," January 1996, pp. 19-22.
Reisch, Michael. 1995. "It's Time to Step up to the Plate: Political Action and the Right-Wing Agenda." *Social Work Education Reporter* 43 (2): 6-9.
Specht, Harry, and Mark Courtney. 1994. *Unfaithful Angels.* New York: Free Press.

chapter **3**

Social Work Values versus Politics

> *A social worker brings to the political process something that's unique, that no one else has. Anyone else can learn how to play games, you know power games. Anybody else can learn how to negotiate. Anybody can learn how to do the power manipulations. Those are techniques and skills that can be learned fairly easy. What the social worker brings is a value system that, if implemented, along with the skills, makes the difference.*
>
> *Maryann Mahaffey*

Policy—whether legislative, executive, or judicial in origin—may be defined as the operationalization or the compromise of a set of values, or both. Values are conceptions of what is desirable that influence the choice of action.

The social work profession, though a field resplendent with values, has, ironically, generally avoided debates over social policy, explaining its apolitical posture by pointing to its "values." The profession has denied that its refusal to politically intervene is, indeed, a political decision. Just as a clinician, after collecting data, may make a decision not to treat a client, so may a politically active social worker make a decision not to oppose a bill or not to support a candidate. If "no treatment" occurs through inattention or neglect, the individual or societal consequences can be dramatic and damaging, regardless of whether this occurs on a clinical or political level.

The centrality of values to the origins and subsequent development of the social work profession preceded any concern with the development of theory or methodology. In fact, one of the most critical arguments in defense of professionalism in social work practice has been that the development of an independent set of norms, specialized helping skills, and humanitarian values enables social service work to remain autonomous, a power with the potential to offset narrow and repressive sectarian political interests.

Critics have argued that professionalism in social work has reactionary consequences. By supporting present societal values it may unwittingly strengthen society's repressive characteristics in the long run. The root of social work values may be a set of potentially conservative, system-conserving assumptions about individuals, society, and social change. Thus it is not that social work values are incompatible in general with politics and the political process, but that these values may be less than compatible with the profession's declared goal of public advocacy for societal structural change.

Although social work values appear to be congruent with practice at the individual or small-group level (micro level), often they have been viewed as contradictory to the values and stances necessary at the larger, macro level of practice, particularly in administration. For example, social workers too often have acted as if budgets and fiscal considerations were not only inconsequential to their programs, but also as if such considerations were inhumane. They seem to take pride in not understanding the issues. Since the 1980s, some social workers have moved to the opposite extreme of becoming too "bottom-line" privatization oriented. Social workers must learn that there is no incompatibility between caring, competence, and humanitarianism, on the one hand, and fiscal efficiency on the other.

This book is devoted to describing and analyzing the politics inherent in social work and the political functions served by social work as a consequence. In some chapters, the roles that social work does or should play in influencing political events are described, but this chapter asserts that social work itself contains political theory and plays a political role. Social work practice, at both micro and macro levels, continuously acts either in support of or in opposition to the major institutions, policies, and values of our society. As such, social work is inherently part of the political process in the broadest sense, in that it is concerned with issues of either social conservation or social change.

Perhaps social work has not always explicitly recognized that any set of values, including those of "professionalization," entails a political position and, consequently, represents a position on the nature of the social order as a whole. "To say that social work is politics is to say, therefore, that social work in its every action represents political activity. Such activity is not limited to the usual arena called politics" (Galper, 1975).

With the exceptions highlighted in the preceding chapter, social workers either have overtly disagreed with this view of the inherently political nature of their work or have been ignorant of it. The vast majority believe that social work is and should be apolitical. A recent national professional coalition (Project Human Serve) aimed at voter registration highlighted this stance. Social workers whose entire professional careers have been devoted to helping the less fortunate gain skills, education, and resources to enhance social functioning were among the opponents of social worker involvement in voter registration drives.

Social workers who are involved in lobbying the legislature and monitoring the process, often have to compromise on products and dollar amounts, but these professionals must be very careful about compromising on principles.

For example, in the last Texas legislative session, I decided to request, in a separate line item from the general mental health budget, a proposal of $10 million for services to children and adolescents. As we moved through the legislative session, it became very clear that we weren't going to get $10 million or anything near that since the legislature was under a great deal of pressure about the budget and, consequently, wanted only to fund programs that we already had in place. I had many opportunities to give up on that line item, but I felt very strongly that if we were ever going to get started in children's and adolescents' programs, we needed a separate line item.

Therefore, we ended up compromising on $2 million. We used that money to fund four programs instead of scattering a few dollars across the whole state for 15 to 20 programs. I didn't compromise on my principles of doing a good service to children and adolescents; however, I did compromise on the amount of dollars and the number of programs. It is important, in my mind, that social workers not compromise on their principles but understand the need of compromise in the political process.

Dennis Jones, MSW
Former Commissioner, Texas Department of Mental Health and Mental Retardation

Indeed, the argument that the profession's values might be compromised has been used to impede the entrance of social workers into the political sphere. It is the intent of this chapter to describe the compatibility of social work values with political action and to suggest that these values often have been misinterpreted. It is also to present arguments showing that in fact these values prescribe and mandate the intervention by social workers in the political arena.

PRIMARY PRINCIPLES: SOCIAL JUSTICE AND EMPOWERMENT

Given the historical analysis in chapter 1 and the debate illustrated in chapter 2, before proceeding to a specific analysis of social work values, a brief discussion of the principles of social justice and empowerment and their connection to the social work profession has been added. The authors offer this as an additional basis for supporting the notion that all social work is and should be political.

As earlier described, there seems to be little disagreement that the founding principle of social work is related to social justice: To the extent that this is and has been true, it represents a posture that redirects and reallocates resources toward a more "just" distribution. Generally, social work has ascribed to the principle that inequities in power, wealth, income, and other essential resources (health care) should not exist unless they work to the benefit of all, including and most importantly, the worse off members of society. In fact, it is around this basic premise that Specht and Courtney (1994) develop their arguments.

If social justice remains a valued principle within the social work profession, then it would appear impossible to argue with a politicized practice, for it is within the realm of budget prioritization at the federal and increasingly at the state level that these decisions, which are clearly value decisions, become focused. Compatible with this social justice principle is an advocacy-based, social change focus. However, many have argued, including the authors, that particularly since the 1970s, social work has been more concerned with the enhancement of the profession and less concerned with the issues of racism, sexism, poverty, and access to health care. However, if the argument continues that social work is politically conservative and that social work values are conservative values, the argument would shift because social work and social workers quite frequently side with the progressive agenda (Sarri, 1992).

The conflict, as Sarri notes, is more likely the result of the dilemma that social work practice exists within social institutions which, whether public or private, are established and maintained by power groups. However, other practitioners, administrators, policy analysts, and educators might not be as constrained. "There is nothing in the tradition, code of ethics, literature, or curricula that explicitly or implicitly defines social work as inherently conservative. But there is no escaping the fact that social work as an institution in society must always reflect the mainstream culture, or that culture will not support it" (Sarri, 1992, p. 49).

For additional perspectives and arguments, Wagner (1990) sets the debate around ideologies of specialization, elitism, and career structures as part of social work professionalism juxtaposed to ideologies of social justice which are clearly compatible with political (or radical) social work. Perhaps the issue, if framed in this manner, is that to do political social work, the social worker cannot view her/his loyalty to the profession or to the institution, but must view her/his loyalty to the political principles and ideologies (Wagner, 1990, p. 5).

The principle of empowerment-based practice appears to be another fundamental principle to frame this chapter. To the extent that empowerment-based practice may either be described as a new or a revived paradigm in social work practice, it clearly connects to a value-based practice.

Empowerment-based practice is based on principles that liberate clients; that achieve reasonable control over client destiny. It is connected to and dependent upon a strength's perspective, a system's perspective, a social justice value base, and a social change model (Pinderhuges, 1994).

Another important aspect of empowerment-based practice, according to Rees (1991), is the connection rather than the separation of policy and practice, and the notion that power does not have to mean dominance, but should and does mean enabling. Thus, "enabling" power is quite consistent with social work values and most social work methodology and thought, and not as contradictory to professionalism. The argument that it necessitates a connection between policy and practice raises conceptual and structural issues in social work education. "Policy" content is mandated within both BSW and MSW curriculums, but policy content generally remains within those distinct courses. Students of the 1990s still complain, "What does policy have to do with what I'll be practicing when I graduate?"

SPECIALIZATION VERSUS SYSTEMIC SOLUTIONS

Among the important elements in any profession are the identification and development of areas of competence within which its members practice; the rights and obligations of the professional's relationship to these stated areas are thereby limited. The reason for this is twofold: to protect clients from a professional's involvement in areas that go beyond the professional's technical competence, and to protect the profession from general and undifferentiated demands made by its clients or consumers. This functional specificity is essential to professions in which great potential exists for intimacy between professionals and clients, because it structures working relationships such that clients view the process and the problem-solving methodology as specific to the problem at hand.

A problem with functional specificity that has long been apparent to the profession is that it creates a tendency, in fact demands, that the professional focus on and engage in only a piece of a client's life, ignoring other problems the person might have. Master's programs have created increasingly numerous, highly specialized areas of practice derived from this idea of professionalism. To the traditional specializations in physical health, mental health, and family and children have been added industrial, gerontological, substance abuse, and renal social work, to list a few.

During the last decade, however, as the number of BSW programs has grown, a countervailing trend has emerged in the discipline, namely a growing concern with the integration and coordination of social services and with the development of generalist practitioners (BSWs) and case managers. Quite clearly, social work has been caught between two competing sets of values: functional specificity versus global or integrated solutions. Given that many clients have multiple problems, sometimes with a single cause, the artificial and narrow focus on one problem that is prompted by specialization may lead to an incomplete resolution. For example, a substance abuser who is also violent in domestic relations may be treated in a residential detoxification program, where the violence may be overlooked or assumed to be the effect of rather than the cause of the substance abuse. Both of these problems also may be the effect of a third untreated problem, such as underemployment.

Inherent in the profession's emphasis on specialization is a more endemic problem: As social problems become the concern of a professional group, a problem-solving arena is created in which both problems and solutions are viewed as technical in nature rather than as structural or political. Improving technology within social work practice inherently limits the way in which problems and solutions can be formulated. The resulting dilemma has been that the profession is unlikely to espouse changes on a broader level that could reorder or reprioritize society or societal values. That is to say, professional social work norms may well act as a set of blinders that induce social workers to prescribe easily implementable, technical solutions to problems that could be better addressed by other means. For instance, as child abuse came to be recognized as a societal problem by social workers, technical solutions based on reporting and investigation systems were most frequently implemented, rather than political alternatives such as adding the "unemployed parent" option to state Aid to Families with Dependent Children (AFDC) eligibility regulations or increasing public support for day care. Although reporting and investigation systems certainly respond to the problem of unnecessary and critical delays in life-threatening circumstances, they are not solutions to the underlying causes of child abuse: poverty, adult isolation, and lack of adequate child care outside the home.

Another aspect of functional specificity that seems on the surface to discourage political involvement is the need to identify "turf." Social work increasingly has attempted (via licensing and classification efforts, for example) to define its role in relationship to other "helping professions" such as psychiatry, psychology, community nursing, recreational and occupational therapy, city and regional planning, and public administration. This has contributed to inter-personal rivalry rather than to building coalitions for the betterment of society. Perhaps even more debilitating than interprofessional rivalry is the existing intraprofessional rivalry between clinicians and administrators, between clinicians in mental health settings and clinicians in health settings or clinicians in school settings, and the like.

One can argue, therefore, that specialization, although necessary to professional definitions and identifications, may be antithetical to some forms of political action. If it is utilized as a clinical tool, however, rather than as an all-encompassing value, it will not be a barrier to political activity.

SELF-DETERMINATION VERSUS COMPROMISE

Self-determination, frequently touted in the profession as the "king" of social work values, is certainly a cornerstone of social work practice. In its ideal form, self-determination gives the client the right and the responsibility to be involved in life choices and, of course, in treatment choices. This value derives from a belief system that imparts to all clients equal human worth and dignity, equal ability to enter into the decision process, and equal rights to determine for themselves the best choice of treatment.

Nonetheless, a number of inherent problems arise in the operationalization of this value. On the clinical level, it assumes that the social work practitioner has the knowledge and agency sanction to adequately and comprehensively present all treatment alternatives. In fact, we know that quite often this is not possible. Particularly among specialists in social work practice, knowledge of treatment alternatives may be limited.

Unfortunately, social work education does not consistently and comprehensively provide information about community resources, eligibility requirements, or accessibility issues. Thus the array of alternatives suggested by the social worker may be artificially and even arbitrarily constrained by lack of knowledge, geographical limitations, or, as earlier noted, problem definition. Social workers also may find themselves in personal conflict with the professed policies of their agency. An obvious example would be a case in which a pregnant teenager is a client of an agency whose restrictions and policies prohibit the discussion of abortion as an alternative. Additionally, referral to an appropriate agency might be prohibited due to any one of a number of eligibility requirements, such as income, gender, age, residence, ability to provide payment for service, or language restrictions. Consequently, the array of alternatives provided to enable and support the value of self-determination often is restricted by the boundaries of a practitioner's knowledge as well as by agency practice (Keith-Lucas, 1963).

Equally important to the operationalization of this value in social work practice is its inherent assumption that all clients can actively engage in self-determination, when in fact many social work clients are unable to choose the best options because they have been unable to negotiate the larger system in an adequate manner. For example, a parent having a child with behavior problems might inappropriately be referred to an agency for counseling because the parent is unaware of the possibility of testing the child for learning disabilities.

Whether we view this failure to be knowledgeable about all treatment options as a personal or structural deficiency, it clearly diminishes the possibility of client self-determination. Whatever the cause—be it the client's age, gender, or emotional or intellectual dysfunctioning—the result is an inability to choose rationally among alternatives that would be in the client's best interest. Young children, the aged, the emotionally disturbed, and the developmentally disabled are the most obvious examples of client groups for whom self-determination may be a meaningless notion. Social work practitioners, therefore, must see that it is well within their professional creed to assume an active responsibility for deciding the best treatment alternative for a particular client or client group. Many practitioners, however, even community organizers and administrators, feel that to make such decisions contradicts social work values by taking away rights from clients and putting social workers in the position of being paternalistic and manipulative.

At the macro level, some social work administrators, researchers, and program evaluators have interpreted self-determination in operational terms that may speak against the long-term interests of clients and the profession. By committing themselves to an unbiased interpretation of data and the presentation of the full array of either funding or programmatic prescriptions, or both, they assume in others—funders, policymakers, and program designers—the same ability to be all-knowing and unbiased that practitioners have assumed in their clients. Unfortunately, administrative and evaluative decisions are not often made solely on the basis of the objective data presented, they are made on the basis of a set of values that may be unstated or unconscious, but nonetheless persuasive.

Social workers entering the political process tend to reveal their discomfort at being in the political arena. They want political candidates, elected officials, and administrative executives to have all available information, rather than a biased and limited perspective, and the freedom to make informed and self-determined decisions. In a political process that has been built on competing political ideologies and values, this approach to macro-level intervention is naive, unrealistic, and too often supportive of the status quo. The problem is not the incompatibility of self-determination and political intervention but the perceived misfit. Although practitioners cannot implement self-determination in a pure fashion at either the micro or macro level, at both levels this value can contribute in important and useful ways to promoting informed and humane decision making.

The number one objective of any political campaign is simple: Get the candidate elected. But at what cost? What if the election is too close to call and any one "hot" issue or unexpected crisis can swing the election to or against your candidate—are you willing to get your candidate elected at any cost?

An anonymous message was left at campaign headquarters three weeks before the election: The opponent, who is married with two grown children and two grandchildren, had fathered his secretary's now ten-year-old child. The information was easily confirmed. Polling showed the race was very close with 38 percent of the registered voters remaining undecided.

The candidate's staff was split on what to do with the information. Some argued that they should release the story a few days prior to the election in a last-minute mailing. The opposition would have no time to respond, while the media would have a field day with this "pro-family values" candidate.

Others thought they should not release the story at all. The "issue" had nothing to do with the campaign and would bring the election to a new low: What did the extramartial affair have to do with the election? What personal damage would the mother and child bear with the resulting publicity? Those in favor said the opponent should be accountable for his behavior, and if there was any such "news" on our candidate the opponent would surely publicize the story.

Personal scandals have been a hallmark of campaigns in recent years. In 1972, vice presidential nominee Thomas Eagleton was forced to reveal he had received mental health care in earlier years—the revelation forced him off the Democratic party ticket. Presidential candidate Gary Hart, a front-runner in the 1988 primaries, was forced to abandon his campaign bid after daring reporters to follow him to prove allegations of his liaisons with women, both of which they did. Former Texas Senator John Tower's nomination for secretary of defense was derailed due to allegations of heavy drinking. Presidents George Bush and Bill Clinton were shackled with reports of sexual trysts.

Even with the history in reveling personal lifestyles and issues, this campaign decided not to release the information concerning the opponent's personal life, even if it did fly in the face of his public "family values" stance. While campaign sleaze might be the hallmark of the 1980s and 1990s electoral process, the prevailing view was that no election is worth winning if it ruins an innocent person's life.

By the way, the candidate lost in a close election: About one additional vote per ballot box would have won the election. However, a young teen, who is getting ready to graduate high school, is not carrying the stigma that could easily have been sewn by a candidate and campaign staff who lost sight of their ultimate responsibility to human decency.

Ira Colby, Ph.D.
Director, School of Social Work, Univerity of Central Florida

EMOTIONAL NEUTRALITY VERSUS CLIENT SELF-INTEREST

Another major premise of social work professionalism is objectivity or emotional neutrality. Social workers are strongly encouraged to become aware of and to control the degree of their emotional involvement with clients. The development and operationalization of this value has been said to represent the essence of the "professional self." Particularly in a profession such as social work, where the primary tool is the social workers themselves, emotional neutrality is required to differentiate professional exchanges from other kinds of person-to-person encounters. Without neutrality, the expertise of the social worker would not be publicly nor legitimately identifiable and sanctioned.

One potentially negative consequence of emotional neutrality is that it may induce social workers to deny or repress emotional experiences or emotional reactions. The isolation and suppression of emotions, however, may only serve to thwart justifiable anger and frustration at the social inequities that clearly are at the root of many client problems. Thus, it may be possible for social workers to intervene with a low-income, multiproblem client and find short-term, ameliorating solutions, and at the same time to ignore the anger they feel toward the societal injustices that created the client's problems. If social workers were to become aware of and to express their feelings of anger at systemic and institutional barriers and inequities, a consensus might emerge that subsequently could lead to cooperative efforts at societal reform.

On a positive note, emotional neutrality may help the worker to continue practicing without experiencing despair or "burnout" in the face of enormous, overwhelming, and depressing social problems. At the macro level, many decision makers (both administrators and legislators) encourage a posture of neutrality because it supports the objective collection, analysis, and presentation by social workers of "hard data." Although collection and presentation of data are functions the professional must perform, restricting one's efforts of these functions may reduce one's effectiveness in being politically persuasive.

In providing legislative testimony, social workers too often have used indices of need, reported gaps in human services, and projected dysfunctions to support their argument for improved service delivery to clients. Although these can be useful elements in a political strategy, what often has been missing is the descriptive, emotionally charged illustration. Torn between a history of breast beating, at one extreme, and case and scientific argumentation, at the other, it may be that social work has swung too far in the direction of objectivity.

Social work lobbyists, for example, might prefer to present aggregate statistics about the probability that a proportion of the elderly in a midwestern state are unable to pay their heating bills, rather than to vividly describe the deaths of two old people due to exposure. The presentation of statistics not only might be less persuasive, but may mask real human suffering and pain caused by a particular inequity. Thus, emotional neutrality serves a useful function in a helping profession, but it should not be interpreted in a way that prevents the expression of justifiable and effective emotions such as anger at social injustice.

IMPARTIALITY VERSUS PARTISAN POLITICS

Impartiality, as a professional norm, means serving clients without regard to race, religion, personal traits, gender, sexual preference, or political ideology. It suggests that professionals should stand above and apart from these differences and be available to provide service equally to all clients. For micro-level practice, it requires social workers to identify in themselves personal values and prejudices that may deter, influence, or mitigate against equal and impartial service to all clients. Impartiality is an essential professional value. However, like the values previously mentioned, it has a potential bias, particularly when applied to macro-level interventions. Predicated on a limited definition of injustice, impartiality can lead to unthinking support of the status quo, especially if equality and social justice are held to be synonymous with equality of opportunity. For example, although social workers supported the civil rights movement and the equal opportunity legislation of the 1960s, many of these measures assume that people start off equally. These laws and the programs they created attempt to guarantee equality of opportunity or of access without necessarily taking into account that people start life in unequal positions. Thus, measures to guarantee equal opportunity, however laudable, do not automatically guarantee equal outcomes for all.

In all societies, ours included, there is a scarcity of valued resources. As a political concept, impartiality, which has given rise to certain guarantees of equality of opportunity, may influence a more equitable distribution or redistribution of resources, by randomizing distribution across racial, gender, income, or geographic lines, but it does not alter the total available amount of a given resource.

For example, the Reagan and Bush administrations repeatedly argued that the federal government and federal budget should not be involved in any form of income redistribution, yet, in reality, income redistribution is precisely what budget and tax programs do. The issue, therefore, is the direction and extent of that redistribution. An impartial stance on income transfer programs may, in some administrations, be tantamount to support of redistribution of wealth to the upper class, which is what resulted from many of the tax changes in President Reagan's 1981 Economic Recovery Tax Act. In fact, in 1990 the richest one-fifth of the population was richer while the lowest two-fifths were poorer, and the gap was wider than it has been since the 1940s.

THE PROFESSIONAL CODE OF ETHICS

Any profession's code of ethics is both formal and informal. In either case, it is the articulation of a set of publicly professed values. The formal code is the written code to which professionals commit themselves on being admitted to practice. Within the social work profession, the formal code is exemplified by the NASW Code of Ethics (National Association of Social Workers, 1979). A coexisting informal, unwritten code carries the weight of the formal code's prescriptions.

Through its ethical code, the social work profession commits itself to certain values as a matter of public record, thereby ensuring the continued confidence of the community and formally obligating itself to client service. This kind of self-regulative code is characteristic of many professions and occupations, both technical and professional, but a professional code usually is more explicit, systematic, and to some extent more binding than an occupational code. As the summary below shows, the NASW Code of Ethics' major principles, as revised and adopted on July 1, 1980, not only specify a set of behaviors but also explicitly support the social work values previously discussed. The sixth major principle states the social worker's responsibility for promoting the general welfare of society. Subsections VI(P)(6) and VI(P)(7) state: "(6) The social worker should advocate changes in policy and legislation to improve social conditions and to promote social justice; (7) The social worker should encourage informed participation by the public in shaping social policies and institutions." A review and comparison of the first code adopted by the NASW and its revision (Gross, Rosa, and Steiner, 1980) notes that the revision contains fewer articulations of this principle and the consequent prescriptions for social workers to engage in political advocacy. But despite the code's omission of substantial coverage of political responsibilities, it does not prohibit or negate such activity.

SUMMARY OF MAJOR PRINCIPLES

I.   The Social Worker's Conduct and Comportment as a Social Worker
    A. Propriety. The social worker should maintain high standards of personal conduct in the capacity or identity as social worker.
    B. Competence and Professional Development. The social worker should strive to become and remain proficient in professional practice and the performance of professional functions.
    C. Service. The social worker should regard as primary the service obligation of the social work profession.
    D. Integrity. The social worker should act in accordance with the highest standards of professional integrity.
    E. Scholarship and Research. The social worker engaged in study and research should be guided by the conventions of scholarly inquiry.

II. The Social Worker's Ethical Responsibility to Clients.
    F. Primacy of Clients' Interests. The social worker's primary responsibility is to clients.
    G. Rights and Prerogatives of Clients. The social worker should make every effort to foster maximum self-determination on the part of clients.
    H. Confidentiality and Privacy. The social worker should respect the privacy of clients and hold in confidence all information obtained in the course of professional service.
    I. Fees. When setting fees, the social worker should ensure that they are fair, reasonable, considerate, and commensurate with the service performed and with due regard for the client's ability to pay.

III. The Social Worker's Ethical Responsibility to Colleagues
    J. Respect, Fairness, and Courtesy. The social worker should treat colleagues with respect, courtesy, fairness, and good faith.
    K. Dealing with Colleagues' Clients. The social worker has the responsibility to relate to the clients of colleagues with full professional consideration.

IV. The Social Worker's Ethical Responsibility to Employers and Employing Organizations
    L. Commitments to Employing Organizations. The social worker should adhere to commitments made to the employing organizations.

V.   The Social Worker's Ethical Responsibility to the Social Work Profession
    M. Maintaining the Integrity of the Profession. The social worker should uphold and advance the values, ethics, knowledge, and mission of the profession.
    N. Community Service. The social worker should assist the profession in making social services available to the general public.

O. Development of Knowledge. The social worker should take responsibility for identifying, developing, and fully utilizing knowledge for professional practice.
VI. The Social Worker's Ethical Responsibility to Society
P. Promoting the General Welfare. The social worker should promote the general welfare of society.

CONCLUSION

Although the values discussed in this chapter are central values in social work, they by no means comprise an exhaustive list. Other important values include confidentiality, service, human worth, and dignity, but these values pose less conflict or confusion for professional social workers than do the ones we have discussed.

There are people who tell me that the ends justify the means. This is antithetical to social work values. Social work values involve people in making decisions that affect their own lives. That means that you get people together and you inform them. Social workers want people to be pleased, but sometimes somebody has to lose, and the question is are you prepared to stand your ground on principle? For social workers the ends and the means must be consistent. Another way to put it: If the method you use to arrive at your ends are dirty, then the end result will be dirty.

Maryann Mahaffey, MSW
President, Detroit City Council

We have attempted to stress the importance and indeed the nobility of social work values. However, two important considerations remain: (1) an inability to operationalize these values into programmatic or legislative objectives, and (2) the leaning of many of these values toward preservation of the status quo rather than social change. It is difficult to imagine that these values are inimical to political strategies or ideologies. However, they are commonly misconstrued as being barriers to political intervention by social workers.

Interestingly, value conflicts can become the center of a political debate within the NASW. Consequently, it is important for social workers in all arenas to make social work values an integral part of any issue or controversy. The following is an example of social work values in a political debate.

Almost my entire career has been in clinical settings. I have often found that I needed to take action on issues which address social workers' ethical responsibility to society.

One such time was in 1981, when I was elected to be a delegate to the National Association of Social Workers' (NASW) Delegate Assembly. This is a body of elected social workers who are members of the NASW whose primary purpose is to set the association's national priorities for the next several years. One of its major functions is to review public policy and develop position statements on social issues for the association to address. Prior to 1981, the Delegate Assembly had given a high priority to the elimination of racism and other forms of discrimination.

Several powerful position papers on these issues had been developed to guide the association in its interaction with the greater community, including state and national legislative bodies. Each elected delegate had an opportunity to review the association's previous priority goals and was asked to rank them in order of importance. The results were circulated to all delegates before the assembly met.

When I received the results of the preliminary balloting, I noticed that the elimination of racism and sexism had been given a lower or secondary ranking. It was clear to me and to those who had elected me that this lower priority was not acceptable.

All forms of discrimination strengthen discrimination toward other groups. If anyone discriminates against women, people will believe that it is acceptable to discriminate against blacks, and others will pick up this postulate and justify discriminatory behavior toward others, like gays or lesbians. As a gay activist, I had been active in the association to impact the NASW to work on eliminating discrimination based on homophobia.

I could not stand by and see the NASW lower its priority on combating discrimination. I made the decision to try to impact the Delegate Assembly to reconsider the ranking.

I understood there would be an opportunity for delegates to rethink their ranking and vote again once the assembly convened, so I set out to lobby my colleagues to change the ranking. I developed a flyer to take with me to the assembly. I wanted to make an impact with it so I invested a little and had it done in a way that would catch their attention. I put a slogan on the flyer which read, "Ageism, racism, sexism, classism, anti-Semitism, and homophobia all have a common root: That common root is to keep the people with power, or promise of power, on top and to keep those who are oppressed in a lesser position." I added another phrase at the bottom: "Please reconsider your ranking of NASW's priority on discrimination."

When I got to the Delegate Assembly, I sought out those who I thought would most likely support my position and organized them to help me. I talked to Jewish people, elderly people, blacks, and Hispanics. They took the flyers and handed them out to people they knew and talked with people they had influential relationships with.

Sure enough, there were those who thought that discrimination had been eliminated. Others argued that other priorities were more important. The group I organized went to every interest group meeting it could, talked at the coalition meetings, and made sure that everyone had a flyer. We did succeed! There were enough people who were concerned, and the priority on combating discrimination was moved back up into the top priorities once again. Although this is an example of political activity within the NASW, it eventually had an external political effect. It directed the organization to lobby and advocate for the elimination of discrimination.

Travis L. Peterson, MSW
Houston, Texas

The intraprofessional debate about whether social workers should be actively engaged in political action committees and legislative lobbying issues, which we will explore in greater depth in later chapters, in large part arises from this perceived conflict between political ideology and professional impartiality.

ASSIGNMENTS

1. Choose one of the social work values mentioned in this chapter. Illustrate first through a casework example, then through a political illustration, the possible contradictions in utilizing this value as a means rather than as an end.
2. Interview three practicing social workers involved in political activity, and discuss why their political activities are consistent with the social work role.

SUGGESTED READINGS

Edelman, Murray. 1974. "The Political Language of the Helping Professions." *Politics and Society* 4 (May): 295-310.
Gordon, William. 1965. "Knowledge and Value: Their Distinction and Relationship in Clarifying Social Work Practice." *Social Work* 10: 32-39.
Levy, Charles S. 1976. "Personal Versus Professional Values: The Practitioners Dilemmas." *Clinical Social Work Journal* 4 (Summer): 110-120.

REFERENCES

Galper, Jeffrey. 1975. *The Politics of Social Services.* Englewood Cliffs, NJ: Prentice Hall.
Gross, Gerald M., Linda Rosa, and Joseph R. Steiner. 1980. "Educational Doctrines and Social Work Values: Match or Mismatch." *Journal of Education for Social Work* 16 (3): 21-28.
Keith-Lucas, Alan. 1963. "A Critique of the Principles of Self-Determination." *Social Work* 8: 66-71.
Mahaffey, Maryann. 1987. "Political Action in Social Work." In *Encyclopedia of Social Work,* 18th ed., pp. 283-293. New York: National Association of Social Workers.
National Association of Social Workers. 1979. *Code of Ethics.* Washington, D.C.: National Association of Social Workers.

Pinderhuges, Elaine. 1994. "Empowerment as an Intervention Goal: Early Ideas." In *Education and Research for Empowerment Practice,* Lorraine Gutierrez and Paula Nurius (eds.). Seattle, WA: Center for Policy and Practice Research.

Rees, Stuart. 1991. *Achieving Power: Practice and Policy in Social Welfare.* North Sydney, Australia: Allen and Unwin.

Sarri, Rosemary C. 1992. "Is Social Work Inherently Conservative—Designed to Protect Vested Interests of Dominant Power Groups?" In *Controversial Issues in Social Work,* Eileen Gambrill and Robert Pruger (eds.). Needham, MA: Allyn and Bacon.

Specht, Harry, and Mark Courtney. 1994. *Unfaithful Angels: How Social Work Has Abandoned Its Mission.* New York: Free Press.

Wagner, David. 1990. *The Quest for a Radical Profession: Social Service Careers and Political Ideology.* Lanham, MD: University Press of America.

chapter 4

Policy Models for Political Advocacy

Social workers have a passion and an understanding of the needs and problems of parts of society that the legislative process, left to its own, will do little for. Understanding the process is key. Don't work at odds with it. Figure out how it works, embrace it—it can be made to work for the very people for whom I believe it was designed—those who have the least.

Sandy Ingraham

One can view, affect, and evaluate the policy-making process in a number of ways. The choice of an appropriate political interventive action should be based on one's evaluation of the policy. Just as a clinician must examine the personal, situational, and environmental elements of a client's problem before reaching an appropriate diagnosis and intervention, the political strategist must holistically examine and then specifically focus in order to determine the appropriate intervention.

The similarity between determining a client's diagnosis and analyzing social policy can prove quite useful. In the same way that a client's presenting problem may initially be incomprehensible, social policy formation can appear complex and mysterious. To gain a clearer understanding of its various components, the client's problem or the social policy must be subdivided. This helps the clinician or the political strategist to identify the various components of the problem, determine the most important aspect thereof, and develop a plan of attack.

Within this clinical model of a generic problem-solving process that cuts across all levels of client intervention are all the steps and processes involved in political advocacy. For the clinician, the first step in the process is to get the client's view of the presenting problem. Intervention then requires a systematic collection of data to either substantiate the client's definition of the problem or to revise it. This data-gathering process, often called the *psychosocial history,* includes collecting information about the client's problems and significant relationships, perceptions of these problems and relationships, and interaction with the community and environment.

Likewise, the political advocate first must come to understand society's definition of the social problem. A needs assessment or social indicators analysis must then be conducted. This includes collecting data about the size and scope of the problem, identifying the primary population at risk, and outlining current policies and procedures that already influence or are influenced by current or new policy goals and administrative regulations.

After the collection of data, a clinician must assess or diagnose the client's problem. This step involves decisions about the scope of the intervention, as well as whether it is change or maintenance that is required. The clinician must decide whether to provide treatment to the individual, to a dyad, or to a group.

On the political level, assessment involves identifying whether the appropriate intervention is administrative, legislative, or judicial, and whether it should take place at the policy formulation, implementation, or evaluation stage. The decisions involved in such an assessment move the social worker, whether clinician or political advocate, to develop the treatment plan or political strategy that seems most appropriate.

Ideally, at this stage each social worker should have an array of interventive models from which to choose. Clinicians can choose from a continuum of models ranging from the psychoanalytic to the behavioral to the client-centered approach. Likewise, political advocates can choose from among interventive approaches that view policy from various perspectives: institutional, rational, elite, group, or incremental. These perspectives will be explained later in this chapter.

Obviously the next step in both the clinical and political processes is execution of the treatment plan or political intervention, followed by an evaluation of the chosen treatment or intervention. This evaluation will result either in a termination of the process or in a repetition of certain steps in the process, so that a new or revised treatment plan or model for political intervention can be chosen.

As the authors have repeatedly noted, the importance of knowledge of policy models, assessment techniques, and evaluative tools are essential for all social work practitioners and for political social work practice. During the past two decades in particular, policy agendas have been set by groups whose values are significantly at odds with professional social work values. Perhaps even worse, many have criticized that domestic social policy development has been in a state of paralysis. If the recent models are not really new answers, but repackaging and window dressing, some group must begin to more effectively find solutions to these social problems (Blau, 1992).

An excellent example of this stalemate or paralysis is national health care. It is a fact that the United States spends more and gets less than any other country. However, with a myriad of proposals from both political parties and many nonpartisan groups, we have reached an impasse. Many proposals, not only for health care but for any social problem, seem to be either so incremental that they will never produce a measurable change in a quick period or so without social vision and humanitarian principles that they spark no support.

Furthermore, since the 1970s, and with increasing rapidity and validity, social programs are being held to an accountability model. While it would obviously be politically incorrect to argue that social services should not be accountable, should not have measures of their success and effectiveness, the primary models that have been promulgated often bear little resemblance or meaning to the social services delivered and the problems being addressed.

In the mid-1990s we have still not satisfactorily differentiated outputs and throughput from outcomes. We have assimilated the language and accepted the funders' demands for empirically validated measures. We have done less to argue these as reasonable and seldom provide meaningful substitute measures. In addition to the fact that substantial amounts of time may be required to generate the less than useful measures (numbers of telephone calls made), what may be worse is that this data becomes an "illusion of productivity" (Gruber, 1991, p. 181). That is, we begin to believe that making x telephone calls or holding y interviews really measures the effectiveness of our social service programs.

So as we have argued previously, social workers must be involved at all levels of policy-making, including model development and the evaluative mechanisms. To argue that policies are inappropriate and evaluative strategies are meaningless is passive and ineffective; to develop policies and evaluative strategies is ultimately to better serve our clients.

As stated earlier, this chapter describes a number of methods by which one can review the presenting problem, develop an appropriate interventive plan, and evaluate that plan within a policy-making framework. It should be evident from our presentation, analysis, and illustrations that the choice of an appropriate political strategy should be preceded by an analysis and definition of the problem, a selection of the appropriate policy model, and a design for policy evaluation. The prescriptions for advocacy, presented in this chapter, support this book—to teach political intervention skills.

MODELS DEFINED

It would be extremely difficult, if not impossible, to develop strategies for political intervention without a clear understanding of the available models from which the political advocate may choose. Just as the caseworker chooses a model because of its appropriateness to the client's problem, taking into consideration pragmatic constraints of time, money, or situation, so too the political advocate chooses from a model that focuses on what appears to be the most critical area for intervention, taking into consideration whatever practical realities the environment, budgets, or political climate might dictate.

A model is a representation of some aspect of the real world designed to yield insight into or to focus attention on a specific segment of it. Models deliberately oversimplify reality in order to permit understanding and to direct intervention. Therefore, models quite necessarily treat some variables as crucial and ignore others in order to appropriately focus attention on a limited and specific array of determinants (Dye, 1981). For example, the psychoanalytic model deliberately excludes such explanatory variables as environmental and interactional data, but it is nonetheless useful in clinical treatment.

Similarly, policy models should simplify and clarify thinking about social policy and political intervention by identifying the important aspects of a policy and the targets of political intervention, and by predicting policy consequences. A useful model should clearly identify the important aspects of a policy using concepts that are testable and have commonly shared meanings. It should be able to explain phenomena, not simply describe them.

Institutional Model

Clearly, much political activity occurs within governmental institutions, such as Congress, state legislatures, courts, and political parties. Technically speaking, a policy does not become a "public" policy until it has been enacted, implemented, and enforced by some governmental institution. The institutional model focuses on policy as the output of these institutions.

This approach may focus on a structural examination of governmental institutions, but to be most useful it must go beyond that to include examination of the linkage between structural arrangements and policy content. This model focuses on questions such as these: Are the policies of federal social agencies more responsive to social problems than are the policies of state or local social agencies? How does the division of responsibilities among mental health services affect the content of social welfare policy? Both of these questions require not only a description of structural institutional relationships, but also a projection of the outcome of the policy as the result of those relationships. When utilizing this model, one effectively focuses on structural arrangements that seem to affect policy outcomes.

For example, most states deliver general assistance to the poor through state or county agencies. However, Indiana still maintains a township trustee system as the vehicle to deliver this service. Consequently, 1,008 separately administered and autonomously directed poor-relief services exist within the state, without any state-mandated standardized procedures for determining eligibility or benefit levels. Not surprisingly, this results in extensive variation across townships and unequal and inequitable service to clients. For several years now, political advocates have sought legislation that would assign responsibility for general assistance to a county-level agency—a structural solution to the problem.

In general, interventive strategies based on the institutional model focus either on altering organizational structures or on choosing an organizational level or division within which to introduce structural change.

Process Model

The process model views policy as a political activity. In contrast to the institutional model, the process model focuses on how decisions are made. According to this view, it is neither the structure of the organization nor the content of the policy that is of primary interest, but rather the activities entailed in the policy-making process. This approach may appear to be of limited use in the analysis of policy, but it is extremely useful to the strategist trying to influence policy.

If, for example, you studied the way in which bills are processed by legislative committees, you probably would obtain information that would prove useful in future lobbying on behalf of measures you support. To do so, you need to determine the types of data and evidence the committee was willing to consider. Do they assign greater weight to written testimony, expert opinion, or empirical data? Do they regard verbal testimony, client or consumer opinion, and experience as valid evidence? Knowledge of the specific types of data considered and the weight given to each might prove to be crucial information to an intervenor.

For instance, as multiple agencies vie for a limited number of dollars, they often have to make presentations to the funding source to support their budget requests. Understanding the decision-making process is essential for successful competition. One Area Agency on Aging, for instance, obtained only partial funding when it presented its budget and position statement at the legislative budget hearings. This testimony was fully supported by empirical evidence on the number of elderly in the area, average income, age distribution, and marital and health status. This information documented the need for funding of home-maker, congregate meals, and medical prescreening services. On the other hand, the local rehabilitation center had not only prepared verbal testimony accompanied by empirically supported evidence of need and documentation of the number of clients served, but the staff also brought to the hearing several paraplegic clients to give personal testimony on the need for extended services. The dramatic emotional appeal of this latter strategy led to full funding of the request from the budget committee.

Additional information useful in this analysis might be information about committee composition, such as the background of committee members and their current positions within the legislature, and knowledge of specific pressures on the committee or on individual committee members, such as the total committee agenda and popular constituent opinions. The strategies likely to be suggested via this model include interventions in the committee process and attempts to influence their outcome most probably through lobbying.

Group Theory Model

Individuals with shared interests commonly group together to strengthen support for their demands. When these demands are made on a governmental institution they become part of policy analysis. Sometimes direct-service agencies with similar goals band together (or cooperate) to strengthen their political clout. The group theory model is characterized by its central focus on interaction between political groups.

Often the group is viewed as a vehicle for transmitting ideas and demands from individuals to the government. In this model, politics is seen as a struggle among groups to influence policy-making. Changes in the relative power of one group vis-à-vis another are expected to determine changes in public policy. The relative influence of a group is related to its size, the resources at its command, its leadership, and its access to decision makers.

About ten years ago there were some scandals about day care offered in people's homes—injury to children and so on. The state legislature finally passed a law saying that if you take care of six or fewer children in your home who are not related by blood, including your own under age seven, you must be registered by the state and inspected for health and safety standards. If you take up to twelve children, you must be licensed, which goes beyond registering and requires inspections.

Detroit has a zoning ordinance stating that a nonconforming use of the land is prohibited. Day-care providers were being closed by the city's building inspection department because they were considered nonconforming to the zoning ordinance. This, coupled with the shortage of decent child care and the fact that many people prefer the smaller units for their children, meant that we had a problem.

I brought together citizens, providers, the Child Care Coordinating Council, and other social services, etc. We talked about the problem: how to do it and what ought to go into an ordinance that would exempt them from the zoning ordinance. We also involved some neighborhood community organizations who were objecting because they bought their houses with the idea that they were buying into quiet neighborhoods with no children and they didn't want the parents parking in front of their houses.

Some providers did not want to be known because they were not registered or licensed and they figured that the city would fine them and close them down. This problem required the use of my social work values of being involved: self-determination, letting the people know all the information, getting the public informed, and then using the problem-solving process.

We did get an ordinance through the city council because I used my community-organizing skills and involved a broad variety of people, a cross section of people, who worked in drafting the ordinance, because I believe in the professional value of letting the people be involved in determining their future.

Maryann Mahaffey, MSW
President, Detroit City Council

In the group model, policy formulation and implementation are the result of negotiations between competing groups. If we were to apply this model in a study of policy-making processes concerning reproductive rights, for example, we would focus attention on the positions taken and tactics used by significant interest groups. Thus, we might examine "right to life" groups and Planned Parenthood coalitions by studying their memberships, tactics, and strategies. We would also be interested in collecting data on the resources available to these groups (such as time, money, or membership) in order to determine why one group may be more successful than another within a given legislative session or have more appeal to a certain constituency.

In the group theory model, the management of intergroup conflict via the establishment of rules (such as a ceiling on campaign contributions) that facilitate intergroup compromise, and the enforcement of such compromises, is seen as the primary function of the political system. Compromise, conflict resolution, or the gaining of victory by one interest group usually are seen as processes that foster the national interest, and the results are said to constitute public opinion. This last assumption, however, is valid only if all groups have or are ensured equal access to power and resources.

Using this model, a policy advocate might try to influence decision making through access to the decision makers or through the control of scarce resources. Intervention strategies could include building coalitions with the controllers of resources or the formation of political action committees. Thus, if a reproductive rights advocacy group was having limited success in legislative lobbying because of its small numbers, active opposition, or public denial of the issue, a possible strategy would be to form a coalition of agencies representing multiple issues. This would provide the advantage of collective persuasive power and might mask the more sensitive or controversial issue.

Elite Theory Model

Elite theory views public policy as largely determined by the preferences and values of a governing elite. Elitists hold that the general population is, in general, apathetic and seldom attempts to make policy or express values. Further, public policy is seen as reflecting the views of the elite, who generally belong to the higher socioeconomic strata and are not representative of the general public.

Consequently, change is slow and the status quo is preserved unless and until societal shifts alter the elite's self-interest. This is not to imply that elites will always work against the general public's best interest, but rather that it is this group who defines the public interest.

Because this model assumes that the general population is either ignorant or apathetic, and views institutions such as political parties as being primarily symbolic in nature, its focus is on elite behavior and preferences. It also tends to assume a consensus among the elite regarding fundamental norms and values.

Using this model, it is possible to argue that even major pieces of social legislation have been introduced or supported by the elite, not by the masses. This model is helpful in examining, for instance, the relative ease with which Medicare and Medicaid legislation was enacted in the mid-1960s compared to the uphill, and as yet unsuccessful, battle over nationalized health insurance. According to this model, the difference is explained by the fact that Medicare and Medicaid affect the upper-income elite only minimally, whereas nationalized health insurance could jeopardize consumer choice and increase health care costs for all, including the elite.

Utilizing this approach, an appropriate strategy would be to convince the elite group of the value of the desired policy change and to work with them to achieve it, possibly by getting elected to public office and becoming "one of them." You would need to advocate not only why the policy is good, fair, or just, but more importantly that it is in the elite's self-interest.

Rational Model

The rational model can also be defined as an efficiency model. That is, a policy is most rational when it is most efficient in achieving maximum benefits. Consequently, what characterizes a rational policy is that the ratio of benefits to costs is more positive and higher than for alternative policies.

The model assumes that costs and benefits of a particular policy can be known, that all policy alternatives are available, that all policy consequences are measurable, and that cost-benefit ratios can be calculated. Further, this model assumes that social values can be defined and weighed.

One of the barriers to an informed, rational choice among policy alternatives is that to eliminate a policy already in place may be extremely costly. Another is that long-term benefits, however predictable, must be weighed against current budget considerations. If, for example, we examine the Women, Infants, and Children's (WIC) program, we see that despite clear evidence that every short-term dollar invested in the program saves three dollars in health care costs in the long run, funding for WIC continues to be stable while food costs have risen and fewer people are served. Thus, since funding is limited, fewer than half of those eligible are served. The only rational explanation for this is that current economic decisions outweigh decisions favoring more efficient, long-range policy outcomes.

The rational model allows us to calculate and evaluate costs and benefits not only on the basis of the group of clients, consumers, or populace directly affected, but also on a larger societal level. Obviously the definition of beneficiaries will determine the cost-benefit ratio of a particular policy.

Using this model, one would compile information and data to be utilized for purposes of persuasion. Arguments showing that the advocated policy change is more efficient, that it enlarges the potential beneficiary group and the long-term positive outcomes of a policy, is a strategy for winning policy changes that will increase benefits.

Incremental Model

The incremental model views current public policy as largely a continuation of past policies marked only by incremental changes. One of the best-known proponents of this model, Charles Lindblom, suggests that decision makers normally do not review the entire range of existing and proposed policies, rank order their preferences among all alternatives, and then make informed choice. Constraints of time, money, intelligence, and politics prevent such a comprehensive, rational approach (Lindblom, 1959).

This model is conservative in that it utilizes existing policies as baseline for determining the range of possible policy change. One of the advantages of this approach is that it is less costly in terms of both the time spent reviewing and projecting alternatives and the costs already invested in existing policies. Consequently, it is a more expedient political model.

Using this model you focus on new or potential policies only in terms of their relationship to existing ones. An example is the addition of an unemployed parent (UP) clause to the Aid to Families with Dependent Children (AFDC) legislation. This clause would enable two unemployed parents to receive AFDC benefits without having to separate. Rather than totally reconceptualizing and dissolving the present AFDC policy in order to enact a guaranteed annual income, some states simply added this UP provision to their AFDC program. Following the incremental approach, one would look for policies not dramatically different from existing ones.

A PROACTIVE APPROACH TO POLICY DEVELOPMENT

The problem-solving strategies utilized in any field are only as good as the theories or models available. Social work does not, however, have one model that is adequate to encompass processes and outcomes as well as the etiology of the social problems to be addressed. Most of the previously mentioned policy models can be characterized as follows:

1. Reactive to crisis and remedial in orientation
2. Residual in response, reflecting a reluctance to intervene
3. Based on existing capabilities of special interest groups to influence decisions amenable to them
4. Supportive of stability and therefore of existing patterns in distribution of resources
5. Only marginally responsive to inequities in society (Humberger, 1977)

These criticisms imply a need for a systemic or holistic approach to the examination of public policy. Humberger suggests a political-economic approach to examining the dynamics and interrelationships among political, economic, and administrative variables that impact the human service field. He suggests that such an approach is useful for both macro- and microanalysis.

Humberger's approach is not significantly different from a systems approach, which, when applied to politics, includes examination of the political system, the external environment bringing pressure upon that system, and the output of the political system, that is, public policy. This approach allows, even demands, that variables be examined in a holistic fashion. It suggests the examination of variables not only as they interact within a particular sector, be it administrative, legislative, or executive, but also as they interact across sectors. For example, a state's decision to mainstream special education children would be viewed as a policy decision affecting the special education sector as well as the social welfare and education sectors, as affecting not only special education students but normal students, and consequently, a broader target system.

A proactive approach not only requires the examination of possible alternatives, but also requires the ability to predict future problems, needs, or issues. Forecasting requires assessing or predicting future conditions and anticipating the behavior of individuals and institutions under those conditions. Demographic projections, simulations, or econometric projections are used, along with the more conceptual approach of developing alternative scenarios.

An excellent example of this model is the efforts of social workers to achieve legal regulation of social work practice. Rather than reacting to public pressure regarding services for the poor from untrained workers, or to action by legislators that might encompass a multitude of disciplines under one regulatory structure, a proactive strategy has been developed. In the early 1970s, for example, the NASW developed a model licensure bill which they promulgated nationally. Almost all state NASW chapters have modified this bill and over two-thirds have successfully lobbied for passage of some form of state legal regulation for social work practice. This effort and others like it have not only protected the quality of services to the public, but also have regulated service providers.

All of these approaches are used to try to project future needs, problems, or both. Developing policy requires a thoughtful examination of future conditions and needs, a realistic projection of future financial and technological resources, and an approach that accommodates these factors. Knowledge of how social institutions and organizations behave and change is needed to anticipate organizational responses to particular policies.

What should be evident about a proactive orientation is its active approach to policy development, its eclectic sampling of a variety of policy models, and its reliance on a systems perspective. Although use of this approach requires finding reliable, current data to use in projecting future problems and needs, it encourages a posture of initiation rather than one of reaction.

POLICY ANALYSIS

While policy analysis skills may be covered in the more traditional policy texts, they should be viewed as an essential component of political skills as well. Policy analysis should be composed of the analysis of the specific issue or issues as well as the analysis of the general political climate (Flynn, 1985).

The more traditional of the policy analysis approaches focuses on the substantive analysis of the issues and on the fiscal analysis of the impact, or lack of impact, of the legislation. However, in including this in a political skills text, it is equally important to focus on the analysis of the political processes and likely outcomes of those processes (Kleinkauf, 1989).

According to Kleinkauf, the substantive issues to be examined include an understanding of the current legislative status of the issue: What are current statutes and regulations—federal, state, or local? What will this new piece add to this? What does the bill propose to do? Once the nature and context of the bill is understood, the analysis should proceed to find out who will be impacted, positively or negatively: What are the implications of no action? Are there any foreseeable unintended consequences of this legislation? Certainly of importance is a consideration of the congruence with social work's mission and value perspective.

Through this initial analysis, the need for additional data regarding the prevalence or incidence of the problem, the current or projected future demand for the service, and the likely supporters or opponents of the bill should be evident. Furthermore, underlying and subtle influences of institutional racism, sexism, and ageism, as well as destructive elements of social control, punitive measures, or regressive redistribution of resources should be examined.

The fiscal analysis should include an examination and documentation of any fiscal analysis completed already. This analysis should include start-up and first-year costs, as well as ongoing costs. The policy analysis should include the cost of new staff, staff training, public information dissemination, and retraining and educating of existing staff where necessary. Hidden costs should be anticipated and "free" services (such as volunteers) or in-kind contributions should not be underestimated relative to other "real costs."

It is important that the social work policy analyst consider the human cost when conducting the fiscal analysis; that is, what would be the cost to current or prospective clients if this legislation were not introduced? Or, put another way, what is the cost of human misery? Also not to be overlooked is the potential cost to other government programs if the current legislation is not enacted.

Additionally the examination of the processes and the likelihood of the bill's passage should comprise the final elements of the policy analysis. An understanding of the assignment to committees may indicate a prediction of the eventual outcome of the legislation. For example, it is commonly understood that the assignment of a piece of legislation to numerous committees increases the likelihood that the bill will die. Conversely, introducing the bill into only one committee, and one whose membership is favorable, is a good sign of quick passage of the bill.

Another indicator of successful passage is the sponsorship of the bill by powerful legislators. Bipartisan sponsorship is an even better predictor. Beyond legislators' support, a thorough analysis should also include an analysis of the bill's support and opposition by community groups and by political parties. The stance of significant community leaders is imperative.

POLICY EVALUATION

Introducing, negotiating, and implementing policies are important aspects of, but do not complete, the policy process. To make informed choices among policy alternatives, an ongoing evaluation of established policies is necessary.

Policy evaluation usually requires a review of programs that flow from the policy being reviewed. Consequently, you must be cautious about judging the merit of any policy on the basis of an examination of only one program. Although evaluation has inherent limitations that arise from procedures such as generalizing findings, it is the authors' belief that policy evaluation is nonetheless superior to judgments made simply on the basis of political expediency, intuition, or organizational pragmatics. The merit of a particular program might be measured through examination of that one program, but the success of a particular policy is best determined by multiple program analyses.

Exclusive use of a single evaluation technique reduces, or narrows, the information that can be gathered about the topic under investigation. This may be necessary because of limitations on data, time, money, and the like, but it will skew in one direction the data collected and the resulting decisions. Consequently, an evaluation that incorporates multiple types of evaluation techniques is more useful and is preferred, all other things being equal.

Effort

To focus on effort as the primary criteria by which to judge the success of a policy means to collect information about what it takes to deliver the policy in terms of staff, equipment, buildings, and so forth. The basic question, therefore, is "How much?"

Data related to effort include costs of salaries, equipment, fringe benefits, travel, rent, utilities, and supplies. Even such tangible costs sometimes are difficult to ascertain or estimate in multiprogram agencies, where proportions of all of the preceding expenses may be attributable to different programs in varying degrees.

Sometimes evaluations of effort may focus on the output of a program. In such instances, collecting data on units of service becomes important. Although this certainly provides information about the numbers of individuals served or the units of service produced, it alone does not measure the effects of a service. This caution is necessary because it is sometimes inferred that units of service produced equals success or problems solved. That is, projected versus actual output of numbers of clients served often is presented to funders as a measure of success even though such statistics do not indicate whether the clients' goals have been met or their problems solved.

Quality

As policies are translated into administrative regulations and procedures, quality control measures often are included. This may be done through separate legislation on accreditation or licensure. In either case, the basic thrust is similar: to evaluate the policy or program on the basis of the quality of services rendered.

Measures of quality focus not on "how much?" but rather on "what kind?" Indicators of a good program might include level of staff training, education, and experience, worker-to-client ratios, or measures of worker performance compliance with other accreditation measures specific to the program, such as the number of square feet per child in day-care settings or a requirement that workers pass a statewide licensure examination. These are meaningful measures of the quality of any policy, but they may lead to inferences that the higher the quality of the program, the more successful the program or policy is. Often this is a questionable and untested assumption. These indicators are central to the analytic focus only if the policy was introduced primarily to enhance quality in specific programs. For example, if staff educational requirements are raised to enhance the quality of professional service, a measure of proportion of staff with higher degrees would be a reasonable indicator of increased quality.

Effectiveness

A third approach to evaluation is to measure a policy's effectiveness. Utilizing this approach, one would ask the central question, "To what extent are the policy/program goals being met?" Although this approach comes nearest to measuring the "success" of a policy, the ability to collect information on program outcomes is certainly dependent on the ability to translate program/policy goals and objectives into measurable indicators of success. Ideally, it also requires the collection of preprogram as well as postprogram data.

This may be the most useful type of information about a policy's impact, but it also can be the most difficult to gather. Programs often operationalize shorter-term goals, leaving the achievement of the long-term policy goal to be inferred. For example, although the goal of detoxification might be to reduce alcohol consumption permanently, the measurable indicator might be taken at the point of termination from the program rather than several years later.

When it is impossible or too costly to collect measurable data on program participants before and after their participation, aggregate statistics sometimes are employed. The reduction in teenage pregnancies as measured by health statistics may be used to evaluate the success of a high school course on birth control or the establishment of a local family planning clinic. In both cases, the inference of causality is untested and the conclusions, therefore, are based on circumstantial rather than direct evidence.

Efficiency

When the primary focus of an evaluation is on cost relative to effectiveness, efficiency is the criterion being used. This type of analysis requires calculating per unit or per client costs for similar programs, consequently facilitating cross-program comparisons. For example, if effectiveness of goal attainment is held constant, it would then be possible to compare a unit of adult day care, home-delivered meals, or adult residential nursing home care delivered by different programs.

The analysis might also include the use of cost-benefit techniques in which benefits are calculated in dollar terms. Thus, the evaluator cannot simply say that 60 percent of an elderly population served by a given nutrition program were properly nourished and maintained or improved in health status. Rather, the evaluator must be able to indicate the worth of this improved health status in dollars. Determining that state and federal governments spent less on Medicaid and Medicare reimbursements as a result of this program would involve translating governmental benefits into dollar terms.

It is even more complicated, but of equal importance, to be able to calculate what these benefits mean in dollar terms to the individual client and to the local community as well as to the government. In the previous example, one might calculate the money saved by an individual client of a nutrition program in terms of lessened medical bills, or the money saved by the community in terms of unneeded ambulance or public health services.

Quite clearly, some benefits are more easily translated into dollars than others. Perhaps one can estimate with some validity the amount of medical expenses saved. Other benefits, such as the saving of a life or prevention of a marital separation, are much more difficult to convert into financial equivalents.

CONCLUSION

An examination of a variety of policy models and evaluative strategies can help one make choices in a more informed manner. Furthermore, by moving beyond theoretical models to prescriptions for professional practice, the practitioner can become aware of the linkage between and importance of both theory and practice. Theory and analysis, without subsequent prescriptions for practice, are of limited professional utility; wisdom gained through practice, without conceptual underpinnings, may be divorced from both long-term knowledge building and generalizations.

In summary, each of the models discussed in this chapter provides specific prescriptive tactics for political intervention. Further, they require skills and interventive strategies related to monitoring, lobbying, coalition building, and the entering of the legislative arena more directly through support of candidates and the holding of political office. These strategies will be described in the next chapter.

As commissioner for the Department of Human Services in West Virginia for eight years under Governor Rockefeller, I found it necessary to constantly monitor the bureaucracy. While the permanent employees of any civil service bureaucracy are extremely important to an organization's strength and ability to keep functioning, like all organizational functions, it needs to be scrutinized. And one mechanism for this scrutiny is the politically appointed person.

For example, I was once faced with the problem of cutbacks in state funding that would reduce a significant proportion of the total personnel. I discovered that the permanent staff of the bureaucracy was cutting back some state jobs, but was mostly proportionately reducing federally funded positions. This did not make any sense to me. The problem was the insufficiency of state funds, not federal funds, and there was money to continue the federal programs. The tenured state people, those who presumed to be around forever, didn't want to destroy the good relationships with their fellow state employees, so they cut the federal jobs. I was able to persuade them that just wasn't appropriate nor was it in the best interest of the clients, and to cut funds only where funds had to be cut.

Any large, public bureaucracy has a lot of rules about personnel, such as who can do the hiring, who can be hired (for example, only the top five on the register), as well as limitations by category. Despite these regulations, I discovered that people who had been in these bureaucracies for a long time could basically hire anyone they wanted—they could change the category or hire in a different category, or even change the classification of the job. They could, in fact, employ anybody they wanted. I got suspicious when I discovered how many relatives of workers there were working in some of the local offices.

I was trying to selectively hire MSWs and BSWs into the department when I was told that the civil service didn't allow for it and there was no classification. I did the same as everyone else did: I found a way around it. I spoke to the personnel service department and found that there was a system to accomplish my objective. I needed to specify a training category for hiring people on what's called the "trainee roster." I would imagine that most civil service systems have something like that. Therefore, I was able to start an Affirmative Action program for professional social workers.

Another time when I used my social work values and knowledge in this job was when someone in the top echelons of the bureaucracy came to me and said that we ought to cut out all chore services (projects under Title 20 or the Social Services Block Grant) that are provided by relatives of the recipients of the services. Their rationale was that these people could probably provide those services without charge, and ought to be doing so— that the state and federal governments shouldn't be paying relatives to provide these services.

Initially this made sense, so we announced that relatives would no longer be reimbursed for chore services provided. I got many letters from chore services providers and other relatives saying, "That's a disaster, you can't do that to us." As it turned out, the program had actually been almost like a cash subsidy, allowing poor families to afford to take care of their relatives. Although it was an unintentional feature of the program, it was actually saving the government money since otherwise these elderly and/ or disabled and ill relatives might have to be institutionalized. This is an example of policy monitoring that may seem reasonable, but unless one checks into the actual implementation of the program first, one could inadvertently destroy the positive utility of the program.

Leon Ginsberg, Ph.D.
Carolina Research Professor
College of Social Work, University of South Carolina

ASSIGNMENTS

1. Choose a current, newly enacted state policy.
   a. Use two of the models to analyze it.
   b. Identify a strategy for changing or modifying this policy as suggested by the model.
2. Identify a potential future problem.
   a. Predict the future extent of the problem.
   b. Describe the type of policy necessary to resolve the problem.
3. Choose a current state policy and analyze it through an efficiency criteria.
   a. Suggest ways of costing out benefits to clients as well as to society.
   b. Describe elements you would include as costs in delivering policy.

SUGGESTED READINGS

Gil, David. 1970. "A Systematic Approach to Social Policy Analysis." *Social Service Review* 44 (4): 411–426.
Sosin, Michael, and Sharon Caulum. 1983. "Advocacy: A Conceptualization for Social Work Practice." *Social Work* 28 (1): 12–18.

REFERENCES

Blau, Joel. 1992. "A Paralysis of Social Policy?" *Social Work* 37 (6): 558–562.
Dye, Thomas. 1981. *Understanding Public Policy.* Englewood Cliffs, NJ: Prentice Hall.
Flynn, John P. 1985. *Social Agency Policy.* Chicago, IL: Nelson Hall.
Gruber, Murray. 1991. "In and Out of the Rabbit Hole with Alice: Assessing the Consequences of Efficiency Prescriptions." In *Efficiency in Social Services.* New York: Haworth Press.
Humberger, Edward. 1977. "A Political-Economic Approach to Human Services." Paper presented at the 1977 American Society of Pubic Administration national conference. Washington, D.C.: Human Resources Administration.
Kleinkauf, Cecilia. 1989. "Analyzing Social Welfare Legislation." *Social Work* (March): 179–181.
Lindblom, Charles E. 1959. "The Science of Muddling Through." *Public Administration Review* 19 (Spring): 79–88.

chapter 5

The Practitioner's Influence on Policy

Social workers cannot afford to stand by and allow others to make policies that we are expected to implement. Social workers, those who have studied and implemented the policies, have seen the effect of the programs and the defects in the programs and know the unfulfilled needs of the people and thus ought to be able to initiate legislative efforts to form new programs or revamp old programs.

Edolphus "Ed" Towns

The general social work practitioner presumably is equipped with a framework and an array of roles that allow for intervention at the macro as well as at the micro level. Policy analysis, policy-making, and political intervention must be a central part of this framework (Pierce, 1984).

As subsequent chapters point out, data on social problems or needs is absolutely crucial to effectiveness in political intervention. A lobbyist cannot sway a legislator on a piece of legislation on day care, for example, without statistics, scenarios, or both, to back up the position, and the practitioner is the best source of such data because the practitioner is on the front line. In contact with clients on a daily basis, the practitioner often develops particular insight into social problems as well as firsthand knowledge of the target population.

The purpose of this chapter is to emphasize the importance of the practitioner, both directly and indirectly, to an array of political activities. Practitioners can have tremendous impact on legislative, administrative, and fiscal decision making simply by utilizing their practice knowledge and clinical data.

> The knowledge and skills students accumulate in social welfare policy and services should prepare them to exert leadership and influence as legislative social advocates, lobbyists, and expert advisors to policymakers and administrators.
>
> *Council on Social Work Education Curriculum Policy Statement, 1982*

It is unfortunate that all social work practitioners do not have within their repertoire of knowledge and skills an array of solutions to social problems, from case or micro level to political interventions. This would not necessarily add additional tasks to the practitioner's role or require the learning of new skills, because the actions involved primarily consist of information dissemination and client empowerment strategies.

INFORMATION DISSEMINATION

Documentation

Regardless of work setting, the practitioner continually encounters unmet needs, social problems, and gaps in or barriers to service. However, recognition of such needs and problems seldom results in collective, public activity by practitioners. More commonly, practitioners treating problems such as marital conflict, poor family communication, or parenting difficulties may look to a new treatment approach, read or write an article, or develop or attend a workshop. Macro-level solutions, such as changing a policy or program, or establishing a new program or agency, seem to come less readily to the practitioner's mind.

No matter what form of intervention a social worker may undertake—community organization, casework, administration, or political activity—the resource most needed and used is information. Before any diagnosis can be reached or community organization strategy developed, information about the client's background and presenting problem or the community's problem and demographics must first be obtained. Intervention in the political arena has the same basic requirement, because the same processes are used by the social worker in the political arena as in case or community work.

Also important is the social worker's daily interaction with clients, not only for the purpose of data collection, but also to facilitate the organization or mobilization of clients in their own behalf. The practitioner's relationship with clients or client groups provides clients with additional insight and motivation, both of which help to enable clients to advocate for themselves.

Social workers, practicing in a variety of settings (hospitals, juvenile homes, the courts, public schools, mental health clinics, and so forth), are in a position to respond quickly and authoritatively when asked about the major difficulties they face in serving clients: lack of time to adequately help people, too large a case load, insufficient resources. Each practitioner is an expert on problems, needs, and resources. Clearly, therefore, the practitioner can become an ideal conduit between those who have problems and needs and those who are politically active. Social workers are also good resources for what works. Unfortunately this doesn't often occur because the practitioner's knowledge and expertise usually remain at the case level. The missing link that would bridge the gap would be to aggregate individual practitioner's diagnoses and data into the kind of information that is necessary in order to function in the political sphere. Part of the solution has now been initiated with NASW's creation in 1986 of the National Center for Social Policy and Practice.

Increasingly, most agencies have some form of system by which to gather data that justifies expenditures to funding sources and describes activities to boards and to the community. Most of these information systems, whether simple and idiosyncratic to the program or highly complex or standardized, are usually constructed to depict or describe the activities of the staff (management information systems) or the characteristics and problems of the clients (client information systems). Consequently, even the most comprehensive and technical of these do not always identify unmet needs or adequately illuminate the overlapping dimensions of a problem.

The practitioner can pull together case statistics and scenarios that clarify, expand, or redefine a problem area in ways that an information system cannot. For example, as the number of teen mothers who choose to keep their babies increases, public school policies need to be changed if teen mothers are to continue their education. Working with individuals, practitioners might find solutions for each young mother. Because the problem is both a social and an individual one, social and political solutions, such as public school policy changes, are needed. Thus, a major requirement of advocacy for policy change is documentation by practitioners of needed services (Briar and Briar, 1982).

Because information systems are initiated to serve either agency documentation or clinical diagnostic needs, it is not surprising that the use of these in political testimony, legislative support, or administrative rule writing and program implementation may appear to be an afterthought. However, as documentation is a primary step in any problem-solving process in social work, systems should be designed for multiple purposes, including clinical, administrative, and political activities. Social work staff at all levels should be able to not only input data but to manipulate it to create categories and groupings that answer many questions, problems, and needs in various dimensions.

If practitioners become imbued with the idea that they have a unique and essential role in the documentation of needs, problems, and resources, they may find the task of "paper pushing" less cumbersome, boring, or unessential. Although their documentation skills and their information are essential to the political process, practitioners themselves do not need to be directly involved as political activists or advocates in order to contribute to political solutions.

Testimony

Given that legislators possess limited knowledge of the wide variety of subjects about which they must make decisions, testimony from the field is an essential part of political deliberations. Here is another opportunity for practitioners to effectively use their experience, expertise, skill, and knowledge to influence decisions made in the political arena.

Presentation at a legislative hearing of testimony using scenarios can have a major impact. Because the practitioner has access to clients who may be affected by a current or future policy, testimony can be enhanced by the inclusion of documented statistics, scenarios, and case illustrations, as well as by the presence of the clients themselves. The practitioner may speak on a client's behalf or have the clients speak for themselves. Either of these tactics can be used in a highly persuasive manner.

Of concern to the practitioner is the client's potential loss of confidentiality and anonymity through the use of client information, client profiles, case illustrations, and the client's presence. The social worker must be cautious about jeopardizing any individual client's privacy.

It is essential to keep in mind the basic principle of client self-determination when decisions are made about a client advocating on behalf of his or her own best interests or on the behalf of other clients. In fact, having clients take matters into their own hands to affect a solution is a recommended part of the helping process. Consequently, the role of enabler is an essential role for the social worker practitioner. If not already aware, clients should be shown that it is possible to implement situational, environmental, political, and organizational solutions to problems, as well as personal solutions. The introduction of macro-level solutions in turn helps to reinforce in clients the idea that their problems may not be caused by their own inadequacies.

Testimony by both the practitioner and the client is an extremely dynamic lobbying tool and is most dramatically done by the practitioners and clients directly affected. It may be more persuasive than the most expensive lobbyist, who, after all, must rely on secondary sources, such as aggregate data or "secondhand" stories. Thus, the client or social worker who can present facts, personal vignettes, and scenarios, and who also is a constituent, can play a significant role for clients and in major policy settings—a role that no other individual or group can fill.

Expert Witness

Legislative committees may request testimony or allow designated time slots for organizations and individuals to give testimony about an issue currently before that committee. Expert witnesses usually are called by invitation, and the expert must hold certain credentials—educational or experiential—to be deemed "expert." Sometimes legislators will undertake trips to seek information, witness events, or experience a particular social problem, so that they can themselves provide this firsthand type of information.

As noted in subsequent chapters, information is crucial to policy-making. It is the practitioner who is the expert on many client needs and problems, far more than the social work administrator or the paid professional lobbyist. The role of expert usually excludes clients, because the term often implies possession of specific educational credentials and a breadth of professional experience. Part of the verification of one's qualifications as an expert might include the ability to project the course of future events if a problem or need were to go unattended, and to show that these predictions have empirically demonstrable bases.

Although, as mentioned, the role of expert witness usually is undertaken at the invitation of a legislative or administrative group, social work practitioners should make themselves more ready to undertake this role and better prepare themselves to serve as expert witnesses if asked.

Written Communication

Writing letters to legislators is another important professional role that practitioners can fill. Many don't realize the potential impact of one letter from a professional. Nor does letter writing take much work: Legislators want to know as concisely as possible which bill one is writing about and the position taken; they want brief documentation for that position and enough identification so that the writer can be contacted for additional information. This type of letter is not difficult to write. Letter writing will be discussed more fully in chapter 5 on lobbying.

Many human service organizations have newsletters or house organs that can and should routinely be disseminated to state and federal legislators and relevant decision makers. The potential payoff in visibility for the organization, its clientele, and the services it provides is well worth the modest investment required. Increasing a public official's awareness of the services an organization provides is as important as is documentation of existing unmet needs. Both pieces of information are essential to informed decision making.

CLIENT EMPOWERMENT

Enabler/Advocate Role

Inherent in the general social work practitioner's functions is the role of enabler or advocate. One of the basic social work principles is to help clients move toward independence from the social worker, to enable clients to define and resolve their own problems, and to help them become self-advocates.

These roles require more than the collection of data and the consequent assessment of the situation or problem. They require the practitioner to imbue clients with the ability to "own" their problems and to identify client strengths for overcoming them. In the role of advocate the practitioner moves from analysis to action, requiring clients to identify resources and assert their rights.

Although the advocate role is most commonly utilized with individual clients to move from case (individual) to class (group), advocacy requires no additional skills other than the ability to aggregate data or mobilize clients. Community organizers build on these basic principles as a practice specialization, but specialization is not required.

Practitioners must not be so constrained by their therapeutic specialization or by an agency's policies on eligibility or service modalities that they become unable to see that macro-level problems require macro-level solutions. For example, an elderly single person who is depressed because of isolation from the community and loss of independence is treated for depression. This may well represent an example of the inability to recognize macro-level solutions. The astute practitioner might also examine community resources to ascertain whether adult day-care centers and accessible transportation are available. If not, practitioners in similar agencies could be queried to see if a sufficiently large client group exists to warrant further strategies, and if so, advocate with them or on their behalf for the development of these services.

An additional benefit of enabling clients to advocate on their own behalf is that it not only gives clients a sense of ability to control their lives, but gives them skills that are useful and transferable to various other situations.

Evaluator/Consultant Role

Thus far we have discussed roles that include and activate clients or involve workers on behalf of clients to seek needed policies and services or to improve inadequate ones. Consequently, we have identified an array of roles, such as testifying and lobbying, that are linked to the external, often political, arena.

Practitioners also are in a central position to identify and evaluate the effects of legislative policies on their organizations and to determine whether the rule-writing and implementation phases have been logically interpreted and consistently followed. Chapter 8 on monitoring describes these processes in greater detail.

Once policies have been passed or services have been introduced or redesigned, the practitioner delivering those services is presumed to be the person best placed and qualified to act as an evaluator and consultant to determine whether new policies or services follow the intent of the legislation. Do the rules prescribe services that will overcome the barriers and issues articulated? Is access assured to the targeted client group? Are clients better off now that the service is available? This is not to suggest that agencies necessarily will invite or encourage this type of critique. However, it is a vital function in policy making and a logical role for the practitioner.

Voter Registration

The central premise of the democratic process is that of freedom of individuals to choose among candidates who represent an array of political ideologies. Voting is the mechanism by which citizens have the opportunity to voice their opinions, make decisions, and elect those who shall represent them. Our system requires voters to be registered before they can vote in an election.

Promoting and enhancing client self-determination is a basic value of social work. Voting is one of the mechanisms that permits the citizens in a democratic nation to have a voice in determining the nation's domestic and foreign policies. Nonetheless, a large proportion of citizens are not registered to vote, and not surprisingly, a disproportionate number of these unregistered voters are social work clients: the poor, the young, the elderly, the unskilled.

It is consistent with social work principles to assist clients to exercise their democratic right to self-determination. One way to do so is to help them register to vote. In the past voter registration activities undertaken by social workers and schools of social work have been opposed by some members of the profession. They argue that registration is a partisan act and therefore is unlike other enabling activities, such as assisting clients to obtain a food stamp identification card, secure necessary documentation to rent an apartment, or file a death certificate so that insurance claims can be processed. Also, arguments have been made, often based on misconceptions about state Hatch Acts, that public employees are prohibited from undertaking voter registration activity.

In reality voter registration is quite legal as long as it is nonpartisan. The National Voter Registration Act of 1993 (also known as "Motor Voter") was enacted to address the problem of declining voter registration and to ensue the participation of all citizens in this country's political process. The act (which took effect in 1995) requires states to register clients at state-funded offices that provide service to people with disabilities and services related to AFDC, Food Stamps, Medicaid, and WIC. In addition, states must permit people to register to vote when they obtain or renew their drivers' licenses (hence the nickname of Motor Voter). Clearly, social workers and human service agencies that have a tax-exempt 501(c)(3) status can participate in voter registration as long as the drive remains nonpartisan. Neither the Hatch Act nor the IRS can prohibit such efforts.

HATCH ACT

In 1939, Congress approved legislation known as the Hatch Act, which limits the political activities of federal employees, employees of the District of Columbia government, and certain employees of state and local governments. The Hatch Act was enacted out of concern that governmental employees were participating in partisan political activities and might cause problems in public institutions. Therefore, the act limits governmental employees' partisan political activities. In 1993 President Clinton signed into law a revision and simplification of the 1939 act. The Hatch Act falls under the authority of the Office of Special Council and they should be consulted for specific questions and concerns. With very few exceptions, all employees in the federal executive branch and employed by state and local executive agencies are subject to the act. A key point to remember is the act is mostly concerned with partisan political activities, which means the election or political action connected to a political party whose presidential candidate received electoral votes in the last presidential election. The Hatch Act is confusing in terms of both who is covered and by its restrictions (Thompson, 1994). The following lists of dos and don'ts should help to clarify permissible and prohibited activities covered by the act.

May register and vote as they chose

May assist in voter registration drives

May express opinions about candidates and issues

May participate in campaigns where none of the candidates represent a political party

May contribute money to political organizations or attend political fund-raising functions

May wear or display political badges, buttons, or stickers

May join political clubs or parties

May sign nomination petitions

May campaign for or against referendum questions, constitutional amendments, municipal ordinances

May not be candidates for public office in partisan elections

May not campaign for or against a candidate or slate of candidates in partisan elections

May not collect contributions or sell tickets to political fund-raising functions

May not make campaign speeches or engage in other campaign activities to elect partisan candidates

May not distribute campaign material in partisan elections

May not organize or manage political rallies or meetings

May not circulate nomination petitions

May not work to register voters for one party only

This summarizes the law governing political activities of governmental employees. Clearly the act does not keep employees from any kind of activity. Social workers who are employed by the government should seek additional information to advocate for social change within the law.

THE EXECUTIVE'S ROLE IN INFLUENCING POLICY

Unfortunately, in the past, social work administrators have been stereotyped as conservative and part of the status quo. Probably a central explanation for this description is that these executives are seen as representatives of recalcitrant and unchanging organizations—the very same ones that are often targets for social work activists (Richan, 1980).

While there has been some empirical evidence to support this stereotype (Heffernan, 1964; Epstein, 1981), research indicates that this perception has changed. In one study of advocacy organizations, for example, it was found that the effective organizations were more likely to have social work administrators than were the less effective ones (Reisch, 1986). In another survey (Ezell, 1989), it was found that administrators devote significantly more time to advocacy on their jobs than do micro practitioners and that these macro practitioners use more of their time for class advocacy. A recent survey (Pawlak and Flynn, 1990) showed that 77 percent of the sample wrote letters and 43 percent talked with officials. About a third used intermediaries in their political activities.

According to Ezell's work, "it appears to remain true that no social workers are very active in political campaigning, litigating, representing clients in hearings, conducting issue research, influencing media coverage of an issue, or attempting to influence administrative rule making. Administrators were significantly more likely to engage in the last three" (Ezell, 1989, p. 13). When asked why they engage in these efforts, the macro practitioners more routinely saw advocacy as part of their jobs and were more likely to belong to other organizations that take stands on public issues.

One potentially simplistic explanation for the administrators' increase in political activity is the growing decentralization of decision making and funding to states and localities and the pressures of an organization to survive. Consequently, social work administrators have, and must, learn to compete effectively in this arena. The "ability to assess the structure and operation of power in an organization and skill in coalition formation are two central attributes of the organizational politician" (Gummer and Edwards, 1985, p. 18). This leadership is most likely to take the forms of working with the state system, redesigning the voluntary sector, mobilizing external constituencies, and pursuing legal options which is externally directed and takes political sophistication (Perlmutter, 1985, p. 4).

Human service programs had developed incrementally in Indiana and by the mid-1980s programs were scattered over at least six state departments, with many operating outside the bounds of any of these bureaucracies. Neither planning, cooperation, nor consolidation were even issues. In late 1983, I decided that the Community Service Council should conduct a needs assessment of the eight-county central Indiana region, funded by the various stakeholders who agreed to do so. I wanted to assure that indirect services such as planning and information and referral were addressed.

An implementation phase followed the completion of the needs assessment, and promoting action on state planning was a priority issue. A prominent businessperson, chair of the implementation phase, arranged a meeting with the governor and his executive staff to talk about inter-departmental planning. While these state officials were not terribly receptive to this concept, they were concerned that some clients were abusing the system and that others were not really being helped due to the lack of coordination among state services. I suggested that CSC should research what other states were doing and provide the governor with a report. Funds for the implementation phase were shifted slightly to provide for this research. After I completed two papers on this topic, I met with the staff director of the statewide human services coalition and the heads of two key human service departments. Although state officials were not extremely supportive, they did agree to fund one position for a planner to work with the Interdepartmental Board for the Coordination of Human Services. Although this position became institutionalized, there still was no attention to statewide structure and policies in the state's human services system.

Thus, in 1987 the United Way of Indiana approached the governor to initiate a statewide public-private strategic planning process for human services. I was a member of "Hoosier Initiative" and we made sure that both candidates in the gubernatorial election were included in the process. Legislation that would lay the groundwork for implementation was championed by CSC and the United Way and passed in Indiana in 1989.

The new governor recognized the partnership achieved through Hoosier Initiative and named me and the three other leaders to four of the seven citizen seats on the interdepartmental board. The state is now engaged in serious study around reorganization and I, as vice chair of the board, will chair the subcommittee responsible for this plan.

Although incremental, the achievements are significant: from a dilemma identified locally to a position held by a coalition made up of diverse constituencies to a state priority. Additionally, my role as an agency executive working from the outside and trying to persuade state bureaucrats what to do has shifted to that of an inside leader, helping the state decide which path to take.

Irv Katz, MSW
Executive Director, Community Service Council of Central Indiana
and Vice President for Planning, United Way of Central Indiana

INFLUENCING POLICY: AN ILLUSTRATION

Sara L. Barwinski, MSW, is currently the Advocacy Facilitator at Lutheran Family and Children's Services in St. Louis, Missouri. She provides an illustration of the process of influencing policy.

Lutheran Family Services is a direct service agency. They, have a variety of services they provide, from very traditional marriage and family counseling to adoption and foster care. I work with the unit that addresses low-income clients, crisis intervention homelessness, case management, and resettlement.

In the early 1980s after the federal cuts, we started seeing more and more homeless families in our own caseloads. It was very frustrating to discover that the people who needed resources after losing their shelter were not receiving food stamps in Missouri. When Lutheran Family Services first started serving homeless families, there was a belief that homelessness was the result of being a skid row alcoholic and that these clients were traditionally served by the Salvation Army. Additionally, most practitioners just accepted that there were no services or benefits for their homeless clients.

It was in 1984 that we really started working with folks in a new way. The fact that I was fairly green in the field was helpful in a lot of ways. I decided to take advantage of the "caseworker training" provided by the Missouri Department of Social Services. I thought that if I was going to work directly with clients in these situations, it would be helpful if I really understood the rules and regulations.

I was confused. I knew that technically homeless people were supposed to be able to get food stamps, yet client after client came back stating that they had been denied food stamps. State officials assured me that the homeless people in Missouri were not being denied food stamps because of homelessness.

Through networking with other state and national organizations addressing hunger issues, I found that, indeed, the federal food stamp program was there for the homeless, but in the streets of St. Louis the homeless were not getting food stamps. I then interviewed clients about the process and their experiences, and then I discovered the problem. The clients were not allowed to apply in the first place! This explained why the state officials at the capitol were saying that there was no problem. They never received any applications, therefore, no problem existed.

At first I wondered whether this was just a problem in St. Louis or whether it was happening in other parts of the state. I found out that it was very common throughout the state not to allow homeless people to apply for food stamps in the first place.

When clients came into the welfare office, the first order of business was to put their names and addresses on a waiting fist from which they could be called to fill out applications. Of course, those with no addresses to put down would never get to the application. They were told that they could not be seen until they came back with addresses. That was the loophole— there was no paper trial, there was nothing that could be legally appealed, and consequently the state was ignorant of their problem.

If you don't have an address, you have to establish residency. This is a matter of concern to the counties, especially in cities like St. Louis, which borders on Illinois. How do the intake workers know whether a person is really a resident of the county? The manual provided no clarification. On the one hand, clients could not be denied because they were homeless. However, clients needed an address to prove residency in the county in order to apply in that county. The issue was not something that the state had previously been challenged to clarify in the manual, as the homeless issue had not been a really pressing social problem until this time.

It was time to take on this issue. The problem that I faced was a lack of paperwork to document or appeal a case to make the needed changes. I needed a client to use as a test case. I didn't think it was wise to use a homeless family because of the possibility of having the children removed from their parents. I needed an unmarried person who was willing to fight the bureaucracy.

I asked one particular client, I'll call him Jeff, a young person who had been through the foster care system. At 18, all of a sudden he found himself on his own, unprepared to do anything. By the time I worked with Jeff, he was 20, had drifted for a few years, and was living on the streets. He agreed to be the test case after I explained the process. He had applied before and been denied. This was important because if we were successful, we wanted others who had been denied to hear of the story and reapply.

I went with Jeff to apply and we used the agency's address to get through that first loophole. When we actually saw a caseworker, we were received with anger when it was realized that Jeff was using the agency's address. I had done my homework and it was going to come in handy. I explained to the caseworker what my real concern was: I wanted the caseworker to clarify their policy and make a decision to either accept or reject the application for food stamps. I had already talked to people at legal services. They were prepared to take legal action, but we needed a formal refusal first. If they accepted the application, then we had a precedent that we could use to change the overall policy.

The caseworker did not want to take the application. I knew that the law was absolutely clear: Everyone had the right to apply and each applicant had the right to a written rejection. When the caseworker asked us to leave, I held my ground and gently demanded his decision in writing. I had with me the names and telephone numbers of the people I had contacted at the state capitol who assured me that this was not happening. I suggested that before he refused to take this application, he might want to call some of them just to check because they assured me that I would not have a problem. He made the calls. He wasn't really happy, but he came back a few minutes later and took the application.

Because Jeff had absolutely no income or resources, it was an expedited food stamp case for the homeless. This meant that legally the state had to respond within the next five days. However, it took seven days before the city office got the approval to issue food stamps.

The state decided to get around the issue of Jeff's not having an address by using the Department of Social Services' county office address and to have Jeff pick up the stamps there. This then established a precedent allowing homeless people the option of either using the county social service office address or other addresses that they could arrange with their caseworker.

Although the system was now in place, we only had one caseworker who knew of the new system. I am not so naive as to think that this action would make a difference for all homeless people in Missouri. It was only the first step.

Next I convened a group of service providers who worked with homeless people from such agencies as Catholic Charities, the Salvation Army, and other groups in town in order to walk them through the process that I had done with Jeff. I explained what the state policy was now and trained them to do the exact same thing with their clients. From that meeting a dozen people or so took homeless clients to the welfare office. This assured me that people were being handled correctly and that other state caseworkers would learn from the experience. Not without problems, it took several months to obtain our goal of having the process well ingrained in the county welfare department so that eventually we would not need to accompany the clients. We met with county officials to discuss the system and to show them that we wanted to help make the new system work. However, I let them know that we were very serious by bringing an attorney from legal services with me. It was all very pleasant, but they knew all along that there was the real potential of a lawsuit. The attorney's presence was like having an iron fist in a soft glove—we came as friends, but let them know we meant business.

At that meeting we identified the main concern, I think a legitimate concern, the establishment of the county of residence. We worked out different ways that would be acceptable as verification of county residency including prior attendance at school in the county, a previous county address, or a previous employer in the county. One progressive approach we came up with was to allow social workers to serve as collateral contacts. We produced a form on which a social worker could state that to the best of the social worker's knowledge, this homeless person, whom our agency has been serving for a certain amount of time, is a resident of this county. This would be accepted as proof of residency for the application.

I had been in communication with people in Kansas City, Springfield, Columbia, and different cities around Missouri, who assured me that this was not just a St. Louis problem. Therefore, it was necessary to formalize the policy change and make it permanent by incorporating it into the manual, which would go out to workers and be included in their training.

To start this next step, we successfully got a policy clarification memo and a manual change that accompanied the memo. The memo clearly stated that homeless people were not to be denied and that they were entitled to receive the stamps at the county offices. A list of the different kinds of verification that could be provided and the mechanisms that could be set up to handle the special situation that homeless people encounter were specified.

To put the final touch on this policy change, I invited state officials to be part of a news conference with us. It was not the intent to embarrass them nor to take legal action, although we were prepared throughout this fight to do so. We felt now was the time to lay the foundation for further efforts on behalf of our mutual clients, and the purpose of the news conference was to announce this new policy. This was a far more effective strategy than blasting them for not rectifying the problem in the first place.

There was another positive outcome from this experience. Including the client Jeff in the news conference, and crediting his collaboration in our efforts, provided an incredible boost for his self-esteem. It is a social work value to empower clients, and I see advocacy efforts to be no exception.

Really, this advocacy effort happened fairly quickly; about six months after Jeff got his food stamps, we had the news conference. Another reason we were successful was the networking with other agencies and the support of legal aid even though we never took legal action.

I guess from a practitioner's standpoint, I could have stayed in St. Louis giving out bags of food and not touched anywhere near the number of people I did by getting this policy changed. This experience taught me how important it is for practitioners to keep tabs on their clients as well as the bureaucracy.

Ms. Barwinski kept up her advocacy efforts on behalf of clients in need of food stamps. Twice she testified before the U.S. Congress on legislation that resulted in the Stewart B. McKinney Act and the Hunger Prevention Act of 1988.

CONCLUSION

It should be evident that the practices and processes advocated throughout this chapter are already in place and part of the intrinsic fabric of social work. As with so many of the skills and techniques discussed in this book, they require only the ability of the social work professional to translate them from the micro- to the macro-level arena of practice.

Furthermore, we have seen that intervention in the policy or political arena need not be direct. Repackaging existing information in a slightly different manner and enlisting other individuals in coalition building or problem identification may be all that is necessary.

The empowerment of clients may be strategically utilized or may occur as an outgrowth of other activities. In either case, it is a core social work principle, not an ancillary function.

ASSIGNMENTS

1. Examine the client data collected by an agency where you are interning or to which you have access. Does the agency collect sufficient information to document a need for new services, policies, or both? If so, explain how. If not, what kinds of information do they need to collect?

2. Through observations made by you in your work with individual clients, generate two research questions that could be tested by having practitioners within the agency collect additional information.

3. Identify an unmet need among your client population and present a political strategy for filling this need. Describe the steps that are necessary steps in the process.

SUGGESTED READINGS

O'Connell, Brian. 1978. "From Service to Advocacy to Empowerment." *Social Casework* 59 (April): 195-202.
Sunley, Robert. 1970. "Family Advocacy: From Case to Course." *Social Casework* 51 (June): 347-357.

REFERENCES

Briar, Katherine Hooper, and Scott Briar. 1982. "Clinical Social Work and Public Policies." In *Practical Politics: Social Work and Political Responsibility,* Maryann Mahaffey and John Hanks (eds.), pp. 45-54. Washington, D.C.: National Association of Social Workers.

Epstein, I. 1981. "Advocates on Advocacy: An Exploratory Study." *Social Work Research and Abstracts* 17 (2): 5-12.

Ezell, M. 1989. "Administrators as Activists." Paper presented at the National Association of Social Workers Annual Conference, San Francisco, California.

Gummer, B., and R. L. Edwards. 1985. "A Social Worker's Guide to Organizational Politics." *Administration in Social Work* 9 (1): 13-21.

Heffernan, W. J. 1964. "Policy Activity and Social Work Executives." *Social Work* 9 (2): 18-23.

Pawlak, Edward J., and John P. Flynn. 1990. "Executive Directors' Political Activities." *Social Work* 35 (4): 307-312.

Perlmutter, F. D. 1985. "The Politics of Social Administration." *Administration in Social Work* 9 (4): 1-11.

Pierce, Dean. 1984. *Policy for the Social Work Practitioner.* White Plains, NY: Longman.

Reisch, M. 1986. "From Cause to Case and Back Again: The Reemergence of Advocacy in Social Work." *Urban and Social Change Review* 19 (Winter/Summer): 20-24.

Richan, W. C. 1980. "The Administrator as Advocate." In *Leadership in Social Administration: Perspectives for the 1980's,* F. D. Perlmutter and S. Slavin (eds.). Philadelphia, PA: Temple University Press.

Thompson, Joanne J. 1994. "Social Workers and Politics: Beyond the Hatch Act." *Social Work* 39 (4): 457-465.

chapter 6

Influence through Lobbying

Legislative advocacy can be at its best when it advances the goals of the advocate, the social work profession, and when it connects to the legislator's concerns.

Patricia Ewalt

In a noisy back room of a restaurant directly across the street from the capitol, a group of legislators continue a debate started earlier in committee hearings. The unresolved issue they are discussing is whether to appropriate additional revenues for services to learning-disabled children or for highway repair and reconstruction.

Several legislators believe learning-disabled children do not deserve special services. In their opinion, the problem of these children is laziness and inattentiveness and therefore the educational system should deal with it as a disciplinary problem. Others believe the money would be better spent on highway and road repair—a significantly more visible project that would affect all constituents.

A lone voice among the group speaks in support of appropriating the funds to the learning disabled, citing physical disabilities as well as difficult home environments. When asked why he takes this position, the legislator describes a child who lives next door to him who has a learning disability and tells how the parents are struggling to pay for private tutors and services.

The others conclude that this is only one example and may be the exception, not the rule. None of the legislators seem to know exactly how many other learning-disabled children are in the state or what problems they and their families face.

Earlier a lobbyist for the highway repair appropriations bill had persuasively demonstrated the degree of popular concern for this legislation, and the number of complaints received about present conditions, and had argued the cost-effectiveness of undertaking these projects now rather than waiting until the next legislative session. The lone legislator sympathetic to the learning disabled's cause, on the other hand, reluctantly admits that he does not know the extent of need and does not have significant constituent support for the proposal. In the absence of additional information or persuasive advocacy, and in light of the legislators' indifference to and ignorance of learning disabilities, the group supports the highway repair bill. In the real world of political processes, decisions are influenced and made by those who work the system in their favor. This chapter discusses what is commonly known as "politicking," or as it is more professionally termed, lobbying.

The term *politicking* is used frequently and indiscriminately. It is sometimes used as a personal adjective: "He (she) is really political." Unfortunately, this usually suggests that the individual is attempting to make contacts and influence individuals in order to enhance a personal position. This may give negative connotations to politicking, suggesting that it is selfish and possibly underhanded.

Indeed, lobbying presumes the persuasive presentation of one side of an issue, primarily to influence decision makers. Because of this, many people, especially social workers, may refuse to participate in what may be viewed as selfish, untruthful, or conflicting practices. However, the American system of government was constructed on the notion of pluralism. In other words, it was designed to encourage and accommodate the expression of conflicting views, group conflict, negotiation, bargaining, and compromise. Lobbying is not a straightforward presentation of all positions on an issue, nor does it have as a goal the enhancement of influence or position. It is our contention that lobbying is a legitimate, fundamental, and powerful practice in a pluralistic society, and that social workers and their clients will continue to lose politically if they do not enter this arena.

Social workers often perceive lobbyists as representatives of special interest groups, failing to realize that they themselves are a special interest group also, with beliefs and values that prescribe goals and positions. Unlike other groups, however, the special interest of social workers always has been society's disadvantaged and disenfranchised members. Thus, the social work profession's special interest is not self-interest, but rather a concern for individuals, groups, and communities who cannot lobby for themselves.

For example, when President Reagan announced in 1979 that the private sector should fill the gap in human service revenues resulting from reduced federal support, no group was in a better position to lobby against this view than were social workers. Yet social workers took little collective action. Although clients of human services certainly have an interest in continuing services, they usually are not organized, knowledgeable, or articulate enough to lobby for themselves.

There are myths about the political process that often discourage social workers from participating in it. One myth is that social workers need specialized training in the political process before they can intervene. They fail to recognize the value of their knowledge and understanding of a community, of individuals, of an individual's functioning within the community, and of group interactions, but this knowledge is the most valuable tool that a social worker can bring to the lobbying process.

Another myth is that a large group of individuals with a lot of money is needed to influence legislators. In fact, there are numerous ways by which a single individual or a few individuals, with the right timing and the right information, can affect social policy. Although it may dishearten many social workers to oppose groups with more resources and money, it should not be cause for retreat.

SOCIAL WORK SKILLS IN THE POLITICAL PROCESS

Because our political structure is both representative and pluralistic, it requires and even demands that some individuals speak on behalf of others and that opposing groups resolve conflicts. The very nature of the political process is one of individual interaction, and this clearly implies the importance of social work skills.

Social workers are trained to understand how individuals relate and interact, how groups form and change, how miscommunication can alienate people from each other and from society, and how motivation affects behavior. Social workers can use this knowledge and their corresponding skills to understand and to intervene in the political process.

In the committee process, for example, a social worker who has background information on the committee members (such as district composition, the members' previous voting records, education, training, and previous professional experience) can observe and understand committee member interactions. In many cases, the social worker will be able to predict what approach and what factors may persuade a given legislator to support the social workers' position.

To be an advocate for the poor requires a kind of lobbying that's different from that which comes to mind when one talks of peddling influence at the state capitol. Social service lobbyists cannot compete with the wining, dining, and campaign contributions of the numerous and powerful lobbyists that have achieved the status of the "third house of Congress." Social workers fail when they play in that league. Our strength and success is in facts and figures, not dinner and drinks.

Sandy Ingraham, MSW
Social Services Consultant
Harrah, Oklahoma

Social workers also receive in-depth training on one-on-one interaction. These skills are certainly transferable to interactions with legislators. Equally important are the other basics of social work, such as knowledge of social problems, social interaction, and the social environment. This knowledge can be very beneficial to the legislator in the difficult task of legislative decision making.

In 1990, while reading a report of the U.S. Public Health Service Act, I noticed that, even though provisions were made for training funds for eleven other health professions, social work was not mentioned at all. I was concerned that social work students would not have access to resources available to other health professions students, for example, scholarships and loans for disadvantaged students and training for health care in rural areas and with people with AIDS.

I had previously made a point of maintaining contact with my senator's office by telephone and mail, as well as by in-person visits whenever in Washington, D.C. Now I wrote to the senator inquiring why social work was not included among the professions funded for training.

As it happened, Senator Inouye has a strong interest in increasing the availability of nonphysician providers, such as social workers and nurses. He is very interested in opening doors for disadvantaged students. And he is very interested in services to disadvantaged populations, including people of color, people in rural areas, and people with AIDS.

Senator Inouye responded that the underlying legislation, the wording that defines health professions, would have to be changed. Social work had not been defined as a health profession. Without this basic change, federal officials would not be required to give consideration to social work training. The senator asked for increased help from the social work profession to bring about the needed change.

The social work profession, represented by the Government Relations Department of NASW at the national office, had already been advocating in Congress for the needed change. The new ingredient at this point was the constituent's request for the senator's advice and help to change the definition, a goal of interest to the constituent, the senator, and NASW.

Consequently, the senator asked for the constituent's as well as NASW's increased assistance to gain allies for the desired change. He gave continuing advice about actions that needed to be taken with members of the Senate and House. NASW implemented the senator's requests and I was able to enlist the assistance of members of an additional organization, the National Association of Deans and Directors of Schools of Social Work.

In October 1992, the Health Professions Education Amendments were passed, including the definition of social work as a health profession.

Patricia Ewalt, Ph.D.
Dean, School of Social Work, University of Hawaii

It should be noted that at certain times and in some situations, the fact that a social worker is not a regular lobbyist can work in favor of influencing a legislator. This is so because the legislator will know that the social worker is lobbying because he or she is truly concerned, has a special interest, and is knowledgeable, not because he or she is being paid to lobby or acting out of self-interest. This should not suggest, however, that it is not important for social workers to build and maintain continuing relationships with legislators.

Throughout this book, we indicate the distinct importance of social work values. It bears repeating that the fact that social workers as lobbyists are less self-interested than are many other special interest groups may be an extremely influential factor. Some have charged that lobbying by social workers to continue or to implement a program is self-serving because such a program creates or maintains jobs for social workers. This argument should not be allowed to cloud the issue. The main reason for lobbying for programs is to provide needed services to people.

THE POLITICAL PROCESS

A formal process exists by which all legislation must proceed. Legislators must follow rules, regulations, and procedures before a bill can be voted on and passed to the executive branch. This procedure includes checks and balances to ensure input from multiple sources and conflict resolution between groups. The essence of the legislative process is making choices between conflicting objectives. Coming to a compromise on a specific piece of legislation can be an extremely time-consuming process. It is true that sometimes a bill can pass through Congress or a state legislature with lightning speed, but usually these are bills that either respond to very critical situations or have great public support.

To influence legislation effectively, social workers must understand precisely how the legislative process works. Each state has its own rules or procedures; the state printing office or state chamber of commerce will have this information or know where it can be obtained.

In general, legislative bodies are composed of committees, each with a separate jurisdiction and substantive area. It is in the committee that a bill is given its most thorough review or reading. A primary method by which committees obtain information is from public testimony; thus, the committee is a key public access point. One individual who acts at the right time with precise and persuasive information can have a tremendous effect on the committee process.

However, there are inherent problems with this process. First, committee agendas can change without notice. Second, committee meetings can be canceled without notice. Third, bills sometimes are not placed on the committee agenda at all. One must keep informed about committee activity and be ready to counteract these problems.

FIGURE 6.1 How a bill becomes law

SOURCE: Reprinted from *Trial Talk*, June 1984.

The key person in the committee quite obviously is the chairperson. The chair has sole discretion over the committee and can choose to present a bill in such a way as to have a tremendous impact on the action taken by the committee. The array of options that a legislative committee can undertake are as follows: (1) report on the bill favorably as is; (2) report favorably, with amendments; (3) report favorably on a substitute bill; (4) report on a bill unfavorably; (5) send the bill to another committee for review; (6) table the bill, or (7) not place it on the committee's agenda.

Depending on the committee's recommendation, the next step is for the bill to go before the first house for full review. At that time, the general legislative climate should be assessed to determine whether a great amount of public support is needed.

From the first house, the bill must proceed to the second house for approval, and finally to the president or governor for signature. This process provides several key points at which intervention can take place.

THE POLITICIAN

The key component within the legislative process is the politician. As legislators, they represent large constituent groups having a diversity of positions, values, and ideas. Politicians vary in age, experience, training, political ideology, and party affiliation. In order to understand the political process, one needs to know not only the rules and regulations, but also the players.

External to but influential in the political process are such other factors as public opinion, media involvement, the activities of special interest groups, and informal coalitions among legislators (such as the black caucus, the liberal caucus, the senior legislators' caucus, and so forth). Knowledge of these factors assists lobbyists in influencing legislators.

Politicians have diverse constituencies to whom they feel accountable. First, politicians are responsible to those who voted for them. Second, they have a responsibility to the population within their geographic district. Third, they feel a responsibility to those individuals who campaigned for them. If politicians are listening to opposing opinions from these diverse constituent groups, decision making becomes difficult.

Another set of concerns involves limitations on the politician's time. Politicians have very little time to go out and seek problem areas and concerns that need correcting. They must rely on individuals, constituents, lobbyists, and others to bring problems to them and to supply them with detailed information about the problems or concerns on which they are working. To further complicate matters, many state representatives have either no aides or only one aide to do research, to investigate, and to advise them. Some have access to staff members hired by the legislative body, but the scope of this assistance is rather limited. Clearly, given the variety of issues that face any one legislator, often there is not enough time or staff to go around, especially when one realizes that politicians frequently are unfamiliar with many issues about which they must make decisions.

Legislators also must deal with constant public exposure. Many hours of work are allocated to understanding and dealing with conflicting views and interests. They must meet with their constituents and with special interest groups, all of whom want to advise them. As a result they may find themselves immersed in such complex social issues as abortion, euthanasia, the death penalty, and domestic violence. The advice and pressure from the groups supporting and opposing these issues often is contradictory.

Furthermore, because any individual who becomes a legislator goes through a very lengthy and costly process to get elected, a frequent concern for politicians is to maintain their position by being reelected. A candidate for the U.S. Congress may spend almost half of a term campaigning and may either avoid difficult and controversial issues during campaign years or assume a popular, noncontroversial position.

Anyone who wants to become an effective lobbyist must have a general knowledge of the factors that influence politicians' behavior. Some individuals become politicians because they want to be in the limelight and to have constant public exposure, some are deeply concerned about issues and want to make changes, and some find themselves in politics because of their family's name and prominent status. These factors may influence how a legislator perceives legislation or acts upon issues; thus, lobbyists must understand them in order to have a total grasp of the politician and the political milieu.

THE INFORMAL POLITICAL PROCESS

Lobbyists must be aware of formal legislative procedures and processes, but they also should be familiar with the informal processes. Usually viewed as "politics," the informal processes actually are individual-to-individual or group-to-group influences, motives, or relationships that affect the outcome of legislation. When attempting to influence legislation, one needs to consider both the formal and informal processes.

For example, one group of legislators trying to push through a bill to create public jobs in order to decrease the unemployment rate may be opposed by another group of legislators who wish to increase a certain defense budget item. These two groups may come together and compromise by creating defense-related jobs, thus enabling both groups to obtain their desired outcomes. It is also possible, of course, for this scenario to result in the defeat of both pieces of legislation.

In addition to caucuses or groupings of legislators by state, by party affiliation, or by issue, other influences exist that can have an informal effect upon legislation. First, the piece of legislation in which you are interested may not have as high a priority in the eye of the public as does other legislation. Second, because legislators may have so many other items to deal with, your piece of legislation may be dealt with only superficially in order to appease you. Finally, legislation will be dealt with by politicians in respect to its possible impact on their careers and reelection.

LOBBYING

Goal Setting

Once a lobbyist understands the formal and informal processes a bill must go through and has a grasp of the players (politicians, aides, other lobbyists), the next step is to formulate a clearly defined goal. One must decide whether to influence already-proposed pieces of legislation, modify present legislation, or develop a new piece of legislation. To enlist others in a lobbying effort, one must have an explicit goal. Whatever the goal, it should be stated clearly and, ideally, in measurable terms so that it is possible to know if the goal has been achieved.

Strategy Setting

Setting strategy is a critical and often neglected part of lobbying. Without it lobbying may be ineffectual. *Strategy* is a plan of action for the achievement of a goal. As soon as the goal has been identified and operationalized, the strategy should be determined.

A parallel can be drawn between strategy setting and management by objectives, where the goal is defined and the various steps to reach that goal are stated. It is clear to all participants what steps are needed in order to proceed to the goal. In the delineation of strategy, any complicating factors or unforeseen obstacles that may delay or block action should be spelled out, and alternative strategies should be developed in case complicating factors or obstacles arise.

For example, legislation is introduced at the state level to restore allocation levels for primary and secondary public education. Passage appears likely, despite the state's fiscally constrained condition, because it is difficult to oppose education for young children. However, the state is plagued by high rates of unemployment, and several mayors have requested the governor proclaim a state of emergency because of the decreasing nutritional level of a large segment of the state's population who are unable to afford adequate amounts of food. This crisis could overshadow concern for public education.

It is impossible to describe all alternative strategies that could be adopted. A strategy must be developed after a review of the policy and the politicians involved, an assessment of the bill's likely trail, an understanding of potential legislative and community climates, and an assessment of what possibilities are realistic for the lobbyists.

One strategy may be to work with and educate key legislators as the legislation is developed, amended, and passed through committees—that is, a strategy of working within the legislative system to overcome resistance and to educate. An alternative and potentially conflict-producing strategy at the opposite end of the continuum is to amass public support and encourage numerous contacts with legislators (Ornstein and Elder, 1978).

Usually it is desirable to first attempt to work within the system and then, when and if opposition develops, to move to an external strategy. A middle approach might be used in a situation in which a piece of legislation appears to have majority support but faces a potential floor debate. In such a case, a letter campaign to the general assembly or the presence of concerned citizens during a legislative session may prove effective.

A social worker/lobbyist should keep in mind several essential concepts. First, it is important to be honest and factual whenever a legislator or legislative aide is contacted. Second, and perhaps more important, it is well to remember that straightforward presentations with data generally provide the most persuasive approach and maintain the credibility of both the social worker/lobbyist and the social work profession. Finally, any presentation should include answers to two questions of critical concern to legislators: (1) What will this proposed legislation cost? (2) What is the social impact of this bill? It is particularly important to anticipate not only the answers to these questions, but, if the costs appear high, to provide information about the costs of allowing the social problem or need to go unresolved.

At the beginning of any lobbying effort, the lobbyist must keep in mind that many checks and balances are built into the legislative process, and that legislators can be influenced in numerous ways. The process is complex, with formal as well as informal variables; hundreds of concerns and points of view are concurrently presented before any legislative body. Thus, a lobbyist must have two important qualities: patience and persistence.

In conclusion, the lobbyist should bear in mind the following guidelines:

1. Know your issue thoroughly. Anticipate the opposition's claims and formulate persuasive counter arguments. Be prepared to provide technical information that will be useful to the politician(s) involved.
2. Identify a core group of committed and effective workers who will lead a coalition of interested groups and individuals who can be called on to write letters, lobby, or publicize the issue.
3. Locate a lawmaker who is sympathetic to your issue and is likely to be effective in advancing the cause, and continue to work with him or her for the duration of the process.
4. Be familiar with the formal legislative structure and the procedural steps a bill must take to become a law.
5. Spend as much time as possible at the capitol, both to answer legislators' questions and to be in a position to intervene effectively at the critical moment, by offering advice or information before decisions have been made. (Michigan Sea Grant Advisory Service, 1981)

In addition to patience and persistence, another extremely important attribute of a lobbyist is the ability to acknowledge the merits of competing proposals. Although a lobbyist's role is to mobilize the strongest and most persuasive arguments for a particular position, when a lobbyist becomes unable or unwilling to acknowledge the merits of an alternative proposal, he or she is seen as a propagandist, and any credibility and eventual utility may be reduced (Patti and Dear, 1981).

FACE-TO-FACE LOBBYING

Social workers who are naive about politicians and the political process may believe that politicians are so powerful that they are unapproachable. It seems easier to them to write letters, sign petitions, or join coalitions than to interact directly with legislators. Nevertheless, legislators need direct interaction and may, in fact, even seek it out from various individuals and groups. They realize that they are very much isolated and protected from what is really occurring in society, and therefore must rely on input from credible sources.

In face-to-face lobbying with a legislator whom the lobbyist has never met, one must establish credibility by identifying who is being represented as well as one's personal expertise and experience. Particularly if the lobbyist is a constituent of that legislator, a basis for rapport may already exist. Having been visibly active in a legislator's campaign is certainly beneficial in establishing a relationship, because campaigns are expensive and politicians generally dislike fund-raising, so they are likely to remember those who assisted and supported them in that process (Mahaffey, 1972).

It is unnecessary to buy a legislator a three martini lunch. Straightforward, factual, and well-presented information is most effective. Although legislative offices and surroundings might be intimidating to the beginning lobbyist, remember that the representative needs your information and assistance. Legislators are extremely busy and often must deal with a multitude of subject areas. Thus, they might switch subjects during an interview. Also, they sometimes deliberately take a contrary stance, but this may be because they want to learn how to argue effectively on behalf of your position.

Developing a good working relationship with a legislator's secretary should not be overlooked. Often secretaries are gatekeepers. As such, they represent a potential access point to the legislator and a channel through which information can be transmitted that may influence the legislator.

Many lobbyists focus their efforts on legislators who share values and goals similar to their own. Although such legislators are valuable, they may not be the most important target of influence (Patti and Dear, 1981). When deciding whom to contact, one should compile several lists: one consisting of legislators overtly supportive of your position, another of those who are explicitly opposed, and a third of those who are undecided. The third list is the one that should be targeted for intensive effort. At the same time, keep in contact with supporters through informative letters, phone calls, and the like.

Before a face-to-face interview with a representative, preparation is in order. Determine what particular issues are of interest, how the legislator approaches certain subjects, and what position he or she has taken on similar legislation in the past. This will allow you to present material in a way that encourages the legislator to listen to your position. Present the information to the legislator, keeping in mind the particular importance of the cost of the proposal and its social implications.

Almost all legislators will grant an appointment on request. However, in dealing with members of Congress, particularly if one is attempting to see them in Washington, time constraints may require that the appointment be with a legislative aide. Do not be dismayed. In most cases, the aides are the ones who formulate policy and persuade the legislator to take a position. When possible, ask for an appointment in the legislator's home district, where committee pressures and other responsibilities are somewhat reduced. Remember that the legislator is in the home district to get constituents' opinions on issues.

Because the length of appointments is likely to be limited, it is an excellent idea to provide written material and supportive documentation. Be sure that this material is as succinct as possible. A copy of all written material should also be provided for the legislative aide. Remember that it is important to utilize case examples from the legislator's district whenever possible.

Obtaining an appointment with state and local officials is usually easier, and these meetings often occur in less formal settings, such as political gatherings, receptions, and in the corridors of the statehouse or county building. However, do not invade the politician's personal life with a confrontation at the grocery store or theater. In all settings, common courtesy should be used and, regardless of the outcome of the discussion, you should thank the legislator for the appointment and for his or her open-mindedness. Follow up the meeting with a thank you letter that includes a synopsis of the position taken by the legislator during that meeting. Finally, follow through with anything that you agreed to do. If you fail to do so, your credibility will quickly deteriorate.

LETTER WRITING

It is commonly believed that letters to legislators are never read. This is a myth. The fact is that they are read most carefully, particularly if they come from constituents. Letters indicate that constituents are sufficiently concerned about an issue to take the time to write (McInnis-Dittrich, 1994).

Letters to legislators should be short, to the point, and credible. Write one or two pages at most. Confine yourself to one subject area or bill. Write different letters for different bills or issues. Legislators are quite busy and long letters are time consuming. However, do not sacrifice clarity and completeness for brevity. Describe your position exactly and, if necessary, provide documentation. State your purpose in the first paragraph and then elaborate in the text. The use of facts combined with personal experiences, whether yours or your client's, is most effective. State the action you want the legislator to take. Whether you want him or her to vote yes or no on a bill or to cosponsor legislation: be specific.

Although form letters, postcards, and telegrams are all read and answered, they don't carry the weight and persuasiveness of a personal letter and should be avoided. These are viewed as efforts by groups and not as opinions of individuals. The more personal the letter, the greater the impact. Handwritten (clearly written) letters on your own stationery are the most effective.

Attitude is important; positive communication works best. Never threaten a legislator: This will be counterproductive and will cause you to lose your credibility and to be discarded as an "angry individual." If you have assisted in a

FIGURE 6.2 Sample letter to communicate with an elected official

SOURCE: Reprinted from James S. Mickelson, *Speaking Out for Houston's Children.* Houston: CHILDREN AT RISK, 1995.

Honorable Elected O. Ficial
Texas House of Representatives
P.O. Box 2910
Austin, Texas 78768-2910

Dear Representative Official:

As a parent of your district, I have a deep, personal interest in H.B. 1001 which will do away with the use of corporal punishment in the public schools. I strongly advocate its passage.

I recently had my son come home from school after receiving three "hits" with a wood paddle from the principal for talking during class. I agree that my child, who is ten, should not be misbehaving. However, children need to learn to follow rules, not learn that you solve a problem by using force. Under current Texas law I have no power to stop the use of corporal punishment on my child.

Please vote for H.B. 1001 when it comes up for a vote next week.

Thank you in advance for your consideration.

Sincerely,

I. Am Right
2424 Most Streets
Anywhere, Texas 77001
713–555–5555

TYPING IS NOT ESSENTIAL, LEGIBILITY IS.

LIMIT LETTER TO ONE PAGE

PARAGRAPH ONE: *Identify yourself, state the subject, state your connection to it.*

REFER TO A SPECIFIC BILL NUMBER. *One issue per letter.*

CLEARLY STATE YOUR OPINION.

PARAGRAPH TWO: *Explain your position, why you feel as you do, present your reasons, use personal examples.*

PARAGRAPH THREE: *Ask for specific action from your elected official.*

WRITE YOUR NAME, ADDRESS, AND TELEPHONE NUMBER CLEARLY. YOUR LEGISLATOR MAY WANT MORE INFORMATION.

campaign or on passage of another bill, remind the legislator of your support in the past and how you are counting on him or her. The legislator should be thanked for considering your views and, if you are comfortable with such a statement, for the hard work the legislator has undertaken on other issues of concern. A short thank you after any vote on a piece of legislation with which you agree will testify to the depth of your interest and may enhance your credibility when other issues arise.

When writing to elected or appointed officials the following forms of address and salutation are recommended:

To: The President

The President
The White House
1600 Pennsylvania Ave., NW
Washington, D.C. 20500

Dear Mr./Ms. President:

To: U.S. Senators

The Honorable (insert full name)
United States Senate
Washington, D.C. 20510

Dear Senator (insert last name):

To: U.S. Representatives

The Honorable (insert full name)
U.S. House of Representatives
Washington, D.C. 20515

Dear Representative (insert last name):

To: Cabinet Members

The Honorable (insert full name)
Secretary of (insert department)
Washington, D.C. (insert zip)

Dear Secretary (insert last name):

TELEPHONING

A telephone call is no substitute for a letter. However, phone calls, timed correctly, can be most effective. Usually 48 hours before a vote is taken is the best timing. The constant ringing of the telephone with people asking for a "yea" or "nay" vote can move an undecided legislator to making a decision.

When calling, you will undoubtedly get a staff member or a receptionist. Simply state who you are and the message you wish to convey: "I would like the representative to vote yes on bill XX. This is important to the many. . . ." Be sure to leave your name, address, and phone number, which will confirm that you are a constituent.

TESTIFYING

A legislative committee struggling to understand the intricacies of a complicated piece of legislation will solicit testimony as a way to gather as much information as possible on various aspects of the legislation in the shortest amount of time. Indeed, if the legislators had endless hours to sit and talk with a variety of individuals, testimony would be much less useful, but because time is limited, testimony provides an excellent opportunity for the general public to have input into a committee's decision. Hearings often are conducted in various parts of the state or nation to ensure access to more people and to a diversity of points of view (Sharwell, 1982).

In the testimonial process the committee listens to statements about the legislation and to information helpful to their decision making. The legislators can ask questions of the person testifying, and any legislator can request that particular individuals appear before the committee or subcommittee to testify. Hearings are an ideal way for the media to gather public opinion, and for individuals to have a tremendous amount of input into legislative decisions (Richan, 1991). The following are some reasons why written testimony should be provided:

- It demonstrates professionalism.
- It shows a more than casual interest in the legislative matter.
- It ensures that the committee record of the testimony will be accurate.
- It can make the oral presentation to the committee more effective, because some of the committee members and the committee staff will read the written statements in addition to listening to the testimony.
- It permits the advocate to say all he or she wants to say in the written statement while still being able to meet the time restraints often imposed on oral testimony.
- It provides flexibility in that the advocate can cover all the issues in the written statement but can highlight points in the oral portion that are particularly responsive to points by opponents.
- It provides greater assurance that media coverage of the testimony will be complete and more accurate, because media representatives can work from the written statement rather than from hastily penciled notes.
- It enables the advocate to inform members of the organization represented and other persons and organizations about the content of the testimony.

- It provides a better record for the advocate's own organization than do notes from memory. (Sharwell, 1982)

If you are asked or plan to testify before a federal, state, or local committee, remember this: The key to effective legislative lobbying is preparation. Although preparation takes a considerable amount of time, it is necessary to increase one's chances of success.

The best recommendation on testifying comes from the Child Welfare League of America's 1987 *Washington Workbook for Child Advocates:*

> Briefly introduce yourself. Tell who you are and what program you're representing. Acknowledge your appreciation to the panel for having the good sense to consider the issue and invite you as a witness. Let them know briefly why they are so smart to have you testify (i.e., how many people you represent, how many people you serve, how much success you have had, or how well qualified you are). This should take no more than one or two paragraphs.
>
> State your goal and outline your major points. In a sentence or two, tell the committee or panel what you hope to accomplish in your statement. Again, be brief. For example, if the subject of the hearing is the threat posed by killer bees, indicate that you are going to (1) tell them how many bees have entered the country; (2) give them some personal examples of people who have been stung; (3) describe the limited success of your state (community) "Ban the Bee" campaign; and (4) offer specific recommendations as to what legislators can do to solve the bee menace. Outlining your major points assures the legislators that you are organized and that your testimony is relevant. This should take one paragraph.
>
> Talk about the problem. Discuss the national (local) significance of the issue and try to relate it to your state and/or community. Even better, try to relate the problem to the states or districts of the legislators before whom you are testifying.
>
> Talk about current efforts to resolve the problem. Describe solutions that are being tried or considered. Has anything worked in various states or communities on an experimental or demonstration basis? Explain why the efforts are insufficient or how they can be improved. This should take about one or two pages.
>
> Offer specific recommendations. Now is the time to list your specific, concise recommendations, focusing on what legislators can do to help solve the problem at hand. Do not tell Congress what the state legislature, city council, or local school board should do. Again, this should take about one or two pages.
>
> Thank the panel or committee and say goodbye. Summarize your major points and tell them how happy you would be to answer questions. This should take about ten seconds!

Do remember that your elected representatives are people too, and they are only people—there is no need to be afraid or to think of oneself as being in court, regardless of how large or imposing the hearing room is.

Don't forget that, as people, your legislators like to be "talked to" rather than "read to." Remember that committee and panel members like to be "talked to" for only about ten (sometimes only five) minutes at a time, so keep your oral presentation brief and conversational. Your hope should be that they will be interested enough in you and your subject to ask you questions after you finish. You want them to become involved in your testimony, an unlikely scenario if you force them to sit through a 20- to 30-minute "reading" of your statement.

Don't spend more time describing your own qualifications or your agency's than you do the problem.

Focus on the specific issue of the hearing; don't give a speech or present a paper you prepared months ago, regardless of how good you think it is.

Don't assume that the panel or committee members are experts. Members of Congress (all legislators) vote daily on a wide variety of issues, everything from water projects to interplanetary space programs. While you certainly don't want to talk down to them, you should also not assume that they know all that you do about the issue at hand. Don't try to tell them everything you know, and simplify, simplify, simplify.

Personalize your testimony—while statistics are helpful, one way to assist elected officials (and get their attention) is to let them know how the issue at hand affects their constituents. A personalized example of someone affected by a problem or someone helped by a proposed solution often carries more weight than the results of ten national studies.

Anticipate ahead of time questions your testimony may prompt and have good answers in mind.

When asked a question or for clarification, answer in a straightforward manner. If you do not have an answer, defer by saying that you would like to answer in writing. Copies of written testimony should be provided not only to committee members, but to aides and the media as well.

LOBBYING AND NONPROFITS

When it comes to lobbying by nonprofit organizations, there exists a myth that this is prohibited and will jeopardize funding. It is true that there are some laws and procedures that an organization, classified by the Internal Revenue Service (IRS) as a 501(c)(3), must follow; but lobbying is by no means illegal or totally prohibited (Hopkins, 1992). Foundations, which are subject to several restrictions that do not apply to nonprofits, can make grants to charities for lobbying and advocacy efforts (Asher, 1995). While there are social and political concerns a nonprofit may face in undertaking a lobbying effort, legal restrictions are too often used to avoid the former. It is recommended that before a lobbying effort is undertaken that might use more than 5 percent of the total agency budget, the law should be reviewed. What follows is a simple summary of lobbying efforts by a nonprofit.

The IRS defines lobbying as the attempt to influence legislation on the local, state, or federal level. This means trying to influence policymakers to vote for or against a certain item that comes before them; for example, approval of a budget. If the nonprofit can "educate" the elected official on the needs for expenditures for a program to remedy a social problem and the specific program budget is not before them to be voted on, then this activity is public education and not lobbying. The rule of thumb is the action of a vote.

The law is clear on how much a nonprofit can spend on lobbying. The law divides lobbying into two categories: grassroots and direct. Grassroots refers to influencing legislation through communications with the general public. Direct is lobbying directly with legislators and their staff (Amidei, 1992). There are two ways that the IRS determines how much lobbying is permissible. First, if the organization includes lobbying as part of their efforts to meet their mission, then the nonprofit may "elect" with the IRS. This is a simple form that tells the IRS that you are lobbying and wish to be reviewed under the "expenditure test." Electing with the IRS gives the nonprofit permission to spend more of their total budget on lobbying. The expenditure test is very precise in determining the amounts allowed. If the nonprofit does not "elect," then the nonprofit is more limited on expenditures and the interpretation of lobbying is done by the IRS. Electing does require more documentation and reporting to the IRS.

Nonprofit organizations must operate within the regulations set by the IRS or they may be categorized as an action organization, losing their tax-exempt status. This, however, should not be construed as prohibiting lobbying efforts. Although the regulation may seem confusing at first, once a clear understanding of the organization's direction and how it fits within the law is determined, the nonprofit can and should enter the political arena to affect change.

CONCLUSION

Lobbying efforts are seen as manipulative and self-serving. However, the reality of the American political system is that these efforts have become necessary to influence successfully of the legislative process.

The social work profession needs to become more astute in the practices and skills involved in lobbying. The various facets of the political process, legislative and committee rules and regulations, and formal and informal decision-making processes have created a milieu that social work professionals have avoided. Lobbying for human service legislation is not self-serving, but rather is consistent with client advocacy.

If more social workers were to acquire the techniques outlined in this chapter, the authors are confident that more humane social policies would be developed and enacted. Lobbying is indeed an essential interventive strategy in social work.

> When working in the political arena, particularly in lobbying, it is important to provide accurate information, to develop trust, and to not overpromise.
>
> *Dennis Jones, MSW*
> *Former Commissioner, Texas Department of Mental Health and Mental Retardation*

This chapter has only touched on the various aspects of lobbying techniques. It is a primer for social workers who wish to advocate for human service goals. The skill with which social workers participate in the political system is an important factor in determining their influence on the formation of social policy. Immense resources neither are required nor will guarantee social workers significant influence in the political arena. Rather, the success of the profession's endeavors will be determined by social workers' ability to utilize both effective lobbying skills and their unique mix of professional skills.

ASSIGNMENTS

1. Learn how a bill becomes a law in your state.
2. Determine when a hearing for a bill you are interested in will occur. Develop a position statement and then testify at that hearing.
3. Develop a position on a current legislative issue and make an appointment with your own state legislator to influence his or her vote.

SUGGESTED READINGS

Mahaffey, Maryann. 1972. "Lobbying and Social Work." *Social Work* 17 (January): 3–11.
Patti, Rino, and Ronald Dear. 1981. "Legislative Advocacy: Seven Effective Tactics." *Social Work* 26 (July): 289–296.

REFERENCES

Amidei, Nancy. 1992. *So you Want to Make a Difference: Advocacy is the Key,* 3rd ed. Washington D.C.: OMB Watch.
Asher, Thomas R. 1995. Myth v. Fact: Foundation Support of Advocacy. Washington D.C.: Alliance for Justice.

Child Welfare League of America. 1987. *Washington Workbook for Child Advocates.* Washington, D.C.: Child Welfare League.

Hopkins, Bruce R. 1992. *Charity, Advocacy and the Law.* New York: John Wiley.

Mahaffey, Maryann. 1972. "Lobbying and Social Work." *Social Work* 17 (January): 3-11.

McInnis-Dittrich, Kathleen. 1994. *Integrating Social Welfare Policy and Social Work Practice.* Pacific Grove, CA: Brooks/Cole Publishing.

Michigan Sea Grant Advisory Service. 1981. *How Citizens Can Influence Legislation in Michigan.* Lansing: Michigan State University Cooperative Extension Service.

Ornstein, Norman, and Shirley Elder. 1978. *Interest Groups, Lobbying and Policy-Making.* Washington, D.C.: Congressional Quarterly Press.

Patti, Rino, and Ronald Dear. 1981. "Legislative Advocacy: Seven Effective Tactics." *Social Work* 26 (July): 289-296.

Richan, Willard C. 1991. *Lobbying for Social Change.* New York: Haworth Press.

Sharwell, George. 1982. "How to Testify before a Legislative Committee." In *Practical Politics: Social Work and Political Responsibility,* Maryann Mahaffey and John Hanks (eds.), pp. 85-99. Washington, D.C.: National Association of Social Workers.

chapter 7

Influence through Organizing Others

Politics is the public side of social work. It is nothing more than the bringing together of people in a public setting to try and solve problems and/or to develop social policy. I think that social workers have excellent skills to build consensus and to solve problems.

Debbie Stabenow

As mentioned in the previous chapter, there is a great deal that can be done by one person to make programmatic changes and policy changes using the skills of lobbying. However, there are beliefs and systems that are so ingrained in the American culture that the only way to bring about social change regarding such policies and national attitudes is to organize the masses. One person can start a movement, but it takes others to fully implement the changes. Such changes occur when one person, like Rosa Parks, initiates an act and brings about a movement such as the civil rights movement.

The preceding chapter on lobbying addressed specific techniques and skills that one or two individuals can use with legislators to have an effect on programs and policies. Much of what was discussed there could be included in this chapter as well. However, the authors see the necessity to address organizing efforts separately because sometimes community attitudes are too overpowering for any single lobbying effort. Social workers have skills and knowledge in the area of community organizing, advocacy, brokering, planning, and evaluating. It is not the intent of this chapter to expound upon an already established body of knowledge, but to state that this knowledge base must be utilized with some of the current trends and changes in mind. Organizing is an option for social workers who wish to affect large scale changes in policy. The old saying that "there is power in numbers" is exactly the message of this chapter. The greater the number and diversity of individuals who are united in support of a policy, the greater the likelihood of making the change.

Organizing others is important because "social developments are part of a total economic and political system—a political economy—in which all strands of life, from the national to local level, intertwine with each other. Most problems that contemporary communities face manifest themselves at the neighborhood level but result from city, state, national, and even international factors. What is most striking, however, is how immune we think we are from the penetrations of the national political economy into daily lives" (Fisher, 1984).

All social changes or movements go through a series of phases. Some movements will take longer at certain phases or may even become stuck in one phase and die. All is dependent upon the economic factors related to the need, societal concerns toward the need, and the effectiveness of the organizing efforts to address the need. All must be present, but one or two factors can dominate to ultimately address the need.

TEN PHASES OF A SOCIAL MOVEMENT

The following phases of a social movement are overly simplified, but are offered for consideration when the need arises to organize others. They are adopted and modified from many sources as early as the works of Lindeman (1921).

Phase one: A consciousness of a need or problem is developed. This may begin with only one person expressing a need. In many cases it comes from a practitioner or client identifying a need or problem that then is expressed to others for validation and clarification of the need. In short, the "idea is born."

Phase two: Consciousness of the need is conveyed to a larger group which incorporates the idea and takes ownership of the issue. This could be a formal organization or institution or an advocacy group that is already addressing a related issue. In some situations, a new group or organization is developed or founded to address this concern.

Phase three: The group that has now adopted the consciousness of need begins to define the need to selected leadership. At this point, the issue becomes more general or the original concerns now include more issues relative to the needs, depending on the amount of fact-finding the group undertakes.

Phase four: The issue now experiences an influx of emotion and the effort to enlist a quick answer to the need. This emotional energy stimulates the next phase and could cause a faction of the group to separate and become the emotional extreme group or spokesperson on the issue.

Phase five: As the issue is presented to more groups, institutions, and individual leaders, an increased presentation of solutions emerge. Hence there are now several approaches to address this new consciousness of need. Additional groups may form supporting their solution.

Phase six: The conflicts between the various solutions emerge and more solutions may be presented which will further the debate. This phase can last for some time given the three factors of economics, societal concern, and the effectiveness of the organizing efforts.

Phase seven: In an effort to sort out the conflicts to the solutions, a phase of investigation may occur. This can be most helpful to the process or it can stall the movement indefinitely. In some situations, this phase may be skipped, depending on the fact-finding efforts or organizers.

Phase eight: The public has open discussion of the issue. This can range from public meetings or hearings, to editorials, to national debates that last for years. Groups with the most influence attempt to secure the support of the public to adopt their plan or solution.

Phase nine: Once there is some testing of solutions and their integration, a practical resolution to the issue can emerge. Efforts to retain something from each practical plan are necessary before the next phase can occur.

Phase ten: Certain groups will relinquish their positions in order to save themselves from complete defeat, and a compromise on a plan occurs which most players will support.

Organizing is not always as systematic as these phases would make it appear, but the course of change from the perceived need to the implementation of a solution requires that all phases be included. If the strategy is well planned and if the social factors are favorable, then change can occur quite quickly. However, all too often, for issues such as civil rights, the elimination of corporal punishment, or a woman's right to choose an abortion, a great deal of effort and time is required before achieving a consensus relative to a solution.

STRATEGY

One variable that affects any organizing efforts to proceed through the aforementioned phases is the strategy that is employed. A strategic analysis is a straightforward, useful way of examining the helping and hindering forces that will impact on any change effort (Staples, 1984). Somewhere between phase two and three, it is important that the group think through how the organizing efforts will be orchestrated. The centrality of a strategy for the organizer is important. Without it, convictions and commitment are nothing but empty hopes. Actions without a strategy are merely ad hoc "targets of opportunity" without any sense of how they fit into some larger scheme.

One question that will arise in developing a strategy is whether to use consensus or conflict methods. A total reliance on a strategy of either consensus or conflict will, in most circumstances, be unsuccessful. In organizing others it is clear that consensus building among groups and individuals is necessary. However, there will come a time in the process when some conflict methods may need to be employed.

Plan everything. Planning skills are very important to impact social policy. Most people think that the legislative process is coming up with a great idea, throwing it into this system, and then sort of nursing it along. What you have to really do is determine what's likely to happen, what kind of problems you're going to face, and plan alternative solutions, alternative approaches. It is extremely important to create an entire strategy before you ever start.

Sandy Ingraham, MSW
Social Services Consultant
Harrah, Oklahoma

Any development of strategy must begin by clarifying the problem or issue. A common statement as to what the need or situation is that should be rectified must be agreed upon. Data must be gathered and presented succinctly for others to digest. The proposed plan or solution must be conclusively stated. Although many organizational efforts are in the best interest of others, it is necessary to clarify or articulately state a contract with those from whom you want support. How will their efforts toward this movement benefit them? All of this should be taken into consideration during the strategy development.

COALITION BUILDING

A *coalition* is a loosely woven, ad hoc association of constituent groups, each of whose primary identification is outside of the coalition (Humphreys, 1979). Social workers, when coalition building, usually seek linkages with those who are most sympathetic to their ideas, values, and philosophies, such as mental health associations and the Children's Defense Fund. But all too often social workers overlook potential alliances with groups which may, on the surface, appear unlikely to be supportive of social work policies. Thus, all aspects of a given issue should be carefully examined to identify points of potential commonality. For example, when Congress was considering an increase in the gasoline tax to generate revenues for the improvement of roads and bridges, this effort was supported by human service professionals because it would create jobs for the unemployed. While this was the central issue that garnered the support of human service professionals, road builders and construction workers also supported the legislation, forming an otherwise unlikely coalition.

The more diversified the groups in a coalition, the more powerful the coalition becomes. However, the greater the diversity, the more vulnerable it is to being splintered by outside and opposing groups. When an organization or coalition is splintered at a critical moment, it can cause loss of support for the legislation, because without unanimity of support legislators may not even bother to discuss the legislation (Mahaffey, 1972).

TECHNOLOGY USED TO ORGANIZE OTHERS

Organizing is overwhelmingly about interpersonal relationships, and social workers are people-focused; however, they often overlook technological developments that can enhance their efforts greatly. With the technological advancements in computers and information handling, much can be accomplished in organizing efforts. With the most recent developments, the potential is awesome. Every 18 months or so a new chip is designed that can do twice as much as the best chip before it. Every decade, computers will be about ten times as powerful as computers at the beginning of the decade—at the same cost (Sterling, 1993). In addition to computers, other technology is available that can help in organizing, such as fax machines, color photocopy machines, and cellular telephones. The learning curve for some software programs and new technologies may seem time consuming given the pressures to take action. However, it is imperative that social workers take the time to learn to use and be creative with these advancements.

Today, word processing is a necessity. This technology enables large numbers of individually personalized letters to legislators or constituents to be produced quite effortlessly. These letters also can be personalized and individualized to address different issues or requests. All members of Congress now use this technology in responding to constituent letters. It is also used by many national organizations to mobilize their members to take action. Broadcast faxing of action alerts is a cost-effective way to contact members and notify them of pressing issues requiring their action. Figures 7.1 and 7.2 are examples of FAX Alerts.

The Internet is the newest tool for organizers. We can now access databases previously unthought of that can give updated information in seconds. For example, one university has set up a comprehensive media page, with a listing of nearly every newspaper in the United States—daily, nondaily, college, and "experimental"—all available on the Internet. Within cyberspace current and up-to-date data is available at very reasonable costs.

In addition to data communications with experts around the world, soon both data voice and visual communication will be common on the Internet. Organizing other groups or members of a coalition can be concluded in a matter of seconds for a fraction of the cost of mailings or phone trees. Utilizing this new network of cyberspace will improve efforts to keep people informed and connected. The time will come when a social worker will be able to access information during a community meeting to answer questions which in the past may have taken weeks to answer and communicate back to the local community. Use of such technology will help social workers bridge the large gap between the technology "haves and have nots" (Raffoul, 1996), a critical issue on the horizon.

S.peak O.ut S.heet

SPEAKING OUT FOR HOUSTON'S YOUTH

children at Risk

Fax ALERT for CHILD ADVOCATES -- February 27, 1995

Action

On Tuesday, the Ways and Means Committee will look at Welfare Reform and restructuring the child welfare programs which is included in the Personal Responsibility Act. Under this Bill Texas will send $865 million to Washington that will go to other states like New York and California. CHILDREN AT RISK will hold a press conference on Monday (11:00 AM) & recommend that Federal dollars to the states be based on the numbers of children. Texas has 7.3% of the U.S. Children but we only get 2.7% for AFDC and 3.5% cut of child welfare dollars. If congress would divide the pie based on child population parity, Texas would gain $865 million. Call or FAX your Congressperson!

VERY IMPORTANT

Contact Rep **Bill Archer's Office**
682-8828   Fax:680-8070
Washington (202) 225-2571
Fax:202/225-4381
    Tell them you want
CHILD POPULATION PARITY
DO IT NOW!!

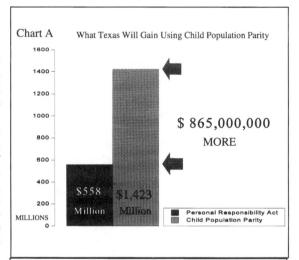

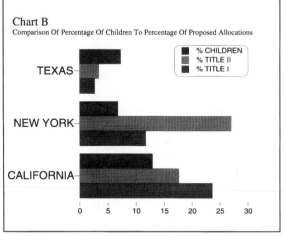

FIGURE 7.1 Example of a FAX Alert

One example of technology in action is the National Network of Runaway and Youth Services, which has a system where they can alert their members if Congress needs to be contacted about an upcoming issue. Members have provided the national office with blank letterhead that includes their signature. When the time comes to send a letter, they can electronically transmit the body

S.O.S.
Speak **O**ut **S**heet

Fax ALERT for CHILD ADVOCATES -- May 17, 1995

WEAPON FREE SCHOOL ZONE SB 840

This bill would prohibit guns within a 1000 feet radius of a school. This bill has passed the

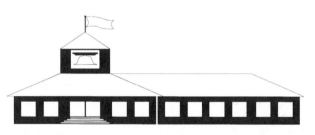

Senate and is going to be voted on in the Texas House Thursday (5-18) morning. This is important now that Texans can carry handguns. If you are concerned about **KIDS AND GUNS** call your representative **ASAP**.

"ASK THEM TO VOTE YES ON SB 840"

FIGURE 7.2 Example of a FAX Alert

of the letter to the national office. The letter is then printed with a personal signature. It is then hand-delivered to the Congressperson within hours of an issue arising.

We should not forget the effects of cable television. On the surface this may not seem to be a method to organize others. But if we look at the fact that a person can see and hear not only Congress, but possibly state and local legislators making actual decisions as they happen, this can be a very useful tool for motivating people to respond to the policy in question. We can turn on cable television and see firsthand what bill is being debated and what the issues of the debate are, at the very moment that it is being recorded in the *Congressional Record.* Take that technology and combine it with the capability to transmit a written document via a fax machine to your representative, and one can literally respond to the comments of a congressperson on the floor of the U.S. House of Representatives by the time the congressperson leaves the floor and returns to his or her office. This is only the beginning. Soon cable companies will have the capacity for interactive communications and over 500 different channels to choose from. Organizers could have videotapes made that members could call up on their television screens (and soon computers) to view.

This kind of technological capability can and will continue to be a critical factor in organizing others and influencing policymakers. The importance of technology for the social worker working to bring about change cannot be emphasized enough. Two common problems arise here. First, the lack of knowledge of the technology and, second, the lack of resources to purchase the technology. If technology can increase an organizing effort by 10 percent, then 10 percent of the organizer's time should be used to learn the new technology to its fullest. If resources are limited, technology should be placed at the top of the list and the organization should make due in other areas. You would not think of starting an effort without a telephone, and now you must see computers (as close to state of the art as possible) as a necessity as well.

"While the future of social work is not totally dependent on changes in computers and technology and their impact on society, it is one opportunity to begin to move the profession into the next century with new vigor and energy. If we can take full advantage of this new product of technology, the personal computer, and put it to use helping us operationalize our vision and implement our mission, perhaps it can be the key to opportunity for the next century" (Raffoul, 1996). The following is such an example of technology and its use in the political arena.

A cable television channel in Nebraska films and broadcasts the legislative activities of the state legislature. When the state is in session, I turn on the television in my office so I can monitor those bills impacting social workers in Nebraska.

Early in the 1989 legislative session I was sitting at my desk with the television on very softly. This is a particularly crucial time to monitor the legislative process because bills are being introduced by senators for the first time. With half an ear, I had been listening to the clerk of the legislature read bill numbers and a short title of each bill introduced.

Suddenly, the television emitted the words "LB949—Repeal the social work certification law" and immediately following that "LB948—Extend the grandfather clause to the social work certification law." I was shocked. The social work community had no idea these two bills would be introduced. Who was behind the bills and why? We had been broadsided without warning!

These two bills galvanized Nebraska social workers. Our response was immediate and effective. One bill was withdrawn by the introducer and the other bill was held in committee.

But the introducer would not accept defeat. Again the television monitored his next tactic. I watched in horror as the senator introduced an amendment to a bill being discussed by the full legislative body. The amendment contained the grandfather provisions of LB948. A sigh of relief came when the chair of the Health and Human Services Committee successfully defeated the amendment.

Television has proven to be an invaluable tool in monitoring the legislative process in Nebraska. Similar tools and resources are available in each state for social workers to use. We just need to be aware that they are available.

M. Jean Andrew,
Executive Director, Nebraska Chapter, National Association of Social Workers

USING THE MEDIA

An important factor in organizing and making issues known is the use of the media. In some cases, without the assistance or attention of the media, a movement may become stagnant. We may view the mass media warily, yet we also know that the media is a powerful force in our society: a force for change (Pertskhuk and Wilbur, 1991).

Social workers need to understand how the media functions, and "work" it just as if it was a legislative body. In media advocacy one must identify the objectives, target an audience, and tailor the message to that audience. As social workers we must learn from other professionals whose expertise is mass communications, public relations, or media consultation. However, a social worker's skills in working with people will pay big dividends if used with those who control the media.

Newspapers

Newspapers are the easiest and the most thorough way to tell your story or to raise the public's consciousness. Letters to the editor are also effective and policymakers read them! Another way to tell your story is in "op-ed" articles. Op-eds—articles that appear opposite the editorial page—can be an extremely powerful and remarkably cost-effective way of getting your message out to a variety of audiences, providing information and shaping opinions (Zeck and Rennolds, 1991). This space is used for columns that address concerns of the community in an editorial or opinionated format. Major newspapers have an op-ed editor to whom you can send your article. Of course, newspapers also cover special events. You can take time to explain the issue to a reporter and give any necessary background information. Editorials, like coverage of media events, are more likely to be included or covered if they are tied in with an issue that is current and of public interest.

Radio

Talk radio can be a powerful force for political action, but more often it works as a forum in which issues can be legitimized as part of the public policy agenda (Aufderheide and Chester, 1990). In this format you can personalize the message and address the issues more in depth than on television. The best example of how effective talk radio can be is illustrated by how right-wing conservatives have used radio to get their message to millions. Talk radio is great for public service announcements (PSAs), which can be helpful in educating the community about concerns or actions that need to be taken. This medium has not been utilized to its fullest by social workers.

Don't Shortchange Texas Children

The Ways and Means Committee, chaired by Houston's Representative Bill Archer has approved a bill (House Resolution 4) that reforms the welfare system and restructures child welfare programs as part of the GOP "Contract with America." This stampede for reform shortchanges Texas taxpayers and children.

   This sweeping reform, titled the Personal Responsibility Act, proposes to give program control to the states. Title I (Temporary Family Assistance Block Grant) and Title II (Child Protection Block Grant) of the bill would cap entitlements and establish a block grant to be distributed to the states.

   Under the proposed legislation, Texas would get $558 million annually for its children. The distribution for these block grants is based on the amount of federal dollars each state had used in previous years. The Title I distribution is calculated by averaging the states' expenditures for fiscal years 1991-1993, for aid to families with dependent children, and Title II by using the amount the states received in 1993. Traditionally, Texas has not concentrated on pulling down the federal dollars because of the federal rules and regulations involved. For years we have been sending money to Washington and getting less in return. Now that the federal rules are to be changed, we still get the short end of the stick. Under this bill, Texas will be able to build programs based on our needs, but we will have to do so without an equitable share of the pie. Texas tax dollars will be used to take care of New York and California children.

   Not long ago Texas became the second most populous state. Additionally, we have a greater ratio of children than most states—to be exact, 5.2 million according to the 1990 census. This means that Texas has 7.3

percent of the U.S. child population. New York has 4.4 million children or 6.8 percent of the U.S. child population. California has long been the most populous state and accounts for 12.9 percent of U.S. children. But New York and California have been spending more than Texas on federally funded welfare programs and, under the new plan, would get a much larger share of the funding pie than Texas. Thus, some of the welfare funds that should go to Texas—under equitable funding—will be going to those states.

This is the intent of the "Contract With America." In Congress' exuberance, an equitable approach to block grants seems to be overlooked. For fairness' sake, Congress should use the formula of child population parity, shifting completely to this priority by the year 2000. By using child population as the formula for distribution of federal resources, Texas tax dollars would be used for Texas children. This would mean an additional $864 million for the state.

Let me be clear about the issue of using our tax dollars for our kids. I am not addressing the size of the pie, but the allocation of the pie. CHILDREN AT RISK is not alone on this issue; United Way of the Texas Gulf Coast and the Joint City/County Commission on Children support this position. Because of our outcry, a provision of $100 million for fast-growing states has been included, which still would be only 12 percent of what Texas alone would receive under child population parity.

It's time that Texans make it known that we want our tax dollars used fairly for our children.

Jim Mickelson

SOURCE: Reprinted from the *Houston Post.*

Inhumane How Texas Treating Its Downtrodden

Amid the barbs of partisan politics over the proposed size and solution to the Texas Department of Human Services' budget deficit is this reality: No cutbacks can be withstood by our state's at-risk populations: our children, elderly, and medically indigent.

While turning away federal dollars is unwise, cutting funds from state-supported programs such as Children's Protective Services and foster care can in no way be considered a solution, since that strategy will only further reduce our ability to help and will ensure a future of even greater problems.

In recent years, Texas has faced this dilemma: Increased stress on families from the economic downturn, which subsequently creates increases in many social problems, while critical public agencies charged with the responsibility of preventing and/or alleviating those problems have had drastic budget reductions.

Private-sector initiatives should be applauded. But these cannot—indeed should not—take the place of responsible government to care for all its citizens. The importance of prevention and early intervention is well understood; so are the realities of systemic and interlocking problems. To allow these conditions to exist for any Texan is not only a terrible statement about Texas, but puts us all in jeopardy.

Unfortunately, our nation trails behind many others in the care of children and at-risk families. Unfortunately too, the data are clear: Even with our "kinder and gentler" focus, poverty is on the rise nationally, disproportionately affecting some (minorities, children, and the elderly). More than half live in a household where at least one member works.

What is worse, in a nation that trails other developed nations, Texas ranks at the bottom compared to other states on all the major indicators of caring for its population: infant mortality, teen pregnancy, high school dropouts, welfare payments, expenditures on child protection, substance abuse.

I am not proud that Texas ranks 46th in what it pays "needy" families on welfare, 45th in what it does to help people with medical needs, 47th in meeting mental health needs, and 49th in terms of services to the elderly. I am not proud that Texas ranks in the "terrible 10" or the "filthy 15" because proportionately our poorest citizens are being taxed much higher than our wealthiest.

The relationship of multiple problems forms an insidious web. Low-income families are likely to be unemployed or marginally employed, have no health insurance, have low rates of completed education, and live in substandard housing. As a consequence (and, I would contend, through no fault of their own), they become imperiled for problems such as substance abuse, teen pregnancy, domestic violence, illiteracy, and chronic unemployment or underemployment.

Any cuts in any programs have an effect on all other services. Reducing or discontinuing services to one population will, without any doubt, increase the demands elsewhere. We in Texas have watched, but not learned from, other states who had the shortsighted belief that social problems were not socially caused, were mutually exclusive, and could be remedied with band-aids.

Texas has always been perceived as a strong state. But we are unlikely to maintain that image with a future labor force that is unskilled and untrained, in the face of enormous and untreated inner-city problems, and in the face of other more accurately descriptive adjectives such as "cruel and uncaring." What is real is our inhumanity to our fellow Texans.

The current projected budgetary deficit for TDHS is in large part the result of effective and much more comprehensive strategic intervention. For that improved intervention I applaud the TDHS chairman, Rob Mosbacher, Jr., its board, commissioner Ron Lindsay, and other executive staff.

The solutions I offer are not "quick fixes." They are not an abrogation of public and social responsibility. They are not the total reliance on privatization and philanthropic "do-gooders." The shortsightedness of current and past legislators and our citizenry is incomprehensible to someone whose life training and experience bring me face to face with the extent and depth of human suffering amid Texas' relative affluence.

The concern of the governor and much of the legislature about the unpopularity of taxes is a narrowly focused definition of taxation and an ill-conceived notion of future economic growth and improved quality of life. For example, if we propose the course of budget reductions in the area of services to the elderly, we will force many of these people back on to families probably already stressed, creating personal economic hardship, a likely increase in family stress, and therefore, increases in elderly or child abuse. Likewise, if we remove funding from quality day care, we will either remove women from the labor force and force them into other public support—Aid to Families with Dependent Children—or create situations in which there are more unsupervised children in our communities who, in turn, may find themselves victims.

There are no easy, quick fixes to human suffering. To disenfranchise a large segment of our population from rights to health care, safe environments, and a minimum standard of living isn't just inhumane, it is shortsighted and ignorant.

I was not born a Texan, but I have twice chosen Texas as my home, based upon a belief that it is a great state. I want to be able to say that Texas is a powerful and strong state because it cares for its own.

Karen S. Haynes

SOURCE: Reprinted from the *Houston Chronicle.*

Television

The most powerful of all the media is television. In order to stimulate the public or to bring pressure on policymakers, the evening news is what you want to use. However, social workers are not knowledgeable or skilled in the use of television. A social worker's best skill is to use words and take time to help a client or community. But in television, time is absolute. After you subtract commercials, weather, sports, and the goodnight comments, a 30-minute newscast is only about seventeen minutes of news (Jones, 1991). Every issue within the profession should have hours of television time devoted to it, but that's not how it works. It is in television that social workers need to learn the "10-second bite." In other words, each message must be effectively delivered in 10 seconds or less. If the story is really big, one might get 15 seconds. Most stories will run for 30 seconds, only a major story gets 90 seconds. When the question is asked and the camera is running, 10 seconds is all you get to get your message across.

Additionally, it must be delivered with as much flair and emotion as possible. Otherwise you'll end up on the editing room floor (Jones, 1991).

EXAMPLES OF ORGANIZING OTHERS

A Competency Issue Becomes Reframed as a Staffing Crisis
In 1987, during my tenure as Assistant Secretary of Children, Youth and Families for the State of Washington, I was asked to represent NASW and its Commission on Families at a national conference of the American Humane Association on the competence needed for child welfare practice. This panel on competencies involved representatives from the American Public Welfare Association and its affiliate, the National Association of Public Child Welfare Administrators, as well as the Child Welfare League of America. This panel shifted from skills to the crisis and the gap between available positions and workers to fill them.

Across the country the vacancy rate was estimated to be as high as one-third. It was here that we pledged to take the crisis to the Children's Bureau. With leadership from the NASW commission, we presented to the Children's Bureau both the crisis and the solution involving the use of Title 4-E funds for training and recruitment of social workers from schools of social work. The response from the child representative at the time (also a social worker) was one of puzzlement and surprise that these funds might be used to prepare social workers for child welfare practice.

Vacancy Rates Symptomatic of the Rising
Challenges Children and Families are Enduring,
Rising Child Deaths, and Fear of the Practice Arena
My own appointment as assistant secretary was the result of a tragic child death in the State of Washington. The Commission on Families heard about the growing crisis in communities across the nation. Commission members carved out an agenda involving the building of a cross-organizational campaign among national agencies, the Children's Bureau, state and local NASW chapters, and units to address reprofessionalization and staffing. The NASW commission held several historic meetings to ground the agenda both in NASW and among the other national associations.

Once the Children's Bureau saw the social work profession's readiness to act, a grant was awarded to host a small national conference. Expecting 25 attendees, the conference attracted over 200 from 40 states representing commissioners of child welfare, deans, directors, and faculty. Eight states were featured for their model partnerships. Within a year, through a Ford Foundation grant to CSWE, 70 to 80 exemplars had been documented.

Many of the strategies drawn upon were good "family-centered practices." Another grant made it possible to host 14 conferences, and by 1993, nationally we were collectively drawing down over $100 million in 4-E funding across child welfare agencies and social work education. Additionally, the Children's Bureau had funded 50 schools to promote training and curriculum building initiatives.

The thrust moved to expanding partnerships with other professions involved with vulnerable children and families. A national conference, cohosted by 14 national associations representing social work, education, and health, attracted more than 300 participants. Voices of consumers of services were heard as presenters and as participants. Attorney General Janet Reno also made an historic presentation on the responsibility that we all share for these most vulnerable children, youth, and families.

Family-Centered Practice Strategies
Used to Build a Movement
Again, like good family-centered practice, unless there is cohesion on how we treat children and families, there will be poor results and we may inadvertently undercut each other. Now that the collaboration movement is building, we are undergoing even greater challenges in the simultaneous renewal and change of health, social service and education, and the counterpart disciples in universities and colleges. What began as a journey to deal with the crisis of recruiting qualified staff in child welfare instead was symptomatic of the need for a much deeper movement and ground swelling in rebuilding our professions and our service delivery systems. My personal role has been to serve as one of the many facilitators of this movement and to nurture and cajole, when I can, as well as to celebrate the many successes and achievements led by colleagues in the country.

Katharine Hooper-Briar, Ph.D.
Chair, Family Studies and Social Work
Miami University, Oxford, Ohio

The Children's Presidential Campaign
It was mid-1987, seventeen months before the presidential election day, when a group of people came together at the Child Welfare League of America (CWLA). We knew that in order to continue to improve the lives of children in this country, the next president had to be sensitized to children's issues. The question we asked ourselves was: "How does one assure that the next president will make children a national priority?" The answer was: "If the public is informed and concerned about the plight of children, then the presidential candidates would more likely respond."

After much thought and discussion I decided that the CWLA would run a campaign of children's issues in conjunction with the presidential campaign. In other words, the issue would be handled similarly to that of the candidates' campaign. Thus, the Children's Presidential Campaign was born.

I had experience with campaigns, having been a state legislator in Massachusetts and having worked for a governor. However, this was the first time that I was running an "issues" and not a "person" campaign. But, like all campaigns, it had to educate and convince the voters to support the issue. Once the presidential candidates embraced the issue, the CWLA would be in a better position to influence whomever the next president was on policies regarding children.

We needed people, time, and money. We had people, mostly league member agencies, but a broader base was needed. We had the time, and we needed to raise money, which we did. The strategy was to create media attention so that the general public would ask questions about children's issues and ask the candidates questions about children's issues, forcing the candidates to make statements on how to address these issues. The campaign targeted not only the media, but the candidates and the general public as well.

The first step was to develop a list of critical issues affecting children which we felt needed to be highlighted in the campaign. We built the campaign around a twelve-point program. The list included such issues as income security, housing, nutrition, child care, and adequate health care for all children, with special emphasis on abused and neglected children, adopted children, and those who are physically and mentally challenged.

To assist in organizing and recruiting, we developed a brochure that outlined the campaign, a newsletter to communicate with our supporters, a fact sheet to educate the candidates, a list of items that member agencies could use to help the effort, and a solicitation approach for money.

We now had all the ingredients of a campaign: time, money, and people. Not only did we use the hundreds of member agencies across the nation, but we sought out others who were interested in joining the movement.

We started with a press conference announcing the Children's Presidential Campaign (CPC). Staff sent out fact sheets, brochures, and information on the CPC to the media and to all candidates who had announced. The campaign was then off and running.

Since the CPC was aimed at the presidential candidates, it should not be surprising that our efforts were targeted at key caucus states and primary states like Iowa, New Hampshire, Florida, Texas, New York, Pennsylvania, and Ohio. There were a number of special events that occurred in these states, starting with Iowa where the media was focusing on the presidential race.

In Iowa, 150 child advocates, adults, and children showed up for a rally at a day-care center to kick off the CPC. The event did attract a fair amount of media interest, and by doing so, we knew that we were on the right track. This initial success was not without an inordinate amount of organizing effort by a local executive director of a children and family agency to assure that there would be a turnout of both the public and the media. In addition to television and radio spots, the Des Moines *Register* ran a strong editorial on the need for a children's agenda by all the presidential candidates.

From Iowa our efforts spread to every targeted state. As the nation focused on each state's race, so went the CPC. One by one each of the targeted states had a special event; each one with its own unique approach. In fact, Oklahoma, not one of the targeted states, had a big event because they wanted "to be part of the action."

There was one event in particular in Texas that received more media coverage than any of the other special events. When one of the CWLA member agencies heard about the CPC, the executive director called together the managing staff of the agency, who felt that this was a prime time for the agency to do something in their community. It was the first time that Texans would be voting in the "Super Tuesday" primary election. Texas was being focused on by the nation as a key state that could influence the primaries.

This group decided that they would hold a presidential debate in the high school gym, which would make a great setting for television. During a meeting with the superintendent of schools, they explained how it would be a great educational experience for the students to see history in the making. It became clear, however, that the superintendent would not support such an event. His rationale was that it was "too political." The agency staff went to the school board. They were met with the same response.

Now, more determined than ever, they developed an alternate plan to have children march on the county courthouse lawns advocating for candidates who supported children's issues. It was a Tuesday, which assured as much media coverage as possible, since Tuesday is usually a slow news day. The date was exactly two weeks before the primary election. The rally would be at noon to make it convenient for the reporters to make their deadlines. Through day-care centers, parochial schools, and the children at the agency, 400 children and 100 adults showed up for the rally. The children made posters which read "We count too" and "America's Future." The children demonstrated to music, yelling "We count too." Not only did these children make a statement about the need for candidates who supported children, but they also told themselves that they are important.

They asked me to speak to the group, along with the mayor and several other folks. Seeing all these young children and young people participating with enthusiasm was exciting and moving. From that one event, 22 media "hits" occurred, not only in the local area but mostly in the urban community 50 miles away. One media hit was an unusual three-minute segment on a major TV channel about the demonstration and the problems facing children. Although the organizing efforts were complicated, particularly when using children, the event was very successful and effective.

In New York a coalition of 19 organizations came together to work on the New York CPC. The New York campaign organized several successful events; however, we experienced one setback. The coalition set up a presidential debate on children's issues, which was canceled at the last minute when the organizing committee realized that the candidates were not really committed to showing. This only proved to us that a continued effort was needed to get and keep children's issues in front of the presidential candidates.

As the presidential campaign swung into the total nation, the CWLA realized that more participation from the general public was needed. We knew from a Harris poll that the public was concerned about child welfare, but we also knew that to get them involved, the approach needed to be simplistic yet effective. After considerable thought and discussion, we realized that postcards, letters, and other such traditional approaches were not going to capture the candidates' attention. After all, there were many groups trying to get their concerns heard, about everything from abortion to gun control to space exploration.

During a brainstorming session the words "platforms" and "planks" kept coming up, which is language often used in campaigns. The idea of a piece of wood or something wooden, like a plank or platform, emerged. The idea of using a tongue depressor was conceived. This would not only catch the attention of the candidates, but also the public whom we wanted to mobilize. The phrase "Put a Plank in Your Platform for Children" became the slogan written on the tongue depressor.

The plan was to use those people who had already signed on to the CPC to host a "Plank Stuffing Party." This effort would quadruple the number of people involved in the campaign and thus broaden the base from child welfare professionals to the public at large. Some 200 persons expressed interest and each was contacted by phone to explain the process. The CWLA would supply the planks, the addresses of each candidate's campaign headquarters, and some sample notes that could be written and sent with the planks. This, then, was the first phase of our public campaign to reach the candidates.

The effort caught on because as people came together to stuff planks, they talked about children's issues. Each participant had an opportunity to have other parties or to find individuals who would stuff planks on their own. The effort multiplied and 300 such parties occurred across the nation, which resulted in about 105,000 wooden planks and personal notes being sent to the presidential candidates.

So successful were the planks that phase two of the planks came after the political parties had nominated their candidates. A new slogan was printed on the tongue depressors: "I'm voting for a children's president." The strategy was to show each candidate that there were a great number of voters interested in children as an issue. CWLA wanted the candidates to talk about their agenda for children. On the back of the plank was printed, "Please send me a copy of your children's platform" and a space for each person to write their name and address.

Phase two had three effects: (1) the candidates knew voters were concerned about children, (2) this then required the candidate to formulate a platform so that it could be sent to the voters, and (3) the voters could see for themselves how the candidate viewed children.

It must be noted that while the CPC was very political, the campaign remained nonpartisan. Never did the CWLA show any favoritism to any party or candidate. We encouraged every candidate to address children's issues, whether they were Republican or Democrat, liberal or conservative. Every candidate was also provided with needed information and technical assistance. Our goal was to get as many candidates as possible talking about kids.

We discovered one day just how successful the planks had been. With only a few weeks left in the campaign, the staff at the CWLA in charge of the CPC received a call from the correspondence officer for the Bush campaign headquarters who asked, "What are all these tongue depressors doing in my office? I have 10 to 15 thousand of them. Just who are you people? Is this some kind of a gimmick?" It was from that conversation that President Bush put together a platform on children and responded to each person who sent a plank.

Soon after the call from the Bush headquarters, another call came from a Massachusetts post office that serviced the Dukakis national headquarters, stating that the planks were jamming the postal machinery and could we stop all these planks being sent.

At the peak of the CPC, both candidates knew that there were voters who cared about children, and indeed some children's issues were discussed during the campaign, like day-care services. Although it may be too early to measure whether the CPC had a significant effect on the presidency, children's issues have certainly become more visible. We are still hopeful that the Bush administration will offer sweeping legislation on behalf of children. Frankly, we never envisioned this would happen right away. We hoped that the campaign would be a beginning in elevating children's needs to a position of national significance. The campaign will pick up where it left off with the next election, to keep the pressure on so that voters will consider candidates who commit themselves to work to improve the quality of life of children and their families.

David S. Liederman, Executive Director
Child Welfare League of America, Washington, D.C.

CONCLUSION

Truly one person can start a movement. In fact, all change is started by one person seeking to inspire the masses to take action. Certainly advocacy has been a central concept within the base of social work practice. Organizing others is one end of the continuum of the political involvement. The intent of this chapter was not to be a primer on organizing, but to point out that such efforts are indeed part of the total political picture. Further, we must not neglect the fact that the use of today's technology can enhance age-old organizing skills. Lastly, it is our hope that we have shown that no issue or social change effort is out of the reach or beyond the skills of social workers to accomplish.

ASSIGNMENTS

1. Watch cable news and send a letter on an issue that has just been debated in Congress.
2. Write an editorial on a subject and submit it to your local newspaper.
3. Join the Children's Presidential Campaign or a similar advocacy effort and monitor the change in policy that the efforts have accomplished.

SUGGESTED READINGS

Jones, Clarence. 1991. *How to Speak TV: A Self-Defense Manual When You're the News,* 3rd ed. Miami: Video Consultants.
Staples, Lee. 1984. *Roots to Power: A Manual for Grassroots Organizing.* New York: Praeger.

REFERENCES

Aufderheide, Pat, and Chester Jeffrey. 1990. *Strategic Communications for Nonprofits: Talk Radio.* Washington, D.C.: Benton Foundation.
Fisher, Robert. 1984. *Let the People Decide: Neighborhood Organizing in America.* Boston, MA: Twayne.
Humphreys, Nancy. 1979. "Competing for Revenue Sharing Funds: A Coalition Approach." *Social Work* 24 (January): 14–18.
Jones, Clarence. 1991. *How to Speak TV: A Self-Defense Manual When You're the News,* 3rd ed. Miami: Video Consultants.
Lindeman, Edward C. 1921. *The Community: An Introduction to the Study of Community Leadership and Organization.* New York: Associated Press.
Mahaffey, Maryann. 1972. "Lobbying and Social Work." *Social Work* 17 (January): 3–11.
Pertskhuk, Michael, and Phillip Wilbur. 1991. *Media Advocacy: Strategic Communication for Nonprofits.* Washington, D.C.: Benton Foundation.
Raffoul, Paul. 1996. "Social Work and the Future: Some Final Thoughts." In *Future Issues for Social Work Practice,* Paul R. Raffoul and Aaron C. McNeece (eds.). Needham, MA: Allyn and Bacon.
Staples, Lee. 1984. *Roots to Power: A Manual for Grassroots Organizing.* New York: Praeger.
Sterling, Bruce. 1993. "Year 2000 & Beyond: Information Technology for Social Work: Vision, Choices, Ethics. In *Proceedings of the Ninth Annual Social Work Futures Conference,* Travis Courville and Paul Raffoul (eds.).
Zeck, Denice, and Edmund Rennolds. 1991. *OP-EDs: Strategic Communication for Nonprofits.* Washington, D.C.: Benton Foundation.

chapter 8

Monitoring the Bureaucracy

Bills are made into laws with good intentions. Those good intentions can become lost in the complex process of rule writing, administrative orders, and budgetary constraints. All can be lost if not monitored.

Ciro D. Rodriguez*

After months of hard work, a social worker who had been lobbying for passage of a bill was informed that the state senate had passed the bill and the governor had signed it. Much effort had resulted in legislative victory. Or had it?

On the contrary, social workers all too often win the legislative battle and proceed to lose the war by assuming their work is finished (Curren, 1982). Legislatures must not only pass bills but fund them, and if they do not fund a bill after passage (as sometimes occurs), that bill effectively is killed. Nor is funding the last of the hurdles. Administrative rules may be written that misinterpret the legislators' intent, or agencies may implement the regulations in a manner that differs from the intent.

The purpose of monitoring the bureaucracy is to ensure that the intent of the legislation is carried out. The social work lobbyist needs to monitor four areas after a bill has been passed: (1) promulgation of rules, (2) implementation and adherence to the rules by agencies, (3) executive orders and administrative changes, and (4) the budget allocation process.

Monitoring should not be confused with lobbying. Monitoring is the process of keeping a watchful eye on the government to see that the legislative intent is carried out, whereas lobbying is the act of influencing legislation. Monitoring and lobbying have some elements in common, yet are distinctly different

---

* Ciro D. Rodriguez has a MSW and is a Texas state representative.

activities. For example, a social worker who discovers an inconsistency between the intent of the law and its subsequent implementation might use the lobbying techniques described in chapter 6 to rectify the situation. The greatest overlap between the two activities occurs when the administrative rules are being promulgated for a recently passed piece of legislation. During this period, a certain amount of lobbying as well as monitoring may take place. In either case, the social worker must develop an interventive strategy, deciding how most effectively to induce others to modify their policy in the desired direction (Dluhy, 1982).

Throughout this chapter we refer to the "intent" of legislation, by which we mean the ultimate goal the supporters of the original bill had in mind. Throughout the entire legislative process, from the initial drafting of a bill to its funding and implementation, various interpretations, modifications, and deliberate misconstruals can result in a program whose characteristics are inconsistent with the original intent of a bill. Consider tax bills: Congress attempts to stimulate certain business or economic activities through tax breaks, but finds that because of regulatory loopholes or misinterpretations, not only have government revenues been reduced, but other unintended tax breaks also have been created.

It is important for the social worker to understand that certain formal and informal steps related to policy adoption and implementation apply to all levels of government: (1) rule writing and promulgation, (2) rule implementation, and (3) budget allocation. In addition, one must be aware of the importance of executive orders and other administrative changes that subsequently may affect program implementation.

Rule writing and promulgation occurs shortly after the bill is signed by the president, governor, or mayor. The promulgation processes usually occur just once, although legislation may be amended, repealed, or replaced at any time, after which the promulgation and implementation process will recur. Administrative orders, agency compliance, and the budget allocation process require more continuous or at least repeated scrutiny. In addition, even after a law has been enacted, a continuous surveillance of the program and the budgetary process is necessary to ensure that the services and benefits that were the intended result of the law are being provided.

The intent of this chapter is to inform the reader about the complex processes that occur after a bill is passed and the effect these can have. Monitoring skills are essential in the repertoire of political interventions. We provide strategies for effective monitoring in the three areas listed previously and indicate how social work skills can be utilized in the monitoring process.

PROMULGATING THE RULES

A law is a mandate from a legislative body that provides guidelines to govern behavior and decision making, while administrative regulations provide directives for the law's implementation. A bill is usually vague in its content.

With respect to monitoring the implementation of policy, I believe that there are three aspects useful for social workers to think about. These are (1) the decentralization of policy-making functions, (2) increased auditing requirements and local public scrutiny, and (3) increases in consumer participation in local decision making. What these three elements mean for professional social workers are opportunities for more direct involvement in policy-making and policy-monitoring activities, having public support for performance as well as fiscal audits, and increased opportunities for coalition building and community organizing.

Dennis Jones, MSW
Former Commissioner, Texas Department of Mental Health
and Mental Retardation

This is to avoid political debates over smaller issues. Additionally, legislators do not have the knowledge to write a bill that would cover every aspect of implementing a program. Therefore, the purpose of rules is to inform both the general public and those who administer the legislation how the law will be implemented and enforced.

Regulations may be perceived as additional policies which transform the legislative ideal into practical design and delivery stages. Regulations usually sharpen and clarify staffing requirements, service provider responsibilities, client eligibility, treatment modalities, and accountability and reporting mechanisms. These regulations are not merely simplistic extensions of the legislation. Indeed, this power to guide the behavior of others and the opportunity to make decisions about the basic allocation of services are powerful tools that can considerably alter the original intent of the legislation.

Public input is always sought during the rule-writing stage, through written commentary directed to the administrative staff engaged in rule writing or at public hearings scheduled by the agency. Usually there is no time limit on how long it can take to write the rules to satisfy all concerned with a particular law. A delay in rule-writing may be a means to weaken or skew the law's intent.

The substance and political importance of public input is weighted by the agency prior to issuing the final regulations (Pierce, 1984). It is possible for the president or a governor to implement emergency rules while awaiting the final draft from the appropriate agency. This possibility can undoubtedly have long-term effects.

The rule-making process varies from state to state and in city and county governments. Procedures articulated in the Administrative Procedure Act (APA), passed by Congress in 1946, are the model most used by other levels of government.

The first decision made in the rule-writing phase is which agency will be assigned the task. On the national level the Office of Management and Budget, under the president, monitors all rule making. Once delegated to a specific division of an agency, agency personnel are assigned to complete the task. Contrary to what is commonly thought, agency personnel do not exist for this function alone. The assignment of rule writing is often added to their other job responsibilities. Regulations reflect the values, knowledge, and expertise of these staff members, as well as any ignorance or unconcern.

Once a draft of the rules has been developed, public input is sought. All rules for the federal government are published in the *Federal Register.* The final draft must be published not less than 30 days before the rules are to be administered. On the local level, one must monitor to determine when and where public hearings will be held and how they will be published.

Now the rules and regulations can be implemented. Once implementation begins, and even after services have been started, the legislative body can make changes in the regulations by passage of an amended bill or by budgetary allocation. Any of these processes can alter or qualify the intent of the initial bill (Curren, 1982).

Within the rule-writing process there are multiple points at which a social worker may find it necessary to monitor and/or intervene. Clearly one point of intervention is with the staff assigned to write the regulations. A weakness of the system is the lack of personnel who understand how statutory design influences program implementation (Gimpel, 1991). An excellent approach at this stage is to set up an appointment with the staff members to provide brief and factual input. A straightforward strategy of showing an interest in the process and a willingness to assist could have a great influence on staff members, since they may have limited knowledge and expertise on the subject of the rules and limited time to complete the task (Curren, 1982). Prior to a meeting, think through and write out a proposal, if possible. These individuals may willingly incorporate your ideas in order to minimize their efforts. Most states require that any input given to those who are writing or promulgating the rules be considered and evaluated.

Providing input at public hearings is another opportunity to influence the direction of administrative regulations. It is essential to keep track of times, dates, and locations of public hearings to ensure that your representatives are present. Written positions or recommendations are important given the time limitations on verbal presentations.

For the sake of illustration, let's assume that a law was enacted to establish a drug treatment program in an inner city. Regulations should specify the types and qualifications of administrators, therapists, and support staff and should establish the targeted clients, eligibility standards, fee schedules, operational procedures, hours, and service parameters. All of these decisions can dramatically affect the services provided by the program. For example, charging a fee for such a treatment would most assuredly be a disincentive to poor inner-city residents and would dramatically reduce the program's effectiveness. Not providing evening or weekend services would have an equally devastating effect. On the other hand, evening hours, drop-in policies, and outreach efforts might improve service delivery and increase program effectiveness.

RULE IMPLEMENTATION
AND AGENCY COMPLIANCE

Once the rules have been written, their implementation must be monitored. This is best done at the beginning, when it is easier to make changes than it is after programs and procedures have become firmly established.

To be sure, there is an inherent contradiction in rules related to human services. In order to ensure that the intent of the law is carried out, it may be desirable to promulgate detailed and possibly restrictive rules. Some degree of flexibility in the interpretation of those rules, however, may well allow the program to address more adequately and equitably over time a variety of individual client concerns and problems, and allow the program to respond to changing client needs as well. Loose regulations may suit the bureaucrat's interest in having administrative flexibility, while easing the agency's drive for political survival (Bell and Bell, 1982). The pitfall is that this flexibility may allow services to change as popular opinions dictate, regardless of recipient needs.

The issues involved in specifying staff qualifications for a particular human service program offer a useful illustration of this type of dilemma. For example, a rigid requirement that only MSWs with mental health training will be acceptable as therapists in a drug treatment program, when applied statewide, may represent an unfairly restrictive qualification if such personnel are not available in all areas of the state. However, the often-used alternative of establishing "minimum qualifications" (e.g., a minimum requirement of a high school diploma or 12 credit hours of human service training) may result in untrained staff providing services and even therapy to program clients.

Monitoring rule implementation is necessary not only to protect the general public's rights, but also to ensure agency adherence to the regulations. Some of the major reasons implementation may deviate from legislative intent are as follows:

1. All agencies, including human service agencies, have vested interests to protect—not only their budgets, but also their organizational structure and general service delivery design. After an organization is established, any modification, whether it be expansion, contraction, or extinction, will create a great deal of resistance. When states enacted child abuse legislation in the late 1970s, strong resistance arose when the responsibility for investigation and reporting was assigned to state public welfare departments or child welfare agencies that already were overburdened.
2. Social agencies, despite the lofty language in their charters and in social legislation, are not necessarily benign with respect to protecting clients' rights. Once reimbursement for the services has been exhausted, the client all too often is disregarded or referred to another agency. When the Title XX amendments to the Social Security Act mandated that 50 percent of all funded services be delivered to current welfare recipients, several states initiated "head hunts" to increase welfare rolls so that they would have more clients to serve.

3. Legitimate differences in interpreting legislative intent can occur. For example, the use of flexible terminology in listing requirements, such as "social work degree or the equivalent," could be interpreted to mean "MSW" but also legitimately could be taken to mean "MSW or MA in psychology or sociology," or even "BA with life or professional experience equivalents."

4. State and federal budgetary oversight agencies have veto power over state agencies when it comes to administrative decisions made in the course of implementing social legislation, and this power is sometimes exercised to the detriment of groups of clients who were intended to benefit from the legislation. For example, mothers in the program often are directed by agencies to find work, when in fact the intent of the law that established the program was to encourage mothers to stay home and raise their children. In such cases, budgetary agencies need to be challenged on their interpretation of legislative intent (Bell and Bell, 1982).

5. Public pressure caused by a misunderstanding of a program might cause legislators, administrators, and agency staff to make changes that ultimately alter the intent and effectiveness of the program. For example, encouraging AFDC mothers to find work, without also providing adequate day care, will result in less adequate care for the children involved than was the case before the program was enacted.

6. The covert purpose of the law differs from the public justification for it, thus complicating the measurement of its effectiveness. For instance, many job training programs for the poor were enacted not to assist people to become economically self-sufficient, but rather to stimulate the economy or reduce welfare rolls.

In sum, agencies may deliberately or mistakenly misinterpret administrative regulations, which can result in deviation from legislative intent at the point of program initiation. Social workers within and without the organizations that administer such programs must monitor and intervene at this stage to ensure consistency with legislative intent. A number of monitoring operations may be legislatively mandated, such as administrative auditing, program review and evaluation, or compliance with quality control measures. Also, state "sunset laws" may require external review of the agency. Getting appointed to an advisory committee with oversight functions is one important and powerful method of monitoring these necessary internal or external review processes.

Budget Allocations

The budget is the clearest and most measurable indicator of governmental priorities. It lies at the heart of the political process and requires a great deal of continuous monitoring (Wildavsky, 1979). Legislators have the opportunity, either annually or biannually, to enhance or undermine the effectiveness of a program or agency via budget allocations. A good example of this occurred during President Reagan's first term of office. The Health Systems Act had received a $1.25 per capita allocation in 1980 but was cut to $0.38 per capita two years later, leaving the agency unable to meet the goals originally established in the legislation.

The size and design of a budget is a matter of serious contention in our political life (Wildavsky, 1979). The budget not only proposes what is to be expended, but projects revenues as well. The federal budget, which can have a deficit, follows an atypical budgetary process since most state, local, and private budgets must be balanced or show a reserve. On the state and local levels, overly optimistic revenue projections by a governor or mayor may cause the administrative branch to react by reducing expenditures in order to maintain a balanced budget. Thus, revenue projections are just as important as proposed expenditures.

Just as flexibility in interpretation of legislation can have both positive and negative consequences, flexibility in how budgets are presented also can have contradictory effects. Budgets may be presented and approved as lump sums for entire state administrative units, by line items, or by departmental functions. If budgetary oversight, approval, and allocation is by line item or by departmental function, legislators can provide more direction and input over agency priorities. A lump-sum budget appropriation process, however, may allow for too much latitude and administrative discretion by the agency chief executives.

The budget allocation process can be influenced in several ways. One way is to influence the type of budget that will be presented and approved. If social workers want extreme latitude, they should lobby for lump-sum budgets. Second, because department heads make funding recommendations to the budget director, the strategy used by the department head can be crucial. For example, if a department head requests an extremely large increase after several years of small, incremental budget increases, this will create legislative interest. If the need for the request is well documented and publicly supported, it may be granted. On the other hand, it is likely that undocumented requests for large budget increases will be disregarded.

As mentioned earlier, budget allocations have a great impact on policy implementation. For that reason, monitoring of the budgetary process is highly important, even crucial, to program maintenance and service delivery. Social workers have both firsthand experience and aggregate data from previous budget cycles on the impact of differing funding levels on client service. This information should be supplied to the legislative budget office before a new budget is proposed. Presented regularly, such information can be used to sensitize fiscal planners to the impact of funding levels on client services and to projections of future demand. After the budget is proposed, the next logical intervention is lobbying the legislature, because after the budget is amended and approved by the legislative branch it is returned to the administrative branch for signature and implementation and further intervention becomes difficult.

The most obvious and yet most controversial issue in budget allocations for human services is to define and operationalize "adequate standards and services."

Operationalization refers to staff size, staff qualifications, caseload ratios, and hours of service delivery. A common value dilemma social work program staff face is how to deliver quality services to all needy clients when funds are limited or decreasing without turning clients away. Although in the short term it is not in the best interest of the client to be denied service, waiting list figures indicating unmet needs can be powerful indicators to legislators of the need for increased funding to expand a particular service.

Administrative Changes or Executive Orders

Once a bill has been enacted, responsibility for the programs it creates rests with the chief executive officer or the department head, who often is empowered to make certain administrative changes. If any changes in the rules are then made, the same process mentioned earlier will be followed. However, there are ways in which administrators can affect a program without changing the rules. One is to recommend a reduced budget.

Another subtle mechanism for circumventing legislative intent is to exercise power over the way responsibilities for the program are assigned. To take an extreme example, assigning program responsibilities to one agency, or to one agency staff member, may signal limited interest in effective program implementation. Likewise, assigning responsibility for the program to an inappropriate agency could predetermine its failure. Therefore, monitoring such administrative actions is a critical interventive task.

Nonenforcement of the rules through administrative oversight is another way to undermine the intent of a piece of legislation. If the law does not include evaluative or accountability requirements or procedures, noncompliance is likely. For example, the Hill–Burton Act required hospitals to provide a percentage of their health care service free to the poor in exchange for federal loans. Under the act, participating hospitals were required to inform poor patients of the availability of the free services. However, because no agency was designated to oversee the hospitals on this point, many hospitals did not comply with the regulation.

Other unobtrusive methods can be used by an executive to alter the outcome of a program: placing a freeze on staff replacements, overloading a specific agency subdivision, rewarding noncompliance, changing eligibility requirements, and reducing publicity and outreach. All of these methods will alter the amount and pattern of services provided.

SOCIAL WORK SKILLS

All of the rule-making and rule-implementing processes mentioned in this chapter require consistent monitoring in order to ensure that the intent of the law is carried out and that the clients targeted by the legislation receive mandated services. Because elected officials, agency staff, public opinion, and society's needs change, social workers must monitor from both outside and inside the bureaucracy. They also need to utilize social work skills to ensure that program goals and services remain appropriate. Although this type of ongoing monitoring is difficult and tedious, it is nevertheless essential and is quite compatible with social work skills as well. The same basic problem-solving approach that social workers use with clients can be employed in monitoring a program: identify the problem, gather information, make an assessment, and develop a plan of action.

Problem identification may seem to be the most straightforward of the stages, because usually it is evident that clients have unmet needs or are falling between service areas. What may not be evident is in which of the stages the fault lies—legislative enactment, program design and delivery, or budget allocation. Once this has been determined, appropriate information can be collected and presented.

Information is the key to effective advocacy. Persuasive information comes in many forms. Quantitative data may be collected and presented, such as the percentage of the population in need, the number of clients served, or the number of population "at risk." Information may be presented comparatively, in the form of data specifying proportions of the population in need or as ratios of clients served county to county or state to state. The same information can also be collected and presented in qualitative terms, by citing case illustrations or by projecting additional problems or future scenarios if the current need is not met.

Regardless of type, information gathered by social workers can increase their ability to influence public officials. Facts collected about community problems will generate questions, identify hidden problems, and support or challenge government policies and explanations. Information also lends credibility to opinions. It also enables one to reveal officials' evasions, question their assumptions, and, if necessary, expose errors or inconsistencies in their figures (Shur and Smith, 1980).

Data can be found in a number of places. The census is a useful resource, and much of the data in it is already cross tabulated, enhancing its utility. For example, one can easily retrieve data on income levels by gender, household size, or occupational status of household head. Guides to the census include the *Census Users Guide,* a more technical book that includes definitions of all terms used in the census.

Another type of information that may be useful for advocacy in the monitoring stages covers program rules, regulations, and procedures is the *Catalog of Federal Domestic Assistance* (U.S. General Services Administration), which contains a complete description of federal programs, including eligibility criteria, application timing and procedures, citations to controlling laws and regulations, and funding available. Many federal programs require states to submit state plans, which may provide data on many areas of interest. Federal law requires that copies of state plans be made available to the public through the governor's office. There are a number of advocacy groups that collect, decipher, and disseminate information on particular subjects and issues. Most public libraries carry a directory of organizations.

Various other sources of data exist: Every two years, the Department of Health and Human Services conducts a national survey of AFDC participants and programs. States must prepare public assistance manuals that describe their rules and procedures for administering AFDC programs. The U.S. Government Printing Office (GPO) publishes almost 300 subject bibliographies. The Washington Information Directory lists organizations working on federal and state-level legislation and programs. Clearly, much of this information is invaluable. However, because increasingly fewer reporting requirements are being enacted, this kind of data collection may no longer be mandated, so much of this type of data will no longer be available to the public (Shur and Smith, 1980).

Whenever secondary sources of data are utilized, the inherent biases in the collection, collation, and analysis must be taken into account. Particularly when using state agency plans and reports, be aware that the need to justify a program may bias the presentation of information. Using census data, government reports, and state plans, both a projection of needs and an assessment of output and outcome can be obtained for the purpose of defending the existence of or expansion of any program or service. After the information is collected and tabulated, the position must be presented in a style and format that is persuasive to those responsible for decision making. For example, stating that 0.003 percent of all children in a particular county were sexually molested last year may be accurate, but is less effective than dramatizing it. You can make this point more effectively by stating that for each member of the six-person committee, 100 children were unwillingly forced into sexual acts by an adult. The general problem is to decide when statistics are useful, which statistics will be most persuasive, and when a more dramatic and personal approach will be more effective.

The final stage in the monitoring process is to develop a plan of action not only for the presentation of information, but also for ongoing monitoring and lobbying to ensure that a particular position is carried through.

A word of caution is in order here: Rhetorical excess and incorrect or purposeful misuse of factual data can discredit even the best lobbyists. Trite phrases can divert attention from the issues. Although personalizing statistics may be a persuasive tactic, sensationalizing them could be detrimental to your cause.

An illustration of monitoring agency compliance with administrative regulations can be drawn from the previously mentioned Hill–Burton Act. With the recent emergence of the "new poor," the need for federally funded health services has greatly increased. One regulation created by the act is that hospitals must post a sign in their emergency rooms and waiting rooms stating that they are Hill–Burton hospitals and that services are available without cost to those without funds. However, many hospitals did not comply with this regulation. It was only through monitoring of hospitals and the threat of a lawsuit by a group of social workers that hospitals were forced to follow through with their obligation to advertise and provide these services to the poor.

A similar example involves a social worker who monitored a state commission that oversaw the implementation of the state's block grants. This person

I got involved when Nixon started cutting social services. When I started graduate school in 1972, there were jobs for every social worker who was graduating. Then in my second year at the University of Oklahoma, all of a sudden programs were being cut. It occurred to me that if the programs were being cut, social work students weren't going to have jobs, and poor people weren't going to get services. I then could see that political influence was needed. I talked the School of Social Work into doing a very creative placement, sort of turning me loose at the state house to see if there was a way to make an impact on that system.

They hooked me up with a local social action agency which had never been involved in state capitol issues, but was very interested in doing so. That was the beginning of a twenty-year career as a political social worker.

Today I have, in essence, a business that is a legislative monitoring, consulting, and training enterprise. It keeps me involved with social service agencies and supports me while I am able to do lobbying, sometimes paid, sometimes just as part of the process that I'm involved in.

On a regular basis, I have about twenty contractors, if you want to call them that. I read all of the legislation that affects social services and summarize it based on what effects it has on social services. This review is sent to the different groups based on their needs. I meet with their boards or associations on their time schedule and have a briefing, helping them figure out how to advocate for themselves.

For example, Monday mornings I meet with the Oklahoma Alliance on Aging. Around the table are representatives from every senior citizen group in the state: AARP, retired teachers, the area-wide aging agencies, and they look at and discuss all of the bills relevant to gerontology. I help them plan what they're going to do to lobby for themselves.

After many years of working, I enjoy an excellent reputation in the Oklahoma state legislature because I put together information and deal with information in an extremely credible way. So most of the time I get asked for information instead of trying to force it on somebody. After a while if you're very consistent and responsive, people will start coming to you and asking. Legislators today come off of the floor to find me and say, "I'm just about to argue a bill on so-and-so, tell me what the issue is here; give me some information." And, you know, all of a sudden, I end up being used as a staff person for every house member and senator who is interested in promoting a piece of progressive legislation.

Sandy Ingraham, MSW
Social Services Consultant
Harrah, Oklahoma

diligently attended every commission meeting to ensure that the commission was complying with the original intent of the legislators. She became so skilled at monitoring individual commission members that she could predict their decisions and individual preferences by their posture, facial expressions, and gestures, and subsequently could alter her interventive style or content. What is not said often can be a clue, as can body posture, gestures, and word usage. Awareness of the external factors affecting committee members or chairpersons can be important in determining the most appropriate interventive strategy. The ability to observe and understand group processes, formal and informal leadership, and committee members' personal goals and ambitions are all essential in effective intervention.

It should be obvious at this point that individuals, either alone or as part of a decision-making body, are the primary actors in all of the monitoring processes discussed in this chapter, from legislative enactment to rule writing to agency compliance. Social work skills and social workers' experiences are tremendous assets in the monitoring stages.

CONCLUSION

Monitoring is the process of overseeing that rules and regulations, budget allocations, and agency compliance are consistent with the intent of the law. Social work skills are very effective in all stages of this process.

Monitoring all of these stages takes time and a great deal of patience, and is probably the most boring of the political interventive techniques, yet it is a necessary step to ensure that the original intent of a piece of legislation is indeed implemented. The effect that an individual can have on the outcome may be even greater than during the initial legislative process. This is not to I say that lobbying for the passage of a bill is not necessary, but many mistakenly think that once a bill is signed, no further advocacy is necessary.

ASSIGNMENTS

1. Choose a recently enacted piece of state legislation and follow it to the agency assigned to write the rules. Obtain a copy of the administrative regulations and assess how closely they appear to follow the intent of the legislation.
2. Identify individuals or formal organizations in your state that monitor human service legislation and implementation. Describe the processes they use.

SUGGESTED READINGS

Albert, Raymond. 1983. "Social Work Advocacy in the Regulatory Process." *Social Casework* 64 (October): 480–481.

Prigmore, Charles S. 1974. "Use of the Coalition in Legislative Action." *Social Work* 19 (January): 96–102.

REFERENCES

Bell, William G., and Budd L. Bell. 1982. "Monitoring the Bureaucracy: An Expression of Legislative Lobbying." In *Practical Politics: Social Work and Political Responsibility,* Maryann Mahaffey and John W. Hanks (eds.), pp. 118-135. New York: National Association of Social Workers.

Curren, H. Patricia. 1982. Speech to the Michigan Political Action for Candidate Election Committee.

Dluhy, Milan J. 1982. *Changing the System: Political Advocacy for Disadvantaged Groups.* Beverly Hills, CA: Sage Publications.

Gimpel, James. 1991. "Congressional Oversight of Welfare and Work: Fundamental Flaws Make Legislative Efficiency Nearly Impossible." *Public Welfare* (Summer): 10.

Pierce, Dean. 1984. *Policy for the Social Work Practitioner.* White Plains, NY: Longman.

Shur, Janet, and Paul Smith. 1980. *Information Resources for Child Advocates.* Washington, D.C.: Children's Defense Fund.

U.S. Bureau of the Census. 1980. *Census of Population and Housing 1980, Users Guide, Part A.* Washington, D.C.: U.S. Government Printing Office.

————. 1978. *Directory of Federal Statistics for Local Areas Guide to Sources 1976.* Washington, D.C.: U.S. Government Printing Office.

U.S. General Services Administration. *Catalog of Federal Domestic Assistance.* Washington, D.C.: U.S. Government Printing Office.

Wildavsky, Aaron. 1979. *The Politics of the Budgetary Process.* Boston, MA: Little, Brown.

chapter 9

Political Action Committees

The role of a political action committee in a membership organization is twofold. It must make complex political judgments and provide tangible campaign support for viable candidates who will advance the public policy interests of the profession. An equally important task is to inform, engage, and mobilize social workers as political leaders in their communities.

Toby Weismiller*

Although social reform and client advocacy traditionally have been viewed as legitimate aspects of social work methodology, organized efforts at political reform by social workers are recent. It might seem self-evident that social workers would need to become politically active in order to affect political reform. Certainly those who have been politically active have done so through such initiatives as testifying, letter writing, or lobbying. It is our contention, however, that collective efforts will prove more effective than individual efforts. For that reason, we endorse political action committees (PACs) as an important and powerful method for affecting social policy and social change.

Political action committees are organizations designed to collect and disperse voluntary contributions for political purposes from members of a special interest group. In order to meet state and federal regulations, they must be independently organized and funded.

Political action committees vary because state election laws differ. Generally a PAC is organized specifically to offer financial support to candidates, to raise funds for donation, and to urge the PAC membership as well as the general public to support candidates endorsed by the parent organization. Special interest

---

* Toby Weismiller is the Political Affairs Director, NASW.

141

groups (business, labor, professional associations, corporate employees) coordinate and systematize these efforts to support candidates viewed as sympathetic to that particular special interest group's positions.

Although PACs are organized primarily to provide financial support to candidates, they influence policy in other ways as well, particularly through coalition building and education and skill development of PAC members. Political action committees are important to candidates who need endorsements and financial contributions when they are up for election or reelection. Conversely, the parent organization assumes that receiving assistance from a PAC may lead a potential legislator, for example, to be increasingly supportive of the PAC's positions in the future (Abrams and Goldstein, 1981). Finally, the principle of collectively organizing to endorse candidates suggests that the support generated will be larger than that given by any single individual and more visible to the candidate.

Political action committees have been in existence since 1972. The recent proliferation of PACs is striking: A grand total of 4,234 business and labor PACs had registered with the Federal Election Commission in 1989. This reflects a 34 percent increase from 1988. Not only have the number of PACs increased, but the amount of money contributed by PACs to congressional election campaigns has also grown. In 1988, $159 million was contributed to federal candidates, a significant increase from 1980 when $60 million was contributed (Federal Election Commission, 1989).

With the growth of PACs, controversy has arisen about the negative aspects of "vote buying." Consequently there has been debate about changing state and federal election laws to limit PAC maximum contributions to candidates or to prohibit them entirely.

In 1976 the NASW created a PAC called Political Action for Candidate Election (PACE) in order to offer financial support to candidates at the federal level. Florida became the first state to create a state-level NASW PAC, followed soon after by Michigan, California, and Indiana. The number of social work PACs has increased, and by the mid-1990s, 45 NASW chapters had PAC operations and PACE was among the highest in money raised of all national PACs. To be sure, NASW's PAC may be slightly different from those sponsored by business and industry. Social work PACs are greatly enhanced by social workers' skills in interpersonal relationships, community organization, and volunteer action.

Table 9.1 compares the top fund-raising PACs with NASW's PAC. During debate in Congress over national health care, for example, the American Medical Association (AMA) and NASW took very different positions. Poor people, sick people, the elderly, and children do not make political campaign contributions, and indeed often don't or can't vote. Thus, a social workers' PAC is a necessary advocacy group, not only for professional self-interest and protection, but for the disadvantaged and disenfranchised as well.

Political action committees eventually may come under greater scrutiny and, perhaps, more legislative regulation and monitoring, but until that time, they are a significant force in the electoral process. In order for human service

TABLE 9.1 Receipts in the 1993–1994 election cycle

Business, Union, and Professional PACs*

International Brotherhood of Teamsters	$ 8,781,083
National Rifle Association of America	$ 6,831,712
American Federation of State, City, and Municipal Employees	$ 4,933,977
Association of Trial Lawyers of America	$ 4,493,211
American Medical Association	$ 4,465,815
United Auto Workers of America	$ 4,335,563
National Education Association	$ 4,330,746
National Association of Realtors	$ 3,429,354
National Automobile Dealers Association	$ 3,090,737
United Parcel Service	$ 2,854,404
Federal Express Corporation	$ 1,389,291
RJR Nabisco, Inc.	$ 1,027,773

Social Work PACs

National Association of Social Workers	$ 505,674
NASW California	$ 31,922
NASW Michigan	$ 19,691
NASW Illinois	$ 18,811
NASW New Jersey	$ 15,696
NASW Oregon	$ 14,296

*These are listed by the sponsoring organization rather than by the PAC's actual registered
name. Federal law prohibits contributions or expenditures in federal elections by corporations,
labor unions, and incorporated trade or membership organizations.
SOURCE: Information gathered from NASW and *Political Finance & Lobby Reporter,* April 12,
1995, Vol. XVI, No. 7, pp. 9–19.

workers to be able to influence the sweeping antihuman service movement, they
also must participate in the process.

This chapter explores in depth why PACs are organized, how they are
utilized in candidate selection and endorsement, and the targeting strategies
useful in distributing available resources.

WHY IS A PAC ORGANIZED?

Those most critical of PACs say they are organized to purchase votes from
candidates. In reality, there are important reasons for the formation of a PAC:
(1) to provide information about candidates and issues to members, and (2) to
better utilize resources. More specifically, this means that a PAC can help
individuals keep abreast of the positions represented by various congressional,
state, and local candidates, thus enabling them to determine what effect the
election of each of these candidates may have on the special interest group.

Further, a PAC can alleviate the indecision that may arise when one attempts to determine how best to use one's own resources (time, skills, money) on behalf of candidate support. This indecision often is compounded by the geographic distance between candidates and the individual, and by the fact that an individual's resources seldom are sufficient on their own to have substantial impact on a campaign or a candidate. A candidate is far more likely to remember the contribution of a group whose endorsement represents approval of one's policies than a number of smaller contributions from several constituents. Furthermore, unlike most individuals, a PAC usually endorses and contributes to many candidates. so its potential influence extends to a much larger segment of the total legislative body than does that of one individual.

The main objective of a PAC is to elect candidates who favor its policies and positions. The many strategies used to accomplish this goal will be discussed later. The resulting actions have several anticipated consequences, the most important of which is to gain a politician's attention after election. Also, because politicians need to be informed about many issues in order to govern effectively, they value people and organizations who can provide them with reliable information. Therefore, the provision and dissemination of information concerning current legislative issues is a central function of one division of NASW—the Education Legislation Action Network (ELAN). ELAN was developed six years before PACE, for the purpose of determining professional positions on current legislative issues, collecting supportive documentation, and lobbying. Now PACE and ELAN work together to develop social policy for both organizations.

Once a candidate sympathetic to a PAC's positions is elected, the political appointment of special interest group members is of obvious benefit in furthering the group's goals. A governor, for example, may make as many as 2,000 appointments, some of which will undoubtedly affect social policy.

PROCESS OF SELECTION

Because it is not unusual for a political candidate to slant a position on a particular issue in order to gain the support of specific groups, often it becomes necessary to determine how a politician really stands on issues that may not be of major campaign interest. In the case of incumbents, the best measurement is action already taken. Consequently, to give a clearer picture of the candidate's position on certain issues, PACs often prepare and publicize a record of the candidate's votes on relevant pieces of legislation—sometimes referred to as the "report card."

In the course of a legislative session, a legislator may cast hundreds of votes. Many of the votes may run along party lines as indications of party support; other votes may be on procedural issues or minor amendments to a bill. These votes are not good indications of position, although procedural votes (e.g., to table a bill) are used as indicators of position when there are no other bills related to a particular issue to monitor. For example, although a vote to legalize abortion is not taken regularly, votes on legislation dealing with physicians' regulations on providing an abortion may provide a measure of the candidate's position.

Not all legislation will be equally important to a particular PAC. A PAC representing social workers, for instance, is not interested in a candidate's position on materials used in highway construction, but would be interested in the candidate's position on a nursing home bill of rights or Medicaid copayment. Clearly the first step is to choose the issues to be used in developing the "report card." Given the great number of votes taken in a legislative session, this is a challenging task. Usually a PAC chooses a limited number of bills that correspond with the organization's goals. Then the records are reviewed to determine the candidate's vote on each issue, noting whether the candidate voted for or against the organization's position (see Table 9.2).

TABLE 9.2 Report card of selected senate incumbents

State/Senator	1	2	3	4	5	6	7	8	9	10	W	A
California												
Feinstein	+	+	−	+	−	+	+	+	+	+	80	80
Boxer	+	+	+	+	+	+	+	+	+	+	100	100
Minnesota												
Durenberger	+	+	−	−	−	−	+	+	+	+	60	60
Wellstone	+	+	+	+	+	+	+	+	+	+	100	100
North Dakota												
Conrad	+	+	−	+	−	−	+	+	−	+	60	60
Dorgan	+	+	−	+	−	−	?	?	+	+	63	50
Oklahoma												
Boren	+	+	+	−	−	−	+	+	+	+	70	70
Nickles	−	−	−	−	−	−	−	−	−	−	0	0
Utah												
Hatch	−	−	−	−	−	−	−	−	−	−	0	0
Bennett	−	−	−	−	−	−	−	−	+	−	10	10
West Virginia												
Byrd	+	+	+	+	−	−	+	+	+	−	70	70
Rockefeller	+	+	+	+	−	+	+	+	+	+	90	90
Wyoming												
Wallop	?	−	−	−	+	−	−	−	+	−	22	20
Simpson	−	−	−	−	−	−	+	−	+	+	30	30

Key: + = voted in favor of NASW's position 4. Budget Reconciliation
    − = voted against NASW's position 5. Defense Authorization
    ? = did not vote 6. Labor, HHS, Education Appropriations
    W = when voting 7. Access to Abortion Clinics
    A = all votes 8. Brady Bill
    1. Family Leave 9. Labor, HHS, Education Appropriations
    2. Motor Voter 10. Surgeon General Confirmation
    3. Cut Welfare
SOURCE: 104th Congress Report Card, NASW, February 1, 1994.

As Table 9.2 illustrates, a further decision must be made in the analysis of the voting record: how to count absences. For example, Senator Dorgan, North Dakota, has a record five in favor, but two absences, on the ten selected issues. Many PACs would consider the absences as negative votes, presuming that an effective senator is one who votes. Before reaching this conclusion, however, it would be prudent to investigate the reason for the absences. After all, the legislator who is absent may have been working diligently on home district issues or may have been ill.

The voting record is a helpful device when dealing with incumbents, but it does not represent the entire record. Other information, such as legislation sponsorship, can assist PAC members. Here caution must be used, because many legislators sponsor bills they know will die in committee in order to secure

FIGURE 9.1   Selected items from PAC candidate questionnaires

1. Congress has introduced a plan that would shift responsibility for AFDC, food stamps, and other social programs to the states. Do you

   _____ Support the proposal in its present form?

   _____ Support the concept, but not for AFDC and food stamps?

   _____ Disagree with the concept?

2. Among federal deregulation proposals are ones that threaten the quality and quantity of health care services by decreasing the number of social work positions in existence. Which of the following best states your viewpoint?

   _____ Deregulation is necessary to achieve cost-effective health care.

   The loss of the quality of services is of more concern to me than the potential
   _____ cost saving.

   The availability of services should be determined by the state rather than by
   _____ the federal government.

3. What, in your view, are the most important problems facing our state?

4. A number of controversial social issues are being discussed now, some of which will come up in the next legislative session. Regardless of what you personally believe about these issues, how will you vote concerning public policy on the issues below?

   a. Because the right to choose abortion is based on a U.S. Supreme Court ruling, will you support Medicaid funding to pay for abortions?

     Yes   No

   b. If a bill permitting prayer in the public schools is reported to the floor of the State legislature, how will you vote?

     Yes   No

5. Do you feel that a family of two can meet necessary expenditures on $290.00 per month?

     Yes   No

6. What is your position on governmental research on AIDS/HIV?

(Hypothetical questionnaire)

political support or appease constituents or special interest groups. Committee votes and activities also may be important, because legislation of interest to the PAC may never reach a floor vote. Other matters to be investigated include the politician's committee assignments and relative power within the legislative body. Consequently, a social work PAC would want to endorse a candidate who chairs the social services committee if that politician's positions are acceptable within the PAC's limits.

Of course, some nonincumbents might be stronger supporters of human service issues than incumbent legislators. Obtaining an understanding of a nonincumbent's position is even more difficult. Often it must be obtained using a questionnaire, an interview, or both. Currently PACE does not use a questionnaire, but requires all challengers to have an interview. A questionnaire (see Figure 9.1) can be open ended, dealing with the candidate's general philosophy, or closed, to identify his or her position on a specific issue or bill, such as the appropriate level of AFDC allowances. The nonincumbent's responses to the questionnaire or interview must then be compared to the record of his or her opponent.

The process of selection is not without complicating factors. A PAC must deal with many political realities, including the fact that in many political districts it is impossible to find a candidate who is totally supportive of the views of the PAC membership. Table 9.3 lists the proportion of Republican and Democratic voters in hypothetical districts. This data may be used in deciding which candidate to target in districts that are proportionally unfavorable to the candidate's party.

Clearly there are times and circumstances when a PAC will endorse a candidate who, on the basis of a voting record, questionnaire, or interview, is not the ideal choice. For example, a PAC might endorse a candidate primarily because of his campaign against a number of candidates whose voting records are known to be unfavorable to human services, or might endorse an incumbent who has a marginal voting record on issues of concern to the PAC but who is considered a "shoe-in." In the latter case, it probably would be wise to endorse and provide at least some support to that candidate. This issue will be further explored later in this chapter.

TABLE 9.3 Proportion of registered Republicans and Democrats by districts (hypothetical)

District	% Registered Republicans	% Registered Democrats
1	60	40
2	50	50
3	25	75
4	10	90

A different type of dilemma exists when all the contending candidates support PAC policies and therefore are considered to be good potential legislators. In this situation PACs will not endorse any candidate for fear of alienating the others who also have taken positions that are favorable to the organization.

Nonendorsement occurs frequently during primaries. Although many people feel that primaries are useless, many important decisions are made at this level. Winning the primary in some districts, for example, the Democratic nomination in District 4 in Table 9.3, is tantamount to being elected. Unfortunately, as important as the primaries are, voter turnout historically has been lower for primaries than for general elections.

CANDIDATE ENDORSEMENTS

Before discussing the variety of candidate endorsements available to a PAC membership, it should be noted that generally the earlier an endorsement is made, the greater the effect a PAC will have on the campaign. A candidate remembers those who helped create the momentum of the campaign. Early money, volunteers, and other support may deter competition, create a "winning attitude" for the chosen candidate, or both, which often induces other PACs to join the campaign. One legislator told a representative from PACE that the $1,000 received sixteen months before a general election had the same effect as $7,000 received two months before the election. Volunteers who join campaigns early have a far greater opportunity to affect policy issues and play a key campaign role. The benefit of an early endorsement is reciprocal, since many candidates will place the endorsements of the sponsoring organization on their campaign literature, thus enhancing the PAC's ability to raise money.

One argument in favor of late endorsements, however, should be acknowledged. The longer a PAC remains neutral in a given race, the more valuable the PAC's endorsement may become, thus increasing the PAC's ability to obtain the candidate's support for the PAC's position on critical issues. The larger the PAC, the more effective this technique.

After a PAC has gathered and reviewed data on all the candidates in a particular race, the members must decide not only whom to endorse, but how. There are several ways in which an endorsement can be made:

1. The PAC can endorse the candidate by stating that the membership organization, for example, NASW, recommends that social workers vote for that candidate. Even though this is the simplest endorsement, it is perhaps least effective from the standpoint of the long-term objectives of the PAC.
2. Services and support can be offered, including mailing and telephone lists. Candidates are aware that the endorsement alone will not guarantee membership votes, but mailing lists and telephone numbers

facilitate the candidate's ability to reach PAC members and to gain their support and labor.

3. A PAC can recruit and assign volunteers from its membership to assist candidates, thereby increasing the effect of the endorsement. PACE has found this to be most effective, because candidates have discovered that social workers have excellent campaign skills. Social workers listen well, are organized, are trained to take a broad perspective, and can work well with a variety of individuals (Wolk, 1981). Some candidates enlist social workers as campaign managers. Also, after an election, social workers often are hired as aides to work out constituent problems.

4. The most important form of support is financial. Campaigns are expensive, and financial support allows the candidate to mold the campaign to the community. As mentioned earlier, not all PAC-endorsed candidates receive financial support. Targeting candidates for in-kind as well as financial support is a more cost-efficient resource utilization method. Many PACs with considerable financial resources provide elaborate in-kind services to a candidate because the Federal Election Commission has set limits on the amount of money a PAC can contribute to a campaign.

TARGETING

A PAC develops a targeting strategy in order to utilize its resources most effectively. Obviously it is relatively ineffective to contribute $5,000 to a candidate who already has more financial support than is needed to run the campaign or who has little opposition. In order to target available resources effectively, a PAC must develop policy guidelines.

In a unique situation, an endorsed candidate chose to use funds contributed to provide internships to enable social work students to work in the congressional campaign. As a result, the students received a great deal of training and a direct understanding of the political arena. This effort provided an excellent way to multiply the political investment. The candidate received the staff support needed, the students learned a great deal, and the candidate learned how valuable social workers are.

Suzanne Dworak-Peck, MSW
President, NCN (NASW Communications Network)
Past President, NASW, and Former Co-Chair, PACE
Los Angeles, California

In developing a targeting strategy, the PAC first reviews the full range of political offices open in the upcoming elections and determines who is likely to be easily reelected or elected. Indeed, many incumbents do not campaign because they already have strong support or no opposition. Whether these obvious winners support human services or not, their races are not targeted because the outcome cannot be changed. The remaining races are examined for candidate compatibility with the PAC's positions. Each race is then reviewed to determine whether the PAC's efforts can have an effect on the outcome and what amount of effort would be required for success. Typical guidelines for a PAC include the following:

1. Targeting supportive incumbent candidates who are in difficulty.
2. Targeting candidates who have the best chance of replacing an incumbent who does not support the PAC's interests.
3. Eliminating incumbents in leadership positions who are opposed to the organization's views on relevant issues.

Another form of targeting is known as "candidate development." This is a strategy by which individuals who are interested in running for office, and who support a PAC's goals and objectives, are helped to develop knowledge of issues and campaign skills. Locating a prospective candidate in a district that offers the best chance for success can be effective. The PAC then supplies the candidate with the maximum amount of financial support permitted and as much in-kind and volunteer support as possible. PACE has always supported social worker candidates. NASW's 1994–1997 program priority states the association will work toward recruiting, training, and supporting social workers to run for elected office at all levels (NASW, 1994).

FALL OUT

The greatest danger to a PAC is "fall out"—quarreling and disagreement. Whenever a decision or action is taken for a large group of people, there will be those who fall out, and PACs must take this into consideration when making decisions to support candidates whose positions on the issues are not completely satisfactory. A PAC must weigh a politically advantageous decision against the potential loss of membership support. Obviously, losing membership contributions will decrease the PAC's effectiveness, but public quarreling or overt support for the opposition are even more divisive. This not only decreases the impact of the PAC's endorsement, but, more importantly, it may become a wedge that could splinter the organization.

Within the human service profession, concern often is expressed about partisan politics. Historically, Democrats have tended to support human services, and social work PACs frequently have found themselves endorsing Democratic candidates only. At times social workers are uncomfortable with the idea of a PAC that exclusively endorses candidates of one party. Some social work PACs

There are often at least two positions that are espoused at a time, like the endorsement of a presidential candidate. One position says, "How courageous, we really are there at the beginning! It's a chance to demonstrate not only our training, but our expertise, philosophy, and values as social workers. If indeed this candidate wins, we will have an important role in shaping this administration or at least taking part in it." The other view says, "You involved us in a campaign in which we really are very visible and if we don't win, it will have a major impact on our ability to operate in the political arena during the next several years." Probably neither of these views is totally accurate. The important point is that these kinds of decisions sometimes need to be made.

Suzanne Dworak-Peck, MSW
President, NCN (NASW Communications Network)
Past President, NASW, and Former Co-Chair, PACE
Los Angeles, California

have sought Republican social workers to serve as PAC board members, thus assuring a nonpartisan ideology. However about 70 percent of NASW members state they are Democrats (NASW, 1995). Most important, however, is to endorse and elect prohuman service candidates, irrespective of party.

The need to make endorsements early may enhance or hamper a PAC's ability to weigh member dissent. Because many members are not politically active until campaigns are well under way, awaiting input from the total membership is often inimical to quick decision making. A PAC must take immediate action in an uncertain and risky environment, and often doesn't have time to poll the entire membership. The case of an incumbent candidate who decided to retire just before the primary presents an interesting example. He was an influential legislator with an adequate prohuman service record and his reelection appeared imminent. This created an excellent opportunity for the PAC to support a prohuman service candidate in an open race, but the urgency of the event made it imperative to make an immediate endorsement, thus risking member fall out.

IDEALISM VERSUS WINNING

A PAC often must choose between a candidate whose philosophical beliefs are compatible with those of the PAC, but who has a poor chance of winning, and a candidate members can "live with" who has a good chance of winning. The wrong endorsement decision in this scenario may determine whether the PAC has a political friend to work with, educate, and influence, or an enemy who

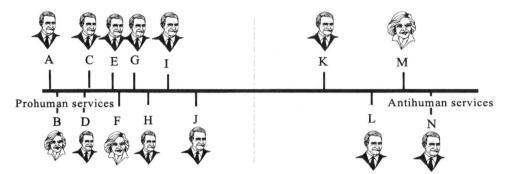

FIGURE 9.2 Primary gubernatorial rankings on human services issues

does not wish to talk or listen. Also, it is in these situations that fall out from membership potentially can be most severe.

In these situations, the PAC must choose between idealism (the best candidate) and winning (the most likely candidate). Figure 9.2 illustrates a continuum of fourteen gubernatorial candidates in a state primary. Candidates are arrayed from left (prohuman services) to right (antihuman services). Candidate A, who most closely agrees with social workers' positions, has run several times but has never gained a substantial proportion of the primary vote. A state senator, Candidate B, also favorable to social work policy issues, received the Citizen of the Year award from that state's NASW chapter and also was chair of the Senate Social Service Committee. However, he had done poorly both in the polls and in fund-raising. The PAC felt it would be most advantageous to reelect him as senator, thus retaining his committee chairship. On the other hand, Congressman F, a six-term congressman with a 50 percent correct voting record, had been instrumental in developing legislation to pool the efforts of union and management in order to save a major corporation. He was perceived by the PAC to be a winner, and was favored in the polls. His organizational and campaign techniques appeared to be professional. Because an early endorsement was important, the PAC decided to endorse Congressman F, although some social workers already were engaged in Senator B's campaign. Senator B pulled less than 5 percent of the primary vote and Congressman F received 50 percent, eventually winning the general election. Thus, the fact that a winner was chosen early ultimately resulted in an ideal candidate for the PAC, because early endorsement allowed access and time to educate the candidate on human service issues.

CONCLUSION

It should be clear that the purpose of a PAC is to financially support candidates who have been or will be supportive of the PAC's position on specific issues. Because this may be construed as "vote buying," some concern exists about the legitimacy of the process. Nonetheless, PACs have proliferated and are contributing substantial dollars to political campaigns. Thus, social workers should be concerned that poor people and people who are in difficult circumstances and do not make campaign contributions are represented.

The social work literature generally has been critical of political involvement by the social work profession and by social workers individually. Although a recent study concluded that social workers participate in the political arena as actively as any profession expects from its members (Wolk, 1981), political activity measured for the study included only traditional, individual methods such as letter writing and testifying. Collective political action and advocacy, although certainly consistent with basic social work goals, seems to have been overlooked and underutilized to date.

Decision-making procedures that determine endorsements may at times run counter to basic social work morals and ethics. Also, lobbying, campaigning, and recruiting voters may require skills and tactics not generally taught within social work education programs—tactics used by PACs may contradict the conventional social work principles of neutrality and client self-determination.

The major purpose of PACE is to achieve legislative successes in the formation of social policy. As long as other special interest groups exert pressure, NASW must continue its assertiveness through organized and collective political participation.

NASW's confidence as an advocacy organization tended to parallel the growth of the political action committee. There was a growing synergy between the two where the chapter's issues provided a basis for candidate selection, and I-PACHS (Indiana Political Action Committee for Human Services) political endorsements "won friends for the social work community." NASW continued to work on a diverse social policy agenda and increased its presence at the legislature. NASW is now a respected actor on the legislative scene and I-PACHS continues to raise and distribute funds for political action.

Irv Katz, MSW
Executive Director, Community Service Council of Central Indiana
and Vice President for Planning, United Way of Central Indiana

---

ASSIGNMENTS

1. Obtain two "report cards," one from a social work PAC and one from another PAC.
   a. Identify any special interest legislation either PAC has chosen in order to examine the legislators' voting records.
   b. Review your state and federal legislators' records.
   c. Determine whether your legislators would be supported by either group and why.

2. Volunteer to work on a campaign (during an election year) or for a legislator who has been identified as being prohuman services.
   a. Identify the process by which a legislator is made aware of constituent issues, such as letters from constituents, pressures from a political party, and so forth.
   b. Identify important constituent issues.
   c. What is the legislator's response?
3. For your local, state, or federal legislator, obtain from an election commission the amount and source of financial contributions donated during the legislator's most recent campaign. Then compare the voting record of this legislator with the sources of contributions to the campaign. Does any evidence of "vote buying" exist? If so, document it and note what might be the most effective way of utilizing this information.

SUGGESTED READINGS

Abrams, Harvey, and Sheldon Goldstein. 1981. "A State's Comprehensive Political Program." In *Practical Politics: Social Work and Political Responsibility,* Maryann Mahaffey and John W. Hanks (eds.). Washington, D.C.: National Association of Social Workers.
Ribicoff, Abraham. 1962. "Politics and Social Workers." *Social Work* 7 (April): 3–6.
Wolk, James L. 1981. "Are Social Workers Politically Active?" *Social Work* 26 (July): 283–288.

REFERENCES

Abrams, Harvey, and Sheldon Goldstein. 1981. "A State Chapter's Comprehensive Political Program." In *Practical Politics: Social Work and Political Responsibility,* Maryann Mahaffey and John W. Hanks (eds.), pp. 241–260. Washington, D.C.: National Association of Social Workers.
Federal Election Commission. 1989. "Final Report: 1988 Election Cycle." Washington, D.C.: U.S. Government Printing Office.
National Association of Social Workers. 1994. *Program Priorities.* Washington, D.C.: National Association of Social Workers.
———. 1995. *Member Political Survey Report.* Washington, D.C.: National Association of Social Workers.
Wolk, James L. 1981. "Are Social Workers Politically Active?" *Social Work* 26 (July): 283–288.

chapter 10

The Campaign

I have found that social work skills were most useful in campaigning. Each of my five campaigns would legitimately be described as grassroots campaigns. In the last one, we ran a campaign that was a full citizen empowerment effort and a good example of organizing techniques.

Ruth Messinger

Whenever you think about a political campaign, you most likely conjure up a picture of bumper stickers, balloons, hats, rallies with impassioned speeches, and cheering crowds. But this is only a small component of what a campaign entails. This chapter provides an overview of campaigning that will encourage social workers to participate in this aspect of the political process. The purpose is not to educate the reader on how to run a campaign, nor to discuss the intricacies of campaign strategy at different governmental levels, but rather to reduce the fears and disillusionments that volunteers, especially social work volunteers, are likely to feel when working on a campaign.

One might ask, "Why is it necessary to become involved in a campaign?" The answer is that it is essential to elect individuals to office who will listen to the concerns of both clients and the social work profession. To have such persons in office makes the social worker's task easier when monitoring and lobbying. For a social worker to have the politician's "ear," the politician needs to know that person put forth a certain amount of effort and time to help the candidate obtain the office. The earlier the volunteer's support, effort, and time is put forth, the greater the return and the greater the influence on the politician. This is not to suggest that one is buying legislative votes. Presumably the reason one works on a campaign is to get into office the kind of person you want as your representative. By being involved at the beginning of the campaign, which is the most difficult stage, as well as in the later phases, one reaps the rewards that come to those who "jumped on the bandwagon" early. Also, such people are much more likely to have the candidate's ear, to be granted access when key issues are discussed, or perhaps to be offered a position than those whose support was given later or perhaps not at all.

It must be remembered that campaigns differ depending on the level of office being sought, the intensity of the issues, and the constituencies that the candidate will represent if elected. Generally speaking, the higher the office, the more complex the campaign becomes.

The object of any political campaign is, quite simply, to win. One must be elected in order to introduce, modify, or vote on legislation. No candidate expects or needs 100 percent of the votes; to win, one must receive only a majority of all votes cast. The remainder of this chapter explains the strategies by which this goal is met, and in chapter 11 some insights on being a candidate will be shared.

COMPONENTS OF THE CAMPAIGN

The campaign is the vehicle that initiates and communicates a consistent message to enough voters to convince a majority to vote for the candidate. Like all endeavors, information, planning, organization, and management are required.

Every campaign has a particular message, or theme, that communicates everything about the candidate: not only occupation, activities, and positions on the issues, but also the nature and substance of the candidate's relationships with volunteers, organizations, and constituents. Consequently, the campaign theme is much more than a slogan, although it can sometimes be captured in a slogan.

Because a candidate's theme transcends all other aspects of the campaign, it should never focus on detailed positions on any one or two specific issues or pending laws, but rather should describe the style of leadership the candidate will provide on issues in general. For example, during a deep recession a gubernatorial candidate's campaign slogan was "Jobs, Jobs, Jobs." Though it may appear that this slogan was rooted in one issue, actually it indicated that the candidate understood unemployment, the problems of the poor, economic conditions, business, the state's budget deficit; in short, everything related to earning a living, including the need for human services. The message conveyed by this slogan was one of hope, and that the candidate was the one who could restore the state to economic health.

Campaign activity, whether by the candidate, paid staff, or volunteers, is designed to convey a consistent theme to as many voters as often as possible. Communication takes place through media such as direct mail, telephone calls, posters or placards, or through personal contact.

However, a campaign must be more than a series of contacts and a hodge-podge of bumper stickers, press releases, posters, telephone calls, and mailings—no matter how frequent, consistent, or effective. Above all, a campaign must establish an emotional connection between the candidate and the electorate, a connection that actually allows people to comprehend the differences between candidates and to choose between them by voting for one. To establish this connection, the candidate cannot rely on the communication of facts alone. Instead, there must be contact with individual voters where they are, in terms of both geography and interest. It must be as persuasive a contact as possible to gain their support on election day (Kleinkauf, 1982). As social workers we understand the power of emotions, and campaigns rely on this fact. The challenge for the campaign is to determine what will generate enough emotion for a voter to vote for the candidate (Reisch, 1993). An example of this emotional pull used by many candidates is crime. Even though the national crime rate has decreased over the last two decades, the emotional fear of becoming a victim of crime is a powerful motivator. The more information you have, the better able you are to tug at the strings that lead a voter to behave as you wish (Selnow, 1994). This may seem unethical to the social worker, yet a basic premise of practice is to start where the client is. In a campaign a candidate must know where the voters are.

In addition to an emotional connection with voters, a campaign must have a strategic management of resources. Irrespective of its level, intensity, or field, the major resources of a campaign are time, money, and people. Because these resources are limited, they must be mobilized, developed, and stretched as far as possible to enable the campaign to contact and persuade enough voters to provide the winning margin.

The amount and utilization of each of these resources is dependent on each of the other resources, as well as on external factors influencing the campaign. For example, when time is short, more people are needed to work on the campaign, whereas tasks can be spread among fewer people when time is plentiful. Alternatively, when money is plentiful, time and people are less crucial.

No matter how abundant these resources are, all campaigns strive to increase the supply. And finally, no campaign can survive without access to all three types of resources.

Time

After the campaign has begun, time becomes limited. The election date represents a deadline that cannot be changed. Therefore, the amount of time available will greatly influence how money and people are utilized. Most election races are about five or six months long. However, the higher the office being sought, the more time the campaign will need to plan strategy, raise funds, and recruit volunteers. Presidential campaigns, for example, now tend to begin as much as four years before election day.

Some campaigns are relatively brief; for instance, when a legislator resigns, dies, or is impeached and a special election is held, or when a primary election occurs in a district where one party predominates. When time is available, money can be raised and volunteer activity can be extended over the full length of the campaign. The longer the time frame, the easier it is to raise funds, plan strategy, or even do with less money and people.

All too often, as election day approaches the working days of the campaign staff and volunteers become longer, with everyone involved working 16- to 18-hour days, 7 days a week in an attempt to maximize use of the time available. Thus, in a good campaign, care is taken that the staff, the volunteers, and the candidate do not become fatigued to the point of feeling disenchanted with the campaign or disconnected from the constituents.

Money

Campaigns are costly. Expenses in a campaign can vary from $5,000 to $15,000 for a local city or county race to millions of dollars for a federal senatorial or presidential race. The higher the office or the larger the district, the greater the campaign costs. In addition, if volunteers are scarce, greater financial resources will be needed to hire or purchase the services necessary to successfully execute the campaign. Cash is the one resource flexible enough to meet any need that may arise. For example, if envelopes must be addressed and the campaign has a large number of volunteers to address them, the money saved can be used on advertising, but if the number of volunteers is limited, the campaign can hire outside help and use the volunteers for a more important task, such as canvassing.

Volunteers cannot help with certain tasks, or lack the skills to do so. For example, a U.S. senator cannot produce television advertising by using volunteers alone. Office space, equipment, and other such necessities cannot always be donated or loaned to a campaign. In fact, if these items are provided by supporters, they are considered campaign contributions and must be reported to the election commission.

The issues concerning campaign contributions and financial reporting were discussed in chapter 9 on political action committees. Suffice it to say that both federal and state statutes are quite precise as to the categorization of in-kind and cash contributions, the permissible amounts of each, and the way in which disbursements are made throughout the campaign. These statutes place ceilings on total campaign contributions and on the amount and type of contribution that can be accepted from any one source.

On numerous occasions, very wealthy individuals have literally tried to buy themselves a legislative seat by using their financial resources to purchase advertising, supporters, and so forth. Often this has been to no avail. Although finances can compensate to some extent for a lack of volunteers, it is difficult to run a successful campaign without community support.

People

Although trite, it is nevertheless true that government in the United States is of the people and by the people. There is no way in our system of government to become an elected official without the help and support of people—both constituents and volunteers.

The people who work on a campaign are crucial, not only to get the work done but also to keep up the image of the campaign. The emotional support, energy, and enthusiasm of volunteers who are also constituents often provide the best advertising possible, especially when it becomes evident that their efforts are contributing to the candidate's momentum and likelihood of success. For example, if 100 volunteers turned out to work on a rally, it would be clear that that many people support and believe in the candidate. The lower the level of the race, the more impressive a large turnout is, because the support of 100 volunteers for a candidate in a county commissioner's race is much more impressive than the same turnout would be for a U.S. Senate race.

Each campaign needs as many constituent volunteers as possible. Efforts have been made to "carpetbag" (to suddenly move into a district and run for office) not only the candidate, but the entire volunteer team. These efforts rarely succeed.

CAMPAIGN MANAGEMENT

A successful campaign not only requires time, people, and money, but it needs these resources early. Therefore, it is in the potential candidate's best interest to make an early decision to run, to find endorsers, and to recruit volunteers. Lining up volunteers, money, and other support early on may deter some competitors and create a "winning attitude" for the candidate, and often will induce others to jump on the "bandwagon."

Essential to the operation of any campaign, no matter how compelling its theme or the candidate's personality, is an effective campaign plan. If the campaign theme is the message to be conveyed to voters, the campaign plan is the sequence of specific activities, all carefully budgeted, by which this message is to be conveyed.

Campaign management begins with a period of research. The necessary research includes a thorough assessment of the name recognition, physical appeal, background, and previous experience of both the prospective candidate and the opposition. It is important to know if the candidate is effective in a debate situation or in front of television cameras. For example, former President Reagan was a master of the electronic media, whereas the strength of his 1984 opponent, Walter Mondale, was in person-to-person encounters.

Additional research must be done on the electorate to determine the demographics of the district. Is it young or old, middle-class or poor? Also necessary is an assessment of the political climate to determine how many candidates will be in the race, whether it will pit an experienced politician against a newcomer, if gender will be an issue, and what the voters are looking for. In lower-level races, this is done by talking with people in the community. At higher levels, comprehensive opinion polls are conducted. To offset any imbalance in time, money, or people, it is necessary to review the resources likely to be available to the candidate.

Because campaigns require the performance of a variety of tasks, it is useful to recruit as many volunteers as possible with skills in interaction, finances, planning, graphic design, and other skills required to run a campaign. An accurate assessment of the volunteers' numbers, skills, and available time must be made at the outset of the campaign, and these resources must be continuously monitored throughout. This allows campaign managers to make the best use of talent and time, and prevents volunteers from experiencing burnout or feeling underutilized.

Following the initial assessment, a campaign plan is developed to tie the resources to specific timed and budgeted programs that will be used to reach voters. If this is done before the campaign actually begins, usually there will be time for laying the groundwork and testing the assumptions of the campaign strategy. All of this occurs before the general public has really started to think about an election.

Campaigns seem to be a hodgepodge of activities, efforts, and loosely organized plans of action, but all successful campaigns actually are highly planned and thought out, while still appearing to be spontaneous. When a campaign appears to be offtrack, volunteers may become frustrated if it does not switch to a new emerging issue or challenge. Campaign strategists must continuously review shifts in the political winds as the campaign progresses. On the other hand, they must be very careful not to change their plans with each political shift. The result of not sticking to a strategy could be a campaign that is wishy-washy and that does not address the main issues, thus failing to persuade the constituents.

In the 1984 presidential election, for example, the Democratic vice presidential candidate, Geraldine Ferraro, was not abandoned by her party's presidential candidate, Walter Mondale, when she was strenuously interrogated by the press regarding her income taxes. Mondale's strategists advised him to take this stance because they felt that eventually the subject would be dealt with adequately and that wavering on this issue might affect the future of the campaign. This is not to say that a situation such as Ferraro's does not hurt a campaign. But in the long run, a sudden shift, such as selecting a new vice presidential candidate, would have been more devastating to the campaign than public scrutiny of one aspect of Ms. Ferraro's background.

The Campaign Manager: Who Really Runs the Campaign?

Often it seems that the candidate is the one who is directing and running the campaign, because indeed it is the candidate who is seeking public office. In reality, however, the campaign is run by the campaign manager, who has an advisory committee to help determine the direction in which the campaign is and should be going. The candidate usually is a member of the committee and has input into major decisions and the general direction of the campaign, but in fact the candidate has only one real function in a campaign: to meet with constituents and win their votes. The management of any campaign plan requires the staffing of at least the following positions: campaign manager, treasurer, volunteer coordinator, scheduler, fund-raiser.

The demands on a candidate's time are so great that the candidate cannot be bothered with the day-to-day elements of the campaign: deciding what should be written on a postcard, who should receive thank-you notes, how a literature drop is to be organized and executed, and the like. But no campaign manager can persuade voters as effectively as the candidate. Thus the candidate's time must be spent talking to undecided voters, not managing people who already are working on the campaign (Kleinkauf, 1982).

A campaign manager is essential to every campaign, regardless of its size. The manager is the administrative officer of the campaign. Because of the responsibilities accorded to the campaign manager, the candidate should have a long-standing relationship with the manager. Effective managerial skills are not enough.

All campaigns also must have a treasurer, someone to see that money is raised, bills are paid, and that the campaign has a solid financial plan. Many governmental reports must be filed regarding the sources of contributions, the amount contributed by each, and the disbursement of campaign funds.

Higher-level campaigns have many kinds of advisors: people who assist with issues, speech writers, schedulers, and in some situations, even wardrobe consultants. In lower-level campaigns, a volunteer or staff person may serve in several capacities, such as volunteer coordinator and scheduler.

Voter Contact

A candidate will have varying degrees of personal contact with voters. The ideal approach is to knock on the door of someone's home, talk to the person about the campaign, and ask for the constituent's support. To have the candidate telephone an individual and ask for support is only slightly less effective. Less-effective means of contact are tactics such as sending a personal note. As in lobbying, the more effort and the more personal the touch, the more effective the pitch.

For many years there were only four basic channels that could be used to contact voters: in-person contact, telephone contact, mail contact, and media contact. Today with the ever-expanding technology, these channels have a greater variety of options for campaigns to get their message across to the voters. Some technical advances allow the campaign to customize a message and target specific voters. One example of new avenues are videotapes of the candidate addressing a local concern that can be used at smaller meetings in people's homes. Electronic mail can be very cost effective, especially as more and more people have access to computers. As technological advances continue more avenues will be utilized. The campaigns that are creative in utilizing new technology will have an advantage.

To repeat, the most effective way to solicit votes is for the candidate to meet one-on-one with individual voters. In lower-level races, more opportunities exist for individual contact with voters than during a presidential race, where it is impossible to shake hands or talk with all potential voters. However, a presidential candidate will "work the crowd," shaking as many hands as possible, because as bizarre as it may sound, the individuals with whom they shake hands probably will be more likely to vote for the candidate than those to whom the candidate presents only an issue statement. In addition, the image of personal interaction is seen by millions in newspaper pictures and on the news.

In-person contact, telephone contact, mail contact, and electronic methods constitute direct contact with the individual voters. As stated previously, this type of direct, systematic, and personal contact with voters is the most effective campaign technique in existence, and voters continue to be most influenced by a personal meeting with the candidate. The second most influential method is when voters meet an enthusiastic and committed volunteer (National Women's Education Fund, 1978). Least effective are media contact, and, in some cases, mail pieces. These are aimed at all voters and therefore are indirect methods. No matter what method is chosen, the contact program must carry the basic campaign theme with an emotional hook, and it must carry it attractively, consistently, and clearly.

Targeting

Targeting is an essential voter contact strategy. The first step in targeting is to identify voters who can be persuaded to vote for the candidate. Second, the emotional hook that will motivate the voter to actually vote for the candidate must be determined. It is unfortunate but true that a large proportion of the people who are of age to vote are not registered to vote. Among those who are registered and will vote, three groups exist: (1) those who will vote for the candidate regardless of any campaign activity (that is, those who vote a party, ethnic, racial, or gender line); (2) those who, for the same reasons, will not vote for a candidate; and (3) those who have not made up their minds. It is toward this last group that a campaign will target its efforts.

The goal of targeting is to concentrate resources where they will be most effective. An effective campaign tries to employ strategies in precincts or with voters that will have the greatest payoff. To determine what message should be directed to certain groups of voters, campaigns rely on public opinion polls. The historical roots of political polling run deep. The first poll may have taken place when the senate divided the people of Athens into two sides of the city, the yea votes on the east and the nays on the west. But polling found its modern voice in the 1930s and 1940s when George Gallup improved sampling procedures. Ever since—despite a few obvious disruptions, such as the infamous Dewey–Truman blunder—polls have been trusted fixtures in political campaigns (Selnow, 1994). It is here that we have seen the greatest impact by today's technology. Although polling is labor intensive, the sophistication of the software and databases are mind boggling to most social workers. Technology has significantly transformed every component of the polling process, from sampling to analysis, impacting the use of public opinion polls in today's campaigns.

Clearly, the more information a candidate has about voters' fears, passions, preferences, and prejudices, the greater success of targeting. Such information allows that campaign to focus on or to avoid topics. With this information the campaign staff can determine where the candidate has the best opportunity to persuade voters, that is, where the undecided or independent voters are concentrated.

As we have pointed out, not every vote is needed to win. A candidate needs only a majority of the votes cast. Consequently, the staff must also determine where they have the greatest potential to increase turnout among voters already committed to the candidate. Efforts to increase voter turnout consist of contacting registered voters about the election and offering such services as babysitting or transportation to and from the voting place if needed.

ISSUES

It is sometimes jokingly said by those who have been involved in political campaigns that nobody really cares about issues. Sadly there is a great deal of truth in this statement. Even in presidential elections, small issues and one-liners can be more effective in persuading people to vote for one candidate over another than the candidate's position on the major issues of the day. The candidate's party affiliation, gender, appearance, and religious or ethnic background also can persuade a voter to support a candidate, and often are more persuasive than a review of the candidate's stance on the issues.

In the campaign process, I found multifaceted skills necessary to social work to be an essential underpinning in my campaign effort. To be frank, all campaigns, no matter how well run or well organized, can be described as going between various states of chaos. The campaign is a dynamic process which must be susceptible to changes from day to day and minute to minute. People who are involved in the campaign process must be able to reorder and regroup quickly to meet changing circumstances and diverse demands. Being able to work within a constantly changing arena, like any good social worker, enabled me to keep the necessary momentum during the campaign process.

By organizing various grassroots organizations to assist in the nuts-and-bolts organizing of the campaign, one maintains close contact with the concerns of the community. This kind of contact with the needs of the community is essential for effective governing. Many people who serve in elected positions lose simply because they lose touch with the electorate. As long as one can maintain contact with various community groups, you will manage to keep abreast and informed of their concerns.

Edolphus "Ed" Towns, MSW
U.S. Representative (New York)

The United States is made up of very diverse people. In this country, there are people from every ethnic background, every country, every conceivable occupation, belief, and culture. Although this diversity poses fewer problems in lower-level races, it still has some effect on election outcomes. In order to obtain the required 51 percent of the votes, candidates attempt to take a neutral stance on as many issues as their ethics allow. On the issue of abortion, for example, some candidates have stated that they are personally against abortion but would allow a woman the right to determine what is done to her body.

Political action committees and special interest groups will want to know how a candidate stands on certain issues and will base their support or opposition upon this information. The public and campaign volunteers can become very frustrated with a candidate who takes a hard stance on certain issues, and this can be as devastating to the campaign as refusing to take any position at all. Also, if a candidate takes one position when talking to one group and a totally opposite position when meeting with another, it can backfire and be more damaging than if the candidate had taken a tough stance or no stance at all.

Because candidates tend to avoid taking positions, especially on difficult issues, the election of a sympathetic candidate does not eliminate the need for postelection lobbying and monitoring.

SOCIAL WORKERS AND CAMPAIGNS

Innumerable skills carry over easily from social work practice to campaigning, the most obvious being communication skills. Social workers are trained to meet people, listen to their problems, and help them find solutions. They know how to manage hostility, how to reach out to shy and quiet people, and how to deal with groups as well as with individuals (Kleinkauf, 1982). Unfortunately, misinterpretations of the Hatch Act and state-level Hatch Acts, fear of agency reprisal, and lack of understanding of how to become involved have kept many social workers from involving themselves in political campaigns. Regardless of the setting in which a social worker is practicing, he or she has numerous useful skills that can be employed in a campaign. Ultimately, through election of sympathetic officials, the social worker's clientele will benefit.

The most important skills a social worker can contribute to a campaign are in the area of interpersonal relationships and listening skills. These can be used in many facets of a campaign, for example, in canvassing a neighborhood for support of the candidate or in working with campaign volunteers and with the candidate.

For most candidates, the entire campaign process is a challenge to their self-confidence, and they must recognize this in order to minimize defensiveness. The social worker's interpersonal skills can be valuable in offering support and reassurance when the candidate is faced with the discouragement that inevitably occurs as the campaign progresses. Just as a candidate needs support, campaign volunteers need reassurance and motivation, which social workers can provide.

Because social workers must deal daily with a multitude of problems and people, their experience can be particularly valuable to a campaign when positions on issues are being formulated. For example, one candidate was going to take a position, in response to public pressure, that all persons convicted of sexual abuse of children should receive a minimum ten-year prison sentence. Social workers with experience in this area pointed out that 70 percent of child sexual abuse occurs in the family, that the abuser usually is the father, that the mother usually is dependent on the abuser and would have to rely on government aid if separated from him, that the child involved would carry the guilt of having sent the father to jail, and that ten years of imprisonment would be quite costly to society. The candidate subsequently reversed his stand and instead supported a rehabilitation program designed to deal with the problem.

Because working effectively with individuals and groups is fundamental to social work practice, social workers will find their professional methods more useful in a political campaign than they might have expected (Salcido, 1984).

A few short years ago, a social worker friend asked how to become involved in a political campaign. "Just call the campaign headquarters and tell them you want to volunteer," I said, noting they will be more than eager "to get you going in the campaign."

Bill said he was somewhat unsure what he could do, "I'm only a child protective services worker, do you think I really can help the campaign? You know, those people are experienced in this kind of stuff."

Skills and roles natural to professional social work practice are also critical and relevant to political campaigns, be they local, regional, state, or national. The core skills of social work, what we can call "people skills," are also central in a political campaign: being able to quickly engage strangers (potential voters), communicate clearly, and listen to questions with understanding and empathy.

Management and planning skills that are part of social work practice, when combined with the professional understanding of people, places social workers in the unique position of being able to contribute in significant ways to electoral efforts: campaign manager, volunteer coordinator, and research specialist are among those campaign functions and roles a social worker can easily fill.

As with Bill, the first step in working in a campaign is to volunteer and this can be done directly with the campaign or with your colleagues. The key is to get involved: Stuffing envelopes and campaign mailers, answering phones at campaign headquarters, canvassing potential voters, and putting up yard signs are among the many tasks social workers can do to help get the right people elected.

Organize other social workers to work one weekday night for the duration of a campaign effort; Tuesday night, for example, will be known as "social workers night." The campaign staff and candidate will be very grateful, while recognizing and remembering your efforts. Be sure to have some campaign buttons made up for your volunteers that identify your group; a good button might say "Social workers for Smith (the candidate)" or "Social workers vote."

Organize a group of social workers to spend a Saturday putting candidate's signs in yards. Start a phone bank, with the campaign's approval, and call other social workers to financially support your candidate. All campaigns need money; raise some funds by using your social work phone lists, for example, NASW unit membership, and ask each person to give $5.00 to the candidate. If you have 200 local members, that $5.00 becomes a $1,000 donation. Be assured the candidate will be extremely grateful to you and your social work friends.

Be creative in your ideas and efforts. Remember, every effort, every dollar helps in a campaign. Today, Bill is an active volunteer in his political party and is far removed from his first, tentative steps in electoral politics.

Ira Colby, Ph.D.
Director, School of Social Work
University of Central Florida

WHAT TO EXPECT WHEN VOLUNTEERING

A committed and enthusiastic volunteer who meets with voters is second in influence only to the candidate. The effectiveness of such contacts far exceeds the influence of advertising and literature. Thus the wealth of many campaigns is a function of the number of skilled, committed volunteers who are involved.

In some campaigns, nearly every task is performed by volunteers, especially when money is a scarce resource. Some volunteer assignments, in addition to campaign planning, canvassing and policy-making, are listed below.

Addressing envelopes
Babysitting for voters or workers
Canvassing (both door to door and telephone)
Clipping newspaper articles
Computer skills of any kind
Delivering news releases
Distributing advertising items at the polls
Doing research, writing, art work, and the like
Driving voters to the polls
Getting out mailings

Leafleting or letter drops

Looking up telephone numbers

Making posters

Mimeographing

Monitoring news programs

Organizing candidate coffees

Organizing fund-raising events

Preparing voter lists

Putting up signs

Recruiting additional volunteers

Running errands

Serving as poll watchers

Serving as messengers

Soliciting contributions

Typing

Often social workers who are just beginning campaign work feel frustrated when they are not allowed a great deal of input regarding issues and public concerns, but instead are asked to do tasks such as those listed above. They feel that their skills are not being utilized to the fullest, that they would rather use their expertise and skills in managing, consulting, and writing issue papers for the candidate. Indeed, a social worker may have these abilities and the ability to play that role in some campaigns. However, it is usually the campaign manager who has established a solid working relationship with the candidate that is essential to a successful campaign.

The best way for a social worker to be accorded more responsibility in a campaign is to become involved in it very early and to establish a good working relationship with the candidate. Nonetheless, regardless of when a social worker enters the campaign, one can make adequate use of other social work skills in conjunction with a variety of campaign tasks, most notably in dealing with people. Tasks may include making telephone calls in response to inquiries or personally contacting constituents. The core of a campaign is interaction with people, and who is better equipped for that than a social worker?

In reality, a campaign is a lot of hard work. It entails many long hours of tedious chores such as those listed above. Many volunteers become dismayed when they work on a campaign because they do so much tedious work, but if the campaign is in tune with the volunteers, they will be shown that what they are doing is an integral part of reaching the campaign's major goal—winning the election.

Social workers understand particularly well the need for balancing volunteer activities, work, and family. However, they must be aware of certain unique characteristics of a campaign in order to survive and be effective. The following are some problems that social workers may encounter within a campaign:

1. The political campaign organization, in contrast to a structured social work agency, is temporary and loosely organized, and as such may not be responsive to the psychological and emotional needs of its workers (Salcido, 1984).
2. Conflicts in values and expectations often exist among the diverse groups and numerous individuals involved in a political campaign. Not all campaign workers (or even the candidate) may really care about human service issues.
3. Some of the political campaign's administrative and personnel problems, such as stress and uncertainty, are so common that they are considered intrinsic to campaign work and left untouched (Salcido, 1984).
4. There is always a lack of time to deal with individual constituents' problems.
5. The many unprofessional activities that must be performed during a campaign, such as licking stamps, can be discouraging to campaign volunteers.
6. Lack of concern within the campaign about issues plus great concern about money can also be discouraging to social work volunteers.
7. The pursuit of one goal, winning the election, leaves both the volunteers and some issues as a secondary concern.
8. Social workers may want the candidate to meet their colleagues, but the candidate, feeling this group is likely to give its support in any event, may consider such a trip a waste of limited resources that could be used to persuade undecided voters.

One benefit of working on a campaign, in addition to having the candidate's ear, is that the social worker will make a great many contacts in the legal, business, and commercial fields, as well as in other areas of the community. As a result of such contacts, one will often discover shared interests and concerns where none might have been thought to exist. A realtor, for example, may be supporting the social worker's candidate for the same reason as the social worker, namely, lack of adequate housing in the community. Such encounters can prove mutually enlightening. The realtor may gain insight into the need for low-cost housing, while the social worker may learn that an adequate supply of mortgage money at reasonable interest rates is needed for families to buy homes.

HOW TO VOLUNTEER FOR A CAMPAIGN

It might seem ridiculous to include a section on how to volunteer for a campaign, but all too often campaigns start quickly with a core group known to one another, and after a brief period volunteer recruitment largely ceases. Later, the campaign becomes so hectic and confusing that volunteers feel lost and unsupported and drop out.

As previously mentioned, it is best to become involved in a campaign very early. In many instances, a good time to make one's interests known to a prospective candidate is January of an election year. Local party offices generally are quite willing to assist volunteers in connecting with prospective candidates.

The best approach is to make yourself known to the candidate or the campaign manager and ask for an assignment. If one has the skills and the desire to do certain jobs on the campaign, that information should be made known. If your interest is not acknowledged, press again for some form of assignment. It must be remembered that given the lack of time and the pressures of a campaign, volunteers may fall through the cracks and not be adequately supported or thanked. A person wishing to volunteer often must persist long enough to make it clear that there really is a desire to help. Volunteers should indicate the number of hours and the level of commitment they are willing to give. In return, the volunteer should be given a clear description of what the job will entail and any deadlines that must be met.

Even if social workers feel their skills and abilities are not being utilized to the fullest, it is wise not to drop out of the campaign. Because of the pressure and the timing of any campaign, the campaign planning committee must be sure that volunteers are adequately dedicated to the campaign and that they can be trusted with major responsibilities. Given the highly sensitive nature of a campaign, the short time frame, and the amount of work involved, candidates must be careful to whom responsibility is assigned. If a key task is left undone, it can badly damage the chances for achieving the campaign's goal.

Finally, it is important to publicize that social workers are working on a particular campaign. Elected officials then will know not only that you assisted in their victory, but also, they and other legislators will know that politically active social workers do exist. Such knowledge may lead the legislator(s) involved to look more favorably upon subsequent lobbying efforts by other members of the social work profession.

CONCLUSION

The campaign is probably the most confusing component of the political process, yet it is at the very heart of it. Participation in a successful political campaign can enhance the effectiveness of subsequent lobbying and monitoring of government agencies and legislation. The campaign offers both excitement and tedious work, and the payoff to the individual social worker and to the profession is much greater than appears on the surface.

Social workers must realize that their skills can be used in various segments of the political arena, but are especially useful during a campaign. There is no greater satisfaction than knowing an elected representative has an understanding of and sympathy for the values exemplified by social work and will respond when a social worker wishes to address, endorse, or recommend a piece of legislation.

ASSIGNMENTS

1. Review different campaign slogans and determine for each what message the candidate is conveying. Surmise from a campaign slogan what positions you think the candidate would have on an issue and then check the position statements to determine if your assumptions are accurate.

2. Volunteer to work on a campaign. After the candidate wins, visit with him or her and talk about an issue that concerns you. Determine if your support is received with a willingness to help on the issue now that the campaign is over.

3. Find a person who wants to run for office and work with the candidate from the very beginning to learn every aspect of campaigning. Then compare responses of your candidate with those of the elected official you interviewed for assignment (2) when you contacted him or her about an issue.

SUGGESTED READINGS

Brager, George A. 1968. "Advocacy and Political Behavior." *Social Work* 13 (April): 5–15.
Kleinkauf, Cecilia. 1982. "Running for Office: A Social Worker's Experience." In *Practical Politics: Social Work and Political Responsibility,* Maryann Mahaffey and John Hanks (eds.), pp. 181–194. Washington, D.C.: National Association of Social Workers.
Salcido, Ramon M. 1984. "Social Work Practice in Political Campaigns." *Social Work* 29 (March–April): 189–191.

REFERENCES

Ginsberg, L. 1988. "Social Works and Politics: Lessons from Practice." *Social Work* 33 (3): 245–247.
Kleinkauf, Cecilia. 1982. "Running for Office: A Social Worker's Experience." In *Practical Politics: Social Work and Political Responsibility,* Maryann Mahaffey and John Hanks (eds.), pp. 181–194. Washington, D.C.: National Association of Social Workers.
National Women's Education Fund. 1978. *Campaign Workbook.* Washington, D.C.: National Women's Education Fund.
Reisch, Michael. 1993. "The Social Worker in Politics as a Multi-Role Group Practitioner." In *Social Work with Groups: Expanding Networks,* Stanley Wenocur et al. (eds.). New York: Haworth Press.
Salcido, Ramon M. 1984. "Social Work Practice in Political Campaigns." *Social Work* 29 (March–April): 189–191.
Selnow, Gary W. 1994. *High-Tech Campaigns: Computer Technology in Political Communication.* Westport, CT: Praeger.

chapter **11**

Social Workers as Politicians

I am the first social worker in the United States Senate. Now I have a caseload of four million Marylanders! And though I am practicing in a different forum, those skills and values I learned as a community organizer in the streets of Baltimore are what make me an effective leader in the corridors of Congress.

Barbara Mikulski

How often do social workers wonder—after helping a teenage mother find formula for her three-month-old child, or after helping a senior citizen pay for an emergency heating bill, or after informing a client that needed services are unavailable—how many other thousands of people may be facing the same problem?

Social workers assist many clients with diverse problems on a daily basis. Athough one obvious career choice—to seek political office—would allow a social worker to multiply his or her efforts a hundredfold, few social workers consider a career as a social worker/politician, even though it can have a far-reaching influence on the development and implementation of social policy.

In the 104th Congress, the U.S. government spent billions of dollars on human services, but only three social workers were members of the 535-person Congress. In addition, although state appropriations for human services represent a large proportion of state budgets, 21 of the 50 state legislatures had no elected members in 1995 who were social workers. However, the number of social workers elected to political offices at municipal, state, and federal levels has doubled in the last five years. In 1993 there were 113 elected social workers known to NASW, which increased by 43 percent to a total of 199 in 1995 (National Association of Social Workers, 1995a) as illustrated in Table 11.1.

171

TABLE 11.1   Selected characteristics of social workers in elected office, 1995

	Women	Men	White	African American
U.S. Congress	1	2	1	2
State legislature	33	28	42	10
County/borough	21	6	19	5
City/municipal	35	18	38	12
School board	36	17	43	7
Other	2	0	1	1
Total	128	71	144	37

	Hispanic	Asian American	American Indian
U.S. Congress	0	0	0
State legislature	6	3	0
County/borough	3	0	0
City/municipal	3	0	0
School board	3	0	0
Other	0	0	0
Total	15	3	0

SOURCE: Reprinted from "Social Workers Serving in Elective Offices 1993," p. 14, published by NASW.

The purpose of this chapter is to help social workers determine whether to consider the social work/politician career role. It must be remembered, however, many aspects of political life will not be discussed here because they are not necessarily unique to the social worker.

The material for this chapter was obtained from social workers who have held or are now holding public office or who have run for an office in the past. The data was obtained by two methods: interviews and questionnaires. The social workers queried held political offices on boards of education, township councils, county or city commissions, state legislatures, and the U.S. House of Representatives. All had obtained an MSW and had some social work practice prior to holding political office. At the time of this research, the National Association of Social Workers did not maintain records on social workers who were employed in political settings, and because of the reluctance of social worker/politicians to acknowledge their social work background (for political reasons), a snowball sampling approach was necessary to identify respondents.

Questions for the interview and questionnaire were designed to determine what unique difficulties and successes social workers have encountered in the role of politician. The questionnaire consisted of 30 questions, 7 of which gathered demographic data, such as age, sex, marital status, and political affiliation. The remaining questions were open-ended and were intended to elicit information about any successes and problems these respondents experienced as politicians that were related to their social work training. For example, the questions posed included the following:

What event(s) led you to run for office?

What, if any, personal stresses or difficulties did you experience either in the campaign or in the office?

If you had it to do over again, would you still obtain a degree in social work? If not, in what discipline?

The following findings are presented not only to summarize the information collected from these respondents, but to provide interested social workers with information useful to them in determining their own interest in and aptitude for a political career.

DECIDING TO RUN

Very few individuals who attend a graduate school of social work intend to become politicians, and few, if any programs exist to teach social workers about politics. As a result, the idea of running for office generally occurs later in a social worker's career and not as a result of graduate specialization.

All of the social worker/politicians who were questioned had been involved in some form of community action or organizing. This is not surprising, since few were clinicians. From these activities they came to realize that their social work background had provided many politically useful skills. Seventy percent indicated they became involved in community organizing because they wanted better solutions to social problems. Eventually these social workers realized that more could be accomplished if they were actually in a political position, thus awakening them to the idea of running for office (Kleinkauf, 1982). Interestingly, all initially discounted the idea of running because they believed that a law degree is necessary for success.

Once awakened to the idea of running for office, many floundered seeking guidance about how to begin. Because there are no formal means of obtaining such training, social workers who wish to enter the political arena need the benefit of informal support and guidance. When asked where they found this, only the younger politicians indicated mentor support; they also stated that few of these mentors were social worker/politicians. AU saw it as advantageous to have assistance from someone who knows the political scene and is supportive of the social worker's efforts.

Ideally that person would be a social worker/politician, but because such people seldom are available, few of the respondents had social work mentors when running for office. However, many are now political mentors to other social workers.

Several problems are unique to social workers who wish to establish a political career.

1. The agencies in which social workers are employed are often reluctant to support the worker's candidacy for political office, citing "politics" as the reason. Private agencies fear alienating any of their

sources of community support. This is particularly true for agencies that rely on community funding. Nor do agency executives want to offend board members who may hold views other than the candidate's on major campaign issues. In state-funded agencies, difficulties arise from state Hatch Acts, which often prohibit this type of employee political activity.

2. Agencies usually do not have the flexibility to allow social workers time to campaign. Attorneys in private practice, on the other hand, may be able to reduce workloads during a campaign, unlike social workers, who generally are in full-time staff positions. Social workers in this situation may be forced to take a leave of absence without pay or to resign in order to campaign, and this can create extreme financial difficulties, since social workers usually are paid less than other professionals.

3. The limitation of personal financial resources, already strained by the necessity of a leave of absence, will restrict the amount of money available to finance a first-time campaign. All of the respondents noted that campaign funding for a first campaign must come from the candidate's own resources.

4. Compared with other professions, the social worker/politician has a limited ability to garner campaign support. Attorneys, for example, often can obtain support from their clients, who frequently represent a potentially powerful group of contacts. Social workers, however, cannot ethically use their clients, nor do their clients traditionally have influence or resources likely to assist one in obtaining an office.

Although this list of obstacles is unique to social workers who run for political office, none of our respondents perceived them as monumental. They did, however, emphasize the need to convince a potential social worker/politician that the goal of political office is worth the effort necessary to overcome these obstacles.

Once a social worker decides to run for office, he or she must be doubly able: determined but also able to withstand losing. This was pointed out by all who had lost an election. Every social worker mentioned the need for determination. Many indicated that difficulty arose because of their belief in a life that balances work and family—a value the social work profession also advocates. This problem, which will be discussed later, also occurred while respondents were in office.

BUILDING A CONSTITUENT BASE

Financial support and volunteer efforts are the key elements in a campaign, and later, for success in office. These indispensable resources are particularly important to social worker/politicians. If money is limited, volunteers become even more important to counterbalance this deficit. Although campaign costs varied, volunteer time, skills, and ideological support were of significant importance to all interviewed.

Although the number of supporters is important, the amount of power these contributions have in terms of income, education, or status is also important. That is, to be elected and to remain in office, one must be connected to a broad spectrum of people. Relating only to selected segments of the population, such as social workers, the poor, or blacks, can easily lead to "labeling" and potential stigmatization. Furthermore, a broad constituent base enhances credibility.

It is well to remember, therefore, that many political issues may fall outside the scope of social work concerns. A social worker/politician must be able to assess ideologies other than those associated with social work. One of the politicians interviewed found himself in the middle of a community conflict between environmentalists and industrial developers over development of a shopping mall. The social work profession obviously does not have a position on such an issue; the social worker/politician formulated his position after assessing his constituents' opinions on this issue.

Given the small numbers in the population who are social workers and the relatively low priority that social workers give to political action, reliance on social workers as a constituent base is unwise, limiting, and potentially harmful to an aspiring social worker/politician. Building bridges to other professions and professional associations, such as lawyers, teachers, and psychologists, is essential for getting elected (Keith-Lucas, 1975).

Social workers may view themselves as being ideologically opposed to many of their constituents—perhaps blue-collar workers, on the one hand, and the upper class on the other. As guardians of the "underdogs," social workers too often have taken a simplistic view of organized labor or the privileged elite as their opponents on social issues. It would be wise to view these groups (and others) as potential collaborators on issues where what is in the best interest of the social work client coincides with the best interest of the general community. Not only is this approach important for getting elected, but generally it is the only way a politician can function once elected.

The emergence in the past few years of the "new poor" or the recently unemployed as a major social problem could well unite organized labor, social workers, and the wealthy to seek solutions that benefit all; that is, solutions that provide incentives to employers to create jobs without reducing wages or increasing taxes. Certainly labor unions and the social work profession have common objectives with respect to this goal.

As mentioned earlier, many of the social workers in our sample had a community organization background. Their grassroots organizing efforts on community issues enabled them to use their experience and personal connections to develop a constituent base. Our respondents included activists in the Civil Rights movement, bloc associations, human service coalitions, and those in significant positions in other candidates' campaigns. Such activities provided many with opportunities to establish linkages, gain experience, and build constituent bases.

Building or expanding a constituent base should not be attempted solely on the candidate's position on key issues. In the tradition of "grassroots organizing," soliciting input on individual and community needs and on the relative importance of community problems are excellent methods for identifying and involving potential supporters.

CAMPAIGNING

A central question that immediately confronts the social worker who decides to run for elective office is whether to publicize a social work background or minimize it in the campaign. Although all the social workers sampled included their MSW degree on campaign literature, few highlighted it as part of a campaign strategy.

One U.S. congressman, however, effectively used his MSW credentials and social work experience in a race against an attorney, convincing the voters that he had "people" experience, whereas his opponent had only "legal" experience. On the other hand, a state representative who chose to emphasize her social work background was unfavorably labeled as a "welfare queen." One's decision is probably influenced by the demographic, political, and ideological characteristics of the total constituency, as well as by the campaign's major issues and the opponent's tactics. For example, if raising AFDC allowances, which would raise taxes, is a volatile issue in a wealthy district, flaunting an MSW may not improve popularity. On the other hand, if legislation is pending to reimburse in-home care of the elderly (Medicaid waiver), and the district is an aged or aging one, a social work platform may be highly attractive.

The question is not whether the social worker/politician should deny the social work identity, but whether the longer-term benefit of election to office warrants emphasizing or minimizing it. As one of the interviewees mentioned, "One should always tell the truth—but not always the entire truth." Related to this dilemma is a second question: Should one always adopt a position consistent with one's social work background, or a position reflecting that of the constituent majority, should it differ from the candidate's own? In a Catholic neighborhood, an avid prochoice stance is unlikely to win votes. This is not to suggest that one's social work training be forgotten, but that the candidate temporarily might need to subjugate it to the immediate goal of gaining office.

In addition to such concerns as one's position on the issues, there is also the matter of campaign skills. The skills most necessary for success, according to the respondents, are varied, and include the following:

1. The "people" skills of listening, responding, persuading, and caring are of primary importance. Historically these are the core generic skills for social work. Regardless of their area of specialization—community organization or clinical—all social worker/politicians interviewed noted the importance of these skills to politicians and emphasized that they

had been acquired during their social work education (Thursz, 1975). If there is something new for the social worker/politician to learn, it is to transfer these skills to nonclients (constituents) and to larger groups.

2. Political skills such as linking, brokering, and advocacy, also part of generic social work training, are invaluable on the campaign trail, where proof may be acquired of the candidate's ability to deliver for the constituency. Again, the only skill development needed may be to transfer these skills from case (individual) to class (constituent) brokering and advocacy.

3. Other important political skills include the abilities to consider alternative solutions to problems and to attempt to achieve consensus during a campaign. A demonstrated capacity to seek multiple solutions to a problem may lead voters to view the candidate as flexible, open to compromise, and creative. Achieving consensus requires skills in group process, conflict resolution, and persuasion: All of these characteristics are essential to success in both political life and social work practice. Several social worker/politicians did note one deficit in social work training, the omission of teaching strategies and skills for dealing with confrontation.

4. Negotiation and mediation are prime political skills that are not incompatible with social work practice. Clinicians negotiate daily with clients to arrive at clinical contracts regarding problem assessment, diagnosis, and treatment. Although political negotiations may seem more underhanded and less open than negotiations to establish contracts with clients in treatment, the negotiation and mediation skills utilized are the same and both are necessary for the achievement of mutually agreeable and beneficial ends.

REALITIES OF OFFICE

Like the general public, social workers often hold misconceptions about the benefits and costs of holding political office. Therefore, we asked our respondents about the realities of being an elected representative. These questions covered changes in the office holder's economic and social status after being elected and the effect on family life. Some open-ended questions about the difficulties, problems, and benefits were included.

Holding a political office received mixed reviews from the respondents, all of whom enjoyed their jobs but reported problems as well as benefits. An obvious benefit is the power to influence decisions. One social worker said what he liked most about his job was "power." An elected representative not only has a vote in policy decisions, but has access to the media and can thereby attempt to increase public awareness of social problems.

A social worker/politician can also sensitize other legislators to human needs. For example, one interviewee related a story about transportation tickets that were being provided in large quantities for use by the county's commissioners. The majority of the commissioners wanted to use them as political chips. The social worker on the commission, however, demonstrated that senior citizens were in need of free transportation, and convinced the other legislators that use of the tickets by senior citizens could be both a sound social policy and good political practice because senior citizens are dependable voters.

It is not unusual for a political candidate with a social services background to believe that s(he) possesses some special insight into the problems their constituency faces. Nor is it unusual for that successfully elected candidate to feel that their election was a public referendum confirming their world view and the implications that view has toward solving societal problems.

Imagine the rude awakening the newly elected official receives when their fellow elected officials (possessing the same egocentric delusional beliefs) do not share the same vision of education, local community, county, state, or national issues. Having served a decade on a local board of education and on a town council, I admit to having suffered from this political hubris. In the spirit of helping others avoid the trauma of this reality, I believe there are five laws all aspiring legislators need to learn. They are

1. New politicians need to learn how to count. Unless your vision for change has the necessary votes for passage, it will fail. Humor aside, this is a profound insight for most new legislators.
2. The United States is not a democracy. The majority does not rule. Rather, this is a representative form of government in which legislators have been chosen to exercise their best judgment. Exercising one's best judgment does not mean following the polls or the crowd in attendance the night of the public meeting.
3. There are no good decisions. Every time policymakers vote they choose from a set of proposals that will harm someone's interests. Hopefully, as an elected official you will choose the least harmful proposal to implement. To illustrate, to protect the spotted owl will increase unemployment in the lumber industry, to save funding for the Center on Substance Abuse Prevention may mean transferring funds from the Safe and Drug Free Schools budget in the Department of Education, and to relax air pollution standards in order to increase industry profits will increase the incidence of lung disease and increase the pollution of the environment.

   Further, consider this situation. The necessary votes to dramatically change welfare programs are there. As a lawmaker, you do not support the act, but you do not have the ability to stop its passage. In exchange for your support and that of your colleagues, the majority of other lawmakers are willing to increase child care support provisions, not punish adolescent mothers and their infants, and provide greater flexibility in administering the program. Do you now support a bill you truly dislike? Not an easy decision, is it? In short, every choice entails a loss.

4. Politics is the "art" of the possible, not the ideal. The phrase checks and balances is most often used to describe the process of our government. To achieve the passage of a budget, an ordinance, or a law requires that numerous bodies concur. To reach the necessary majority often means compromising the original language in the motion. For the elected representative, it may mean exchanging support on another issue that is important to a fellow elected member. The business of government, because of this inclusionary process, is messy. Still, no other system, as respectful of the rights of others, has evolved.

5. Remember most, that "good" politicians increase the possibilities. Representative government means that all constituents have the opportunity to provide input into the legislative process. To avoid the paralysis that would otherwise accompany this reality means that politicians must be willing to negotiate and be willing to find ground upon which a majority can stand.

Thomas P. Gullotta, MSW
Former member of the Glastonbury Board of Education
and Vice Chairman of the Glastonbury Town Council
Glastonbury, Connecticut

One difficulty noted by the respondents is the need at times to compromise social work values for political necessity. An example of such a compromise was described by a state representative who had been working unsuccessfully to change the juvenile code. During a past legislative session, a bill was introduced, with the urging of the Sheriffs' Association, that would have imposed limits on the incarceration of juveniles. The Sheriffs' Association's motive was to reduce costs and overcrowding in the jails. The social worker/politician's motive was to prevent the jailing of juveniles. The social worker/politician supported the bill because the solution, although not ideal, was a great improvement over existing practice.

Two constant problems for all politicians are keeping current on social issues and responding to the continual demands and problems of constituents. An overwhelming majority of respondents indicated that they had little difficulty in these areas, for which they credited their social work training. Many remarked on their success in this area in comparison to that of nonsocial worker politicians.

Some may think that lawyers would have an advantage in the legislative arena. That is true. Although lawyers may be better able to decipher and discuss "the law," that doesn't make them better at politics. You see, politics really has more to do with service to people than with the letter of the law or with the type of bill enacted.

Before you get to the point of bill proposals, floor debates, or legislative language, you have to understand the needs of the people. It is in being able to understand the needs of the people and translate those expressed and inchoate needs into bills and laws which will serve the people. If you can't communicate and have open exchanges with the people, you will never know what they want. Social workers have the ability to communicate and to create an atmosphere where others can communicate.

Edolphus "Ed" Towns, MSW
U.S. Representative (New York)

Before running for office, many of the interviewees believed that a law degree was necessary for political success. Several felt that some courses in law would be helpful, and recommended that schools of social work offer some course work to enable social workers to become more politically active (Jankovic and Green, 1981; Miller, 1980). Only one respondent wished he had pursued law instead of social work, and, parenthetically, that particular respondent had been treated mercilessly during the campaign because he was a social worker.

One of the myths dispelled by the respondents was that economic status is greatly improved after election to office. The reader may be skeptical, as were the authors; however, when the expenses of the campaign and of maintaining an office are deducted, one's net worth seldom increases. The general public may feel that politicians are overpaid, but in reality, social work administrators receive salaries comparable to politicians. Politicians must attend fund-raising events in return for support received during the campaign and must join many organizations in order to expand their constituent bases. These additional expenditures often offset any salary increase. Also, social workers, unlike attorneys, cannot anticipate an increase in paying clients after leaving political office. Improving one's short- or long-term economic status is not likely to be an incentive for a social worker contemplating this career choice.

On the other hand, politics does offer the prospect of high social status, in clear contrast to the relatively low status accorded social workers. Thus, although improved economic status may not be an incentive or reward for the potential social worker/politician, improved social status may be. Seventy-five percent of the respondents reported enhanced social status as a result of contacts and invitations received once they were in office. Despite the public's apparent distrust of politicians, they are, in fact, regarded as community leaders and persons of influence and power.

On the surface, political life appears glamorous, and indeed it may be, but in reality, there are many nonglamorous aspects. The respondents confirmed that the job requires hard work and long hours to maintain one's position. The hours invested in political life, particularly during the campaign, strain the social worker/politician's personal life. Public exposure and scrutiny intensifies this strain. Furthermore, the demands to attend social events, glamorous or not, should be met, and constraints on family activities must be accommodated. One respondent noted that her family could not participate in any federally funded project, thus prohibiting her child from using the public swimming pool.

Although these strains are not unique to social worker/politicians, they are particularly relevant to them because of the profession's emphasis on interpersonal relationships. We did not investigate the effect of such stress on family and marital relationships; however, it is evident from the responses of the interviewees that a spouse must be committed to this career choice for it to succeed.

A number of alternatives to holding elected political office also offer an opportunity to define social problems and initiate appropriate solutions. Two of the most common roles that offer such an opportunity are legislative aide and administrative appointee.

RECOMMENDATIONS

We asked our respondents to advise social workers interested in pursuing a political career. Their recommendations to individual social workers included the following:

1. Obtain experience in precinct politics, campaigning for another candidate, lobbying, or any combination thereof.
2. After gaining basic experience and building a constituent base, the potential candidate must be willing to ask for financial and personal support.
3. Candidates cannot be falsely modest about their qualifications and must be comfortable with ideological conflict and confrontation. Compromise and political savvy should be exercised.
4. Social worker/politicians must be cautious about taking exaggerated liberal positions and must be aware that acting in the best interest of the client or community may require the short-term compromise of social work ideals and values in order to achieve longer-term societal reform.
5. The decision to emphasize or minimize one's social work background must be considered on an individual and constituent basis.

Our respondents also offered some advice concerning social work education and organizations:

1. Social work education should include content on political and legislative processes from an action-oriented perspective, not only a historical, descriptive approach. Content on class advocacy, a highly valued social work ideal, should be reintroduced into all courses.
2. The policy course should include experiential and skill-based assignments and be designed for both graduate and undergraduate students.
3. Social work organizations should become more politically active and aware. They should promote political advocacy as a legitimate professional role. Client data, which may be useful in supporting or opposing legislation, should be obtained.
4. Social work organizations must investigate most closely the legal and regulatory constraints on political activity and organizational members in order to dispel myths about these obstacles.

All good politicians could use a little help from their friends, and in this day that means having access to computers, modems, and the Internet. The following locations on the world wide web are excellent sources for help and information. To search the web using keywords type http://webcrawler.com/webcrawler/webquery.html. An excellent spot on the web that will lead the searcher to a wealth of information from government sources: http://www.folk.med.pitt.edu/gov.html. Finally, state and local government information can be found at http://www.yahoo.com/government/states.html.

Thomas P. Gullotta, MSW
Former member of the Glastonbury Board of Education
and Vice Chairman of the Glastonbury Town Council
Glastonbury, Connecticut

CONCLUSION

It is clear from our research that social worker/politicians recognize a congruence between political and social work skills. The vast majority of those questioned, whether they came from a clinical or a community organization background, were positive about the appropriateness and logic of social work education and training as a basis for political life. Why social workers do not pursue this career choice in greater numbers, therefore, remains a mystery.

Although the pitfalls and difficulties of political office were recognized, almost all of the respondents indicated that they wished to continue in politics and probably would do so. Although social work schools and professional organizations could initiate programs to facilitate this career choice for more social workers, the final choice, of course, rests with the individual.

Legislators' Caucus Forms

"Seven social workers who serve in state legislatures throughout the country came together recently to form a caucus to help bring social work expertise to state legislatures at a time when delivery and funding of social services is likely to shift from federal to state and local levels.

"The seven social work legislators gathered at a breakfast meeting hosted by NASW and the National Conference of State Legislatures that was held in Milwaukee last July [1995].

"The new caucus was spearheaded by state representatives Alexander Santiago (D) of Hawaii and Elliott Naishtat (D) of Texas who noted that many more social workers are seeking legislative office to have a more direct impact on policies. NASW has identified 60 social workers who hold legislative offices. Other social work legislators present at the July meeting were state representatives Jorge Luis Garcia, an Arizona democrat; R. Mont Evens, a Utah republican; Patricia Thibaudeau, a Washington democrat; and state senators Allyson Schwartz, a Pennsylvania democrat, and Maggie Tinsman, an Iowa republican.

"Invitations will be made to other social work legislative staffs to attend the next caucus meeting at the National Conference of State Legislatures meeting in St. Louis next year [1996]."

SOURCE: Reprinted from *NASW News*, September 1995.

Despite the respondents' differences in timing, previous experience, and choice of first political activity, the common and recurring recommendation they gave to potential social worker/politicians is that the only absolute prerequisite for success is to get involved. Further, the evidence is conclusive that there is no reason for social workers to expect their entry into politics to be anything but successful.

On the night I won election to the United States Senate, I gave a speech in which I thanked everyone in the room. And then I looked directly into the camera and said, "Gee, Dad, I know you're watching. I'm sorry you can't be here, but I love you, and I thank you for everything you've done for me."

You see, my father was in a nursing home in the final stages of Alzheimer's disease. He could not be with me that night because of his illness.

I had gone through quite a learning experience. I went from Congresswoman Mikulski—knowing about Alzheimer's from briefing memos, hearings, and even touring great facilities like Johns Hopkins—to Barbara Mikulski, daughter, coping with the disease in my own family.

As our family went through this, I became determined to take our personal situation and our personal tragedy and turn it into positive action. I vowed I would not only learn about it, but I would know it, I would feel it, and would do something about it.

As a social worker and a feminist, I believe you make the personal political. That is, you take the personal experiences that you live through, in terms of day-to-day experiences, and then extrapolate them into national policy.

When my father became so ill that we needed to put him into a nursing home, I discovered the issue of "spend down." The cruel rules of our government became very apparent. Those regulations required that you "spend down" all of your assets to the meager sum of $3,000 before the government would step in and help.

Essentially, those rules penalized the good guys, the families who had saved all their lives for retirement. Because it put them in the same situation as the spendthrifts, those who spent all their money on round-the-world cruises or gambling trips to Atlantic City.

No one should have to deal with the fact that after a lifetime of building lives together, saying they were one family, one name, one bank-book, one checkbook, that, because the rules administered by a social service agency say so, suddenly it becomes "his money" and "her money."

My family was fortunate, we had strong bonds and a strong faith. But it wasn't just my family, the people I would talk to every Sunday at the nursing home all told of how they went from being middle-class to being pauperized.

My proudest accomplishment as a United States senator was getting legislation passed that lessened the burden of "spend down." My spousal anti-impoverishment bill restored the good-guy bonus, and lets couples keep more of their assets when one of them faces prolonged nursing home care.

If that had been the only change I ever made in my political career, I would still know that I had helped hundreds of people live better, more secure lives.

Barbara Mikulski, MSW
U.S. Senator (Maryland)

I was first elected to the Michigan House of Representatives in 1979. I was aware that the Michigan Friend of the Court system, the arm of the court that handles issues related to children and divorce, was not working well, especially for the children, and needed reform. After discussions with my colleagues in the House of Representatives, I found that none of them wanted to touch the issue. I was told by seasoned legislators that, indeed, it was a law that needed to be rewritten, but it was too emotional an issue since it related to divorce, custody, visitation, and child care payments.

Although it was a law that had not been rewritten since it was passed in 1919, and despite the fact that a lot of constituents complained that child support was not being paid and visitation orders were not being honored, it was viewed as a political loser. There seemed to be no way of bringing consensus from what appeared to be opposing factions of mothers, fathers, attorneys, and judges. Furthermore, the most important and most harmed group in this issue, and the group which had no political power, was the children.

It needed to be done, so I decided to test my social work skills. To start, I used a basic principle of the profession. I began by determining where the client groups were, with a process of hearings, just to listen to what people had to say about the system. I spent hours listening to people talk about their particular problem. After that, I put together a very large task force of all the interested groups and spent even more time listening to people. At moments the emotions were extreme. For example, one father, trying to make a point, started banging his shoe on the table telling me: "You can't understand this because you haven't been through the system." There was so much emotion and so many viewpoints and issues that the process took many months. My staff became frustrated with the process of letting people verbalize their complaints. The staff kept telling me that we were not doing anything, nor getting anywhere.

I knew the need for ventilation and I discovered that there were common patterns and common problems. Finally, all agreed that the system was not working. This agreement was the common ground on which to build. The task force started listing issues which we had been hearing and started to get more specific and more practical. We began to hone in on exactly what could be done and on some specific solutions.

Because of my social work background as a caseworker, I was knowledgeable about families and had a holistic perspective. I also had one basic question that I kept in the forefront as we went through this process: "What is in the best interest of the children?" It wasn't the child's fault that their parents were divorced; they still have the right to be cared for financially, the right to a relationship with and the emotional support of both parents. The goal of this reform had to protect and foster their interests.

It was important to have a multi-issue package developed to gain the necessary votes to make it a law. If I brought a package to the legislators that only strengthened child support enforcement, it would have been viewed as an anti-noncustodial bill. On a practical level, I was aware that most noncustodial parents are fathers, that most legislators are men, and that some of these male legislators pay child support. Consequently, such a single issue approach would not gain the necessary support.

However, it was clear that custodial parents needed child care payments to be made in the best interest of the children. So we included a process to increase the rate of payment. On the other side, noncustodial parents wanted to be assured of visitation and had provided examples of the withholding of visitation, which is also not in the best interest of children. Thus, we included penalties, including jail, for withholding visitation.

Another vocal constituency in this issue were the judges, who disliked these cases because they were asked to make decisions on custody and other issues that they felt unqualified to make. They wanted it out of the judicial system. Therefore, another part of this proposed legislation included a system of automatic administrative enforcement and mediation to work out as many problems as possible before a judge became involved.

However, ironically, at first the attorneys didn't want automatic enforcement and mediation because that meant that people didn't have to hire an attorney every time a problem occurred. However, these concerns looked too self-serving for them to oppose the new changes on these grounds. A compromise was struck, allowing attorneys to do mediation as well as others.

It took two years of work, but in 1982 a package of bills to reform the Friends of the Court system became law. These changes have placed Michigan in the number one position for collecting child support in the country. Michigan was also the first state with specific enforcement requirements for visitation.

I now have quite a reputation among my colleagues for being able to bring together diverse and competing groups to reach a solution.

Debbie Stabenow, MSW
Former Michigan State Senator

Postscript

Various pieces of the Michigan law had been adopted by the federal government under the Reagan administration in 1984. Other states around the country are using the Michigan model and either have pilot projects or have implemented similar legislation. Ms. Stabenow, who received her MSW from Michigan State University, has received national recognition for her work on the Michigan Friends of the Court reform legislation.

ASSIGNMENTS

1. Examine the local positions in your community to which officials are elected and determine which would be the most viable one for a social worker to hold. Note the reasons for your choice.

2. Attend a city or county council session to determine whether you would have the expertise to deal with the issues on their agenda. If not, what education, training, or experience would enable you to do so?

3. Work on a candidate's campaign. Analyze the tasks necessary for thorough organization and running of a campaign.

SUGGESTED READINGS

Mathews, Gary. 1982. "Social Workers and Political Influence." *Social Service Review* 56 (December): 616–628.
Ribicoff, Abraham. 1962. "Politics and Social Workers." *Social Work* 7 (April): 3–6.

REFERENCES

Jankovic, Joanne, and Ronald K. Green. 1981. "Teaching Legal Principles to Social Workers." *Journal of Education for Social Work* 17 (Fall): 28–35.
Keith-Lucas, Alan. 1975. "An Alliance for Power." *Social Work* 21 (March): 93–97.
Kleinkauf, Cecilia. 1982. "Running for Office: A Social Worker's Experience." In *Practical Politics: Social Work and Political Responsibility,* Maryann Mahaffey and John Hanks (eds.), pp. 181–194. Washington, D.C.: National Association of Social Workers.
Miller, Jill. 1980. "Teaching Law and Legal Skills to Social Workers." *Journal of Education for Social Work* 16 (Fall): 87–95.
National Association of Social Workers. 1995a. "More Social Workers Hold Office." *NASW News* (40): 2.
National Association of Social Workers. 1993b. "Social Workers Serving in Elective Offices." Political Action for Candidate Endorsement. Washington, D.C.: National Association of Social Workers.
Thursz, Daniel. 1975. "Social Action as a Professional Responsibility and Political Participation." In *Participation in Politics,* J. Roland Pennock and John W. Chapman (eds.), pp. 27–34. New York: Lieber-Atherton.

chapter 12

Some Final Words on Being an Advocate

> *No one is the master of any craft in a day. A craft is mastered through the fine tuning of skills with experience over a lifetime. Since politics is of and for the people, social work provides an admirable apprenticeship for politics.*
>
> *Karen S. Haynes and James S. Mickelson*

Now that you have read the book and are convinced that social work skills are indeed relevant in the political arena and that social workers can and should be involved in policy formulation to affect change for their clients and for society as a whole, you may be asking yourself, "Where do I start? Should I write a letter to my representative or should I run for office? Can I really have an impact?" We assume that you may be asking these questions because we asked similar questions as has everyone who has entered the political field.

We have tried to provide answers to these questions through several mechanisms. We have included assignments at the end of chapters 2 through 11 as a mechanism by which you can choose the level of involvement that is comfortable for you. Additionally, because we learned that social work politicians needed mentoring and role models in order to "jump in" and learn the political arena, we have incorporated throughout the book vignettes of social work professionals using their basic social work skills in the political arena. We have provided additional suggested readings and references.

We also know through our own experiences that once a social worker becomes involved in the political arena, the opportunities and challenges are there from which to choose. We also know that social workers must themselves remove the barriers to becoming involved. But, just in case this isn't enough, we're ending this book with some final words of encouragement and advice.

DO SOMETHING

Not one of the social workers mentioned in this book who has affected change has not at some time in their lives asked themselves, "How do I get started?" We believe that the best answer is simply, "Jump in."

I advise them all to jump in and learn and use their power and influence in the political arena, just as they would in other sectors, and to encourage their clients to use their power in the same way. I do that all the time with my clients.

Travis L. Peterson, MSW
Private Practitioner
Houston, Texas

To get started, change your ideas of "political intervention." We are not suggesting that you become registered human service lobbyists, or run for political office, or even write your legislator once a week, although we hope some of you think about all of those. Political activism takes an array of forms,

---

There is the stereotyped perception among many, especially social workers, that if one becomes involved in the political arena, you have compromised; ipso facto, you have dirtied your hands. They say, "Gee, that's politics, and politics is tainted." I see the needs of our clients and say, "Taint enough."

Dennis Jones, MSW
Former Commissioner
Texas Department of Mental Health and Mental Retardation

Whether social workers feel it or not, they have a very specialized training in the political arena and we need to get in touch with that.

Suzanne Dworak-Peck, MSW
President, NCN (NASW Communications Network)
Past President, NASW and Co-Chair, PACE
Los Angeles, California

and once incorporated becomes an integral part of our everyday professional selves. Regardless of the amount of experience a social worker has in the political arena, every time a new challenge is confronted the question will arise where to start. A rule of thumb that is no different than in clinical practice is the earlier the intervention, the greater the influence. Jump in at the first indication of a social injustice or an opportunity to make a difference.

BE PREPARED

Do not become cynical about the "unsolvable"—poverty, physical abuse, chemical dependency. Rather, take those finely tuned skills of assessment, partializing, and goal setting, and begin where it's doable—with people. Another rule to remember is people influence people, and who but social workers are better equipped to influence people. Social workers understand and embrace people from all walks of life. Here is another advantage since the greater the diversity of support, the greater the influence.

> If a student is interested in eventually running for elected office, my advice would be to work in the political sector first. There are a growing number of elected officials whose constituent services are run by social workers. These are perfect places for social work students to have a field placement or to use as an entry-level position to enter the political arena. Such practice as doing constituent work, public policy work, or working in a government agency can be a real strength when you run for office some day. The experience of suddenly being a candidate and being expected to know something about 132 issues is really hard to duplicate unless you spend some time in and around government. My point is that a legislative staff person to an elected official ends up with an extraordinary range of information that's useful to actually running for office.
>
> *Ruth Messinger, MSW*
> *Manhattan Borough President*

Stop thinking about them, whoever "them" is—your legislator, your delegation—as the powerful, and yourself as the weak. Start thinking of yourself as the tough and the powerful and them as the weak, and you will have a very different perspective on what is going on. Think for a moment of how weak and ineffec-tive those legislators would appear if they were the direct line workers with these multiproblem families trying to create self-esteem, find resources, instill hope where there is none.

Social workers are "high touch," not "high tech" by nature. As a profession we have not embraced technology. However, the technology revolution has impacted not only social workers and our clients, but all of society. To compete in today's political arena we must not only utilize information technology, but we must be creative with it for the greatest impact. Information is power, and modern computers have greatly enhanced our ability to store and process large amounts of information, and with that comes the capacity to synthesize and create new information (Gingerich and Green 1996). Make no mistake that the "opposition" to social justice will utilize this technology to their advantage.

As social workers we are trained to be open to other's thoughts and feelings, and we are trained to be accepting of differences. We often go out of our way not to hurt, insult, or block communication. This of course is valued among our colleagues as well. We mention this because, as social workers, when we enter the political arena we need to remember the rules of the game, and that the goal is to win. Yes, compromise and win-win solutions are always desirable, however, bringing about change causes not only anxiety but loss for someone, regardless of the overall social benefit. All this means is that social workers must have a "thicker skin" in this arena than all the other areas of practice. Further, change is difficult to bring about, and the successes, although pleasant, are few and far more incremental than ever hoped.

You need to view it as a credible and extremely effective career option. One in which you can make substantial changes. The failures are pretty hard, but the victories are tremendous. There are ways to make it pay, have a good career, and be doing substantial social reform at the same time.

Sandy Ingraham, MSW
Social Services Consultant
Harrah, Oklahoma

To be candid, advocacy is not for wimps. The message is we can't bring about the change if we are worried about our opponent's feelings. This may seem frivolous to state, but the authors have encountered social workers that worry more about "rocking the boat" or "blocking communications" than they do about the people who are suffering from bad public policy. We, of course, must use our skills to our advantage; nevertheless, we must also remember that if someone is not in agreement with an advocate's actions then real change is not being proposed. Like it or not the rules of the game have been set. We may be able to change these rules as our efforts in the political arena increase, but not without entering the game as it is played today. Be comfortable with not always being liked or with perceptions that you're always angry; that's okay.

People should not think that you have to study law in order to go into politics.

Ruth Messinger, MSW
Manhattan Borough President

SPEAK OUT

Speak out always and at all times whenever and wherever misinformation or continued stereotyping takes place. Feel empowered and know that you know the facts, the truth. You will find more opportunities than you thought to get your message across. One easy trick to use in elevators, buses, and restrooms is to find someone you know and begin, "Hey did you see what the Senate Human Resources Committee did yesterday?" Your friend may wonder why you are doing this to them. Why you are putting them through this in front of all of these people? This friend/colleague hopefully, will say, "No, what did they do?" "They did something yesterday that could affect every working family in America, and I bet most people don't even know it." By now, the rest of the people in the subway (train, bus, elevator) are listening attentively (Amidei, 1992).

Leadership is a state of mind. It is not a position paper on every issue, or an empty slogan. So how do we create a leadership role? First, really listen to people and the stories of their lives. We can't create an agenda out of conventional Washington analysis or think-tank memos; hear what people are saying—the innate wisdom of the neighborhoods. Second, have a defining economic and social purpose. You cannot be an effective leader with a void in the center that is filled with the latest polls and tidbits from media consultants. The purpose of leadership is to create an opportunity structure that helps people to help themselves, not with guarantees but with earned opportunities. Third, policies should attach consequences to behavior. We should reward hard work and honesty, and we have to assert the truth that there is a cost to pluralism. We do not live in a no-cost democracy. Fourth, we must hold to the habits of the heart, the great traditions of neighbor helping neighbor that built this country. And we have to be committed to helping people who have been left behind. Finally, we must empower people. We must always lead the way toward equality and human dignity.

Barbara Mikulski, MSW
U.S. Senator (Maryland)

Do it in checkout lines. When you overhear people talking—like two women talking about those lousy welfare mothers who had left their young kids at home alone—interrupt them and say, "Do you know what the cost of day care is? Do you know any jobs where you can bring your three-year-old?" Give them something to think about.

You can do it at professional meetings of all kinds. For example, at a school district meeting, educators were talking about an experimental school built for public housing students with a few new academic ideas and some high-tech stuff, making a point that this would surely "get these families off welfare." A good advocate cannot sit quietly. Educate them about the complexity of these families' problems and the variety of interventions beyond academic that are necessary.

You want to be an advocate? You want to speak up? You want to get people's attention? Do it anyplace. It doesn't make any difference where you speak out. Get the message across. An essential ingredient to political advocacy is disseminating information and we have a great deal of the real information, and information is a powerful tool. Speak out and use it.

JUST SAY NO

We should have learned something from the Reagan era. We don't have to just take it when changes in policies or regulations mean that our practice, principles, or philosophy are jeopardized. Just say no. In privatized models, in budget reshaping and downsizing, we have too often changed professional roles to volunteer, agreed to higher caseloads, or cut technology or professional develop-ment from our budgets. While we understand that social workers may have to bend some, we must know when it's too much. We must remember that it may be in the long-term best interest of our clients to refuse to do more with less.

The authors were astonished during a workshop to address shrinking budgets to hear a social worker present a "creative" idea of staff spending their Saturdays for staff meetings, without additional compensation, to allow the staff to handle even more cases. This presenter never discussed the question of the effects on the staff or the effects of burnout. There comes a time when it is better to say no than to do the job with insufficient resources.

Social workers are ideally equipped to deal with the problems of a nation. I cannot think of any educational underpinning better suited to a career in government and politics than social work. Whether you see the use of a background and training in social work as a helpful thing in the field of politics may well depend on how you see politics. I think the definition of politics that I understand is the one that holds that politics is merely the way we decide who gets what, when they get it, and how much they can expect. In essence, politics is a means through which resources in society are divided. There are few who know better about the disbursement of resources than social workers. We see the effects that the adequate and inadequate disbursement of resources has on the lives, health, and well being of people every day.

Edolphus "Ed" Towns, MSW
U.S. Representative (New York)

YOU CAN MAKE A DIFFERENCE

Social work skills should be relied upon. Remember always that there are times you will win and times you will lose. Whether it is a vote on the floor of your statehouse or a candidate's election, never get discouraged when you lose or become overconfident when you win.

Keep a sense of humor because politics can be erratic, crazy, perplexing, discouraging, as well as rewarding and stimulating. It is all right to take a rest, find a new way of working, or slip into the background for a while, but so long as others are in need it will never be all right to give up (Amidei, 1992).

Don't be overwhelmed. There are many examples of only a couple of people who have had an impact. One social work advocate, the CEO of a two-person child advocacy organization, was concerned about the block grants that the 104th Congress was proposing. Congress was moving fast. How could one person make a difference? The social worker began to ask questions, then collected data on how much the state would receive if block grants were funded on former allocation levels versus number of children in the state. The result was that children in his state would really suffer. This two-person organization held a press conference where they proposed a child population parity formula. The idea was well accepted by the media and others supported the issue. In a few days the social worker received a call from the press secretary of the House Ways and Means chair requesting more information. Several weeks later the U.S. House Ways and Means Committee set aside $100 million to top off the funding levels for the "fastest growing states." Not yet ideal, but the children that the social worker was advocating for benefited.

Know that you're one of the good guys. A favorite analogy of ours is often told by one of the best advocates we have met, Nancy Amidei:

A good advocate is like those two good guys in the old cowboy movies, stuck up on a hill all by themselves. They're hopelessly outnumbered, and they don't stand a chance because down in the valley there is a horde of bad guys. These bad guys are mean and ugly, and they are riding hard toward the hill. So what do the good guys do? One of them gets behind a rock, gets a couple of stones, and starts making a lot of noise. The other one gets a big stick and starts whipping up a big cloud of dust. Pretty soon the bad guys down in the valley hear all that noise and rumbling; they see the huge cloud of dust and think, "Oh, no, they've got us outnumbered," and they turn around and run. Even if there are only two of you, one of you should get out there and make as much noise as you can, while the other whips up the biggest possible cloud of dust. That's how our side is going to win. (Haynes and Mickelson, 1991, p. xii)

CONCLUSION

To come full circle from where we began, we believe that the roots and essence of our profession compel us to enter the political arena; to do anything less would be an aberration of our historical mission and place us in an indefensible posture in the future. Social work will need to compete with many other interests in the public and legislative arenas.

We must compete effectively and consistently with the skills and technology necessary to support the advocacy efforts for our clients. We trust that this book has helped to provide those and that you will be a more effective advocate as a result. "When the combined efforts of both micro and macro practitioners focus on the needs of clients, social justice for all will be achieved" (Mickelson, 1995, p. 99).

SUGGESTED READING

Amidei, Nancy. 1992. *So You Want to Make a Difference: Advocacy is the Key,* 3rd. ed. Washington, D.C.: Office of Management and Budget.

REFERENCES

Amidei, Nancy. 1992. *So You Want to Make a Difference: Advocacy is the Key,* 3rd. ed. Washington, D.C.: Office of Management and Budget.
Gingerich, Wallace J., and Ronald Green. 1996. "Information Technology: How Social Work is Going Digital." In *Future Issues for Social Work Practice,* Paul R. Raffoul and Aaron C. McNeece (eds.). Needham Heights, MA: Allyn and Bacon.
Mickelson, James S. 1995. "Advocacy." In *Encyclopedia of Social Work,* 19th ed., pp. 95-100. Washington, D.C.: NASW Press.

Glossary of Legislative Terms

This glossary of legislative terms defines words and phrases frequently used in the legislative process. It is compiled from a variety of state and federal pamphlets.

Adjournment sine die. "Adjournment with a day." It marks the end of a legislative session because it does not set a time for reconvening.

Administrative bill. A bill proposed or favored by a governor.

Adoption. Approval or acceptance; usually applied to amendments or resolutions.

Agency bill. A bill proposed by an executive agency.

Aide. Legislative staff member, hired or appointed to perform clerical, technical, or official duties.

Amendment. Any alteration made or proposed to be made in a bill, motion, or clause thereof by adding, changing, substituting, or omitting.

Amendment, Constitutional. Resolution passed by both houses that affects the Constitution; requires approval by voters at a general election. *See also* Referendum.

Appropriate. To allocate funds.

Appropriation. A legislative authorization of money in a specific amount for a specific purpose. Funds are allotted to the agencies by the budget agency after the appropriation is made by the general assembly.

Approved by governor. Signature of a governor on a bill passed by the legislature.

Assembly. The legislature, made up of a certain number of members; elected from districts apportioned on the basis of population.

Author. The member who introduces a bill in the house of origin. *See also* Sponsor.

197

Bill. Proposed law presented to the legislature for consideration.

Bill analysis. Brief summary of the purpose, content, and effect of a proposed measure.

Bill, emergency. A bill to take effect upon signing by a governor or president.

Bill, prefiled. Bills prepared and filed prior to the opening of a regular session.

Bill room. A room where bills may be studied. Other useful legislative material for reference purposes is also available in the bill room.

Bill, vehicle. A bill that is introduced by title only. Because some legislation is complicated to write, for example, a school-aid distribution formula, it may not be ready to file by the filing deadline. The chairperson with responsibility for that measure files the bill under a very broad title to ensure its timely introduction.

Bills, special order of. An order by the legislative body to consider and reconsider a matter that has been before the legislative body at one time.

Bloc. A group of legislators who have certain interests in common and who may vote together on matters affecting that interest (also called a caucus).

Budget. An estimate of the receipts and expenditures needed to carry out programs for a fiscal year.

Budget agency. An executive agency that prepares the budget document for the governor or the president.

Budget bill. A bill specifying the amounts approved by the general assembly for each program of state government.

Budget committee. A committee of legislators that acts in an advisory capacity to the budget agency between sessions of the general assembly (also called appropriations committee).

Budget, executive. Suggested allocation of state money presented by the governor for consideration by the legislature.

Calendar (House). A daily list prepared by the speaker of the bills eligible for second and third readings that day.

Calendar (Senate). A daily list of all bills eligible for second or third readings that day.

Chair. Presiding officer or chairperson.

Chamber. Official hall for the meeting of a legislative body.

Clerk of the House. The chief administrative officer elected by the members.

Code. A systematic and complete compilation of the laws on a given subject. A code supersedes all prior acts on the subject.

Committee, ad hoc. Committee appointed for some special purpose. The committee automatically dissolves upon the completion of its specified task.

Committee chair. A member appointed to function as the parliamentarian head of a standing or special committee in the consideration of matters assigned to such committee by the legislative body.

Committee of the whole. A parliamentary device by which the entire membership of one house sits as a committee to consider legislation. Like other committees, it reports its recommendations to the house.

Companion bill. Two or more bills dealing with related aspects of the same topic (also called tie bar).

Concurrence. Action by which one house agrees to a proposal or action that the other house has approved. A proposal may be amended, adopted, or returned to the other house for concurrence.

Concurrent resolution. A statement of the attitude or feeling of the two houses not having the force of law.

Conference committee. A bill may be passed by both houses, but in differing forms. If the house of origin objects to the version passed by the second house, a special committee is appointed by the leadership of each house to reconcile the differences.

Constituent. A citizen residing within the district of a legislator.

Constitutional amendment. A change in the provisions of a constitution by modifying, deleting, or adding portions.

Constitutional majority. A constitutional majority is a bare majority of all members of each house, not merely the majority of members voting on a given issue.

Contingency fund. Money appropriated by the respective houses for incidental operating expenses.

Convene. The meeting of the legislature daily, weekly, and at the beginning of a session as provided by the constitution or law.

Convention, constitutional. The assembling of delegates for the purpose of writing or revising a constitution.

Convention, joint. The assembling of both houses of the legislature for a meeting.

Cosponsor. One of two or more persons proposing any bill or resolution.

Day certain. Adjournment with a specific day to reconvene.

Debate. Discussion of a matter according to parliamentary rules.

Digest. A brief summary of the contents of a bill which must be attached to the bill before introduction.

Dissent. Difference of opinion; also, to cast a negative vote.

District. The division of the state represented by a legislator. These can be designated numerically or by geographical boundaries.

Division. A method of voting.

Division of question. Procedure to separate a matter to be voted on into two or more questions.

Do pass. The affirmative recommendation made by a committee in sending a bill to the floor for additional action; do pass as amended means a committee recommends certain changes in a bill.

Effective date. A law becomes binding, either on a date specified in the law itself or, in the absence of such date, within a certain number of days specified by the constitution or law.

Emergency clause. A phrase added to a bill to make it effective immediately after passage and signing by the governor or president. Laws normally become effective after copies of the acts are distributed to the clerks of the circuit courts.

Enabling act. A statute that makes it lawful to do something that otherwise would be illegal. In some states, the legislature enacts a law that becomes operative only on the adoption by the people of an amendment to the constitution.

En bloc voting. To consider in a mass or as a whole; for example, to adopt or reject a series of amendments by a single vote.

Engrossing. This is a procedure for incorporating any amendments and checking the accuracy of a printed bill.

Ex officio. Holding two offices, one of which is held by virtue or because of the first; for example, the lieutenant governor is also a member of the Senate.

Executive committee action. The formal recommendation of a standing committee on any proposal referred to such committee for consideration.

Executive session. A session excluding from the chamber all persons other than members and essential staff personnel.

First reading. To read for the first of three times the bill or title for consideration.

Fiscal note. States the estimated amount of increase or decrease in revenue or expenditures and the present and future fiscal implications of pending legislation.

Fiscal year. An accounting period of one year.

Floor. That portion of the assembly chamber reserved for members and officers of the legislature and other persons granted the privilege of the floor.

Gallery. Balconies over the chamber from which visitors may view proceedings of the legislature.

Governor's proclamation. A means by which the governor may call an extra or special session.

Grandfather clause. Laws providing new or additional professional qualifications often contain a "grandfather clause" exempting persons presently practicing the affected profession from having to comply.

Hearing. A session of a legislative committee at which witnesses present testimony on bills under consideration.

House. The federal legislative body more commonly known as the House of Representatives; the lower house of the General Assembly.

House of origin. The chamber in which a measure is first introduced is known as its house of origin. A bill is filed either with the clerk of the House or the secretary of the Senate, is numbered, and is assigned to a committee. One can determine from a bill's number its house of origin. Numbers given to legislation introduced in the House are preceded by HB (House bill). Numbers assigned to Senate bills begin SB (Senate bill).

Immediate effect. Legislative action to render a law effective at an earlier date than the normal course of events would allow. For example, "Takes effect upon" is usually written into the bill.

Introducer. One who presents a matter for consideration. Cointroducers are those who subsequently sign a bill or resolution. The primary introducer is the first-named of several introducers.

Introduction. The formal presentation of a bill or resolution for consideration.

Journal. An official chronological record of the action taken and proceedings of the respective houses.

Law. A bill passed by both houses and signed by the governor or president. A bill also may become law if each house, by majority vote, overrides the governor's or president's veto.

Legislative study committee. Frequently an ad hoc committee is established with membership selected by the leadership to work on a controversial subject between sessions in the hope that legislation acceptable to both houses can be developed.

Lobbyist. A representative of a special interest who attends sessions of the legislature to influence legislation.

Majority leader. A member of the house chosen by members of the majority party as their leader and floor spokesperson.

Majority party. The party having the greater number of members in the legislature of either house.

Majority whip. A member of the House or Senate designated to perform certain functions, usually of a partisan nature.

Members elect. Members who are elected but who have not taken the oath of office or are not officially serving.

Members present. Refers to those members who are actually present at a daily session.

Message from the Senate or House. Official communication from the opposite house read into the official record.

Minority leader. A member of the minority party designated to be the leader.

Minority party. Party having the fewest members in the legislature or either house.

Minority report. A report that reflects the thinking of the members not favoring the majority position on action on an issue.

Minority whip. A member of the legislature designated to perform certain functions, usually of a partisan nature.

Minutes. Accurate record in chronological order of the proceedings of a meeting.

Motion. Formal proposal offered by a member of a deliberative assembly.

Motion, main. A consideration of a bill is a main motion. Consideration of an amendment to that bill would be a subsidiary or secondary motion. Consideration of a bill may be postponed. Consideration of an amendment to that bill generally cannot be deferred to another day when the body is to continue its deliberations on the bill because the body in the meantime may dispose of the main questions.

Motion to reconsider. A move that places the question in the same status in which it was prior to the vote on the question.

Nondebatable. Subjects or motions that cannot be discussed or debated.

Officers. That portion of the legislative staff elected by the membership; for example, the Speaker of the House or the whip.

Out of order. Business that is not conducted under proper parliamentary rules and procedures.

Pair or pairing. An arrangement between two members of a house by which they agree to be recorded on opposite sides of an issue and to be absent when the vote is taken.

Parliament inquiry. Question posed to the chair for clarification of a point in the proceedings.

Party caucus. Each party convenes all its members to elect leaders and establish party positions on specific issues. Party discipline can be very strict, and on certain major issues individual legislators are discouraged from taking independent positions. The party leadership can exert strong influence.

Party leadership. Within the legislature, party leadership consists of the majority leader (in the House called the Speaker and in the Senate the president pro tempore), the minority leader, and their whips. They are elected by their respective caucuses.

Passage of bill. Favorable action on a measure before either house.

Per diem. Literally, per day; daily expense money rendered to legislators and personnel.

Petition. A formal request submitted by an individual or group of individuals to the legislature.

Plank. Statements on issues that form the foundation of a political party's platform.

Platform. The principles and policies of a political party.

Point of order. Calling attention to a breach of order or rules.

Postpone indefinitely. A means of disposing of an issue by not setting a date to again consider same.

Postpone to a day certain. To defer consideration to a definite later time or day.

Precedent. Interpretation of rulings by presiding officers on specific rules; also unwritten rules that are established by custom.

Prefile. List of all bills, amendments, and resolutions filed before a session convenes.

President of the Senate. By constitutional enactment the lieutenant governor; title of the person who presides over the Senate (may vary by state).

President pro tempore. The majority floor leader in the Senate who presides in the absence of the president of the Senate.

Presiding officer. Person designated to preside at a legislative session.

Previous question. A motion to close debate and bring the pending question or questions to an immediate vote.

Printout. A copy of material printed by high-speed computer.

Procedures. Rules and traditional practices of the respective houses of the legislature.

Promulgation. A proclamation of a governor declaring that the acts of the general assembly have been distributed as required by law.

Proof of publication. A regulation requiring the journal to show that the legislature has determined that notice of intention to apply for passage of any local or special law was published in the affected community the required number of days prior to introduction of the proposed law.

Public acts. Enacted acts.

Public laws. Legislation enacted into law. A bill, as passed by both houses of the legislature, that has been enrolled, certified, approved by the governor, or passed over the governor's veto, and published.

Publication clause. Section incorporated in a bill to enable legislation to become effective on a specific date.

Question, privileged. Those questions which, according to rules or by consent of the assembly, shall have precedence.

Quorum. The number of members of a house who must be present for the body to conduct business.

Ratify. To approve and make valid.

Reading. Presentation of a bill before either house by the reading of the title; a stage in the enactment of a measure.

Reading, first. A bill is read aloud on the floor of the House or Senate by title only and is assigned to a committee by the Speaker or the president of the Senate.

Reading, second. After a committee finishes its work on a measure, it may report it out of committee. Copies of the legislation are printed and distributed to all members of the appropriate house. At this juncture, called the second reading, debate takes place in the chamber and a bill can be amended, killed, or passed.

Reading, third. A bill is reprinted with second-reading changes incorporated. Its title is read for a third time. At this point a two-thirds majority is necessary to amend the bill. A final vote is taken and the legislation either passes or fails.

Ready list. List of all proposed legislation reported out of committee and ready to be placed on the agenda.

Recall (a bill). Request by a house that the other house or the governor return a bill, usually for a corrective amendment.

Recede. Withdraw from an amendment or position on a matter.

Recess. Intermission in a daily session.

Recommit. To send back to committee for further investigation or to another committee.

Reconsideration. A motion which, when granted, gives rise to another vote annulling or reaffirming an action previously taken.

Record. By custom, members of a legislative body often request that the record show a statement or that it be recorded a certain way. These requests, if approved, are entered in the journal and are said to be "on the record."

Referendum. A vote at the polls for the purpose of allowing the wishes of the people on a subject to be expressed. A referendum may be held on any issue.

Referral. The sending or referring of a bill to committee.

Regular order of business. The established sequence of business set up for each legislative day.

Regulation. A rule or order of an agency promulgated under the authority of a statute passed by the legislature.

Rejection. An action that defeats a bill, motion, or other matter.

Rerefer. The reassignment of a bill or resolution to a committee.

Repeal. A method by which legislative action is revoked or abrogated.

Representative. A member of the House of Representatives.

Rescind. Annulment of an action previously taken.

Resolution. A document expressing the sentiment or intent of the legislature, governing the business of the legislature, or expressing recognition.

Resolution, joint. A form of legislation used to pose amendments. Joint resolutions do not become laws and do not require signature by the governor.

Resolution, Senate or House. Same as a concurrent resolution except it is the expression of one house.

Revenue. Yield of taxes and other sources of income the state collects.

Revised code. Statutory laws of the state.

Roll call. The recording of the presence of members or the taking of a vote on a bill.

Roster. Booklet containing names of members, officers, employees, and a list of standing committees and districts of each house for the current session.

Rules. Regulating principles, methods of procedure.

Rules, joint. Rules governing the relationship and affecting matters between the two houses.

Rules, standing. Permanent rules adopted by each house for the duration of the session.

Rules, suspended. Temporarily setting aside the rules.

Rules, temporary. Practices usually adopted at the beginning of each session until standing rules are adopted, generally consisting of the standing rules of the preceding session.

Rules, waive. A procedural step used to forego a rule in order to speed the process of enactment of a measure.

Second house. A house other than the house of origin.

Secretary of the Senate. A nonmember officer of the Senate elected or appointed by the members to serve as chief administrative officer.

Section. A portion of the codes; sections are cited in each bill that propose to amend, create, or replace same.

Segment. A portion of a bill.

Select committee. A special committee of legislators, members of the Senate, or members of the House.

Senate. The upper house of the General Assembly, consisting of 50 members.

Seniority. Recognition of prior legislative service, sometimes used in making committee assignments.

Session. Period during which the legislature meets.

Session, daily. Each day's meeting of a legislative body.

Session, extraordinary. Special session called by and limited to matters specified by the governor.

Session, joint. Meeting of the two houses together.

Session, regular. The annual session at which all classes of legislation may be considered.

Simple resolution. An expression of the sentiments of one house on matters related to that house. A simple resolution does not require action by the other house.

Sine die. Adjournment without a day being set for reconvening. Final adjournment.

Speaker of the House. The presiding officer of the House of Representatives, chosen by the members.

Speaker pro tempore. Substitute presiding officer, taking the chair on request of the Speaker in his absence; elected by the body.

Special order. Matter of business set for a special time and day.

Sponsor. A member who agrees to introduce and support a bill in the second house after its passage by the house of origin. *See also* Author.

Standing committee. Regular committees of the legislature set up to perform certain legislative functions.

State the question. To place a question before a legislature for its consideration.

Statutory committee. A committee created by statute.

Stopping the clock. Practice of lengthening the hours of the legislative day, irrespective of the passing of the hours of the calendar day.

Strike out. Delete language from a bill or resolution.

Stripping. The entire contents of one bill may be deleted and a completely new measure inserted under the title of the old bill. It is a technique employed to resurrect a measure that may have died in committee.

Substitute. An amendment that replaces an entire bill or resolution.

Sufficient seconds. The support of the number of members required to make certain motions and procedures.

Supplemental appropriation. Adjustment of funds allocated over the original allocation.

Table. A means of disposing of a bill or other matter for an indefinite period of time.

Term. Duration of office of an elected official.

Title. Statement of the general subject of a bill.

Unanimous consent. Usually requested to suspend rules for a specific purpose.

Unfinished. Business that has been laid over from a previous day.

Uniform and model acts. Legislation recommended by various national groups for passage in all or several states. Uniform acts are prepared by the Conference of Commissioners on Uniform State Laws and are intended to be adopted verbatim by the various states. Uniform acts are prepared by numerous organizations to serve as guides for state legislation and may be modified to suit each individual state.

Veto. The president's or governor's disapproval of a bill passed by both houses of the general assembly. The governor is allowed a set number of days to sign or veto a bill or allow it to become law without his signature. Bills vetoed during a session must be returned to the house of origin for reconsideration and vetoes may be overridden by the vote of a constitutional majority in each house.

Veto override. To pass a bill over the president's or governor's veto.

Voice vote. Oral expression of the members when a question is submitted for their determination. Response is given by yeas and nays and the presiding officer states the decision as to which side prevailed.

Vote, division and rising. To vote by a show of hands or by standing.

Vote, en bloc. To dispose of several items, such as a series of amendments, by taking one vote.

Vote, record. A roll call vote in which members answer to their names and announce their votes yea or nay. Each vote is recorded in the journal.

Vote, roll call. Individual votes of members are recorded in the journal.

Vote. Formal expression of the will or decision of the body.

Whip. An elected member whose duty it is to keep the rest of the members informed as to the decisions of the leadership.

Withdraw a motion. To recall or remove a motion according to parliamentary procedure.

Without recommendation. A committee report that is neither favorable nor unfavorable.

Yeas and nays. Recorded vote of members on an issue.

Yield. The relinquishing of the floor to another member to speak or ask a question.

Index

About the Authors

KAREN S. HAYNES

Dr. Haynes is currently the president of the University of Houston-Victoria. She is on leave from her position as Dean of the University of Houston Graduate School of Social Work, which she has held since 1985.

She has authored articles on political social work and published other books including *Women Managers in Human Services* (1996, 1989) and *Invitation to Social Work* (1994). She was the first chair of the Indiana Political Action Committee for Human Services in 1978 and the co-creator of the first Students Day at the Texas Legislature in 1992. As dean she helped create the only graduate program in the nation with a political social work concentration.

She holds a Ph.D. from the University of Texas at Austin; a Masters of Social Work degree from McGill University in Montreal, Quebec, Canada; and an A.B. degree from Goucher College in Baltimore, Maryland. During her 25 years in higher education, she has presented numerous addresses on advocacy within which she continuously admonishes that "all social work is political."

JAMES S. MICKELSON

Mr. Mickelson is the President and Chief Executive Officer at CHILDREN AT RISK, a local children's (class) advocacy organization in Houston, Texas. He also is an adjunct professor at the University of Houston's Graduate School of Social Work. As a mayoral appointee to the Joint City/County Commission on Children, he serves as vice-chair. In addition he serves on many boards and committees addressing the needs of children.

He has authored many professional articles and contributed the section on advocacy for the *Encyclopedia of Social Work,* 19th edition. Mr. Mickelson has contributed numerous editorials to local newspapers. In addition he has written and lectured about "youthism," the discriminatory treatment of children, which he sees as a major factor contributing to the plight of today's children.

Mr. Mickelson received a B.S. degree from the University of Southern Colorado and a Master's in Social Work degree from Wayne State University. His 20 years of social work practice in child welfare has been combined with political action to assure social justice for children. He has been described by a high school student as "the man in the grey suit with a fire in his gut for children."